MW00607447

CRUCIAL CHRISTIANITY

CRUCIAL CHRISTIANITY

AN ETHOS THEOLOGY FOR THE THIRD MILLENNIUM

Indexed Edition

G.C. Dilsaver, P/M, PsyD, MTS

ISBN# 978-0-9993607-5-0

Imago Dei Press

ImagoDeiPress.com

*To the Sweet, Sorrowful Mother
of Christ the King Crucified,
and to My Wife & Children,
the Most Gracious & Undeserved Blessings
of this Same Blessed Mother*

CONTENTS

PREFACE

There is no crisis in the Church at this dawn of the third millennium. Rather there is a crisis *between* the Church and the universally pervasive Western culture. This predominant Western secular order—be it statist, corporate, or popular—is intrinsically anti-Christic. This is because it is a cultural order that came into being by the very rejection of its Christian cultural matrix that was Western Christendom, and in doing so rejected the Gospel itself. As such, the universally pervasive and predominant Western cultural order has as its very specific difference an enmity towards true Christianity. Irrefutably, there is an epic crisis in this third millennium of Christianity, but it is one that entails the individual Christian, the family and community in which he resides, and the living out of the Holy Faith in the midst of a virulently and irredeemably hostile macro-culture.

But there is no crisis *in* the Church. There is no crisis in papal authority, much less in Catholic teachings; for these are but red herrings, distractions from the real crisis and thus deflections from the real opportunity to survive and thrive as Catholics in the third millennium. For the authority of the Church derives fundamentally not from her papacy but from her infallible Deposit of Faith. This Deposit of Faith has over two thousand years been unpacked fully via the Magisterium; thus for all intents and purposes, all dogma has now been definitively pronounced. It is these infallible truths, more certain and discernible than ever before, that are ultimately authoritative; indeed the heeding of these truths via an informed Catholic conscience must be adhered to even if it means disobeying a pope. The result being that the papacy and the Magisterium are rendered less immediately impactive than ever before, for that papacy and Magisterium have over the millennia successfully worked themselves out of their most important job: that of infallibly defining Catholic truths.

While there is no crisis in the Church, what is occurring in the Church, and not without some trauma, is the necessary deconstruction of obsolete, even if at one time functional, ecclesial structures. As per God's providential unfolding of salvation history, this deconstruction is allowing the countenance of Holy Mother Church to shine forth unencumbered by no-longer-needed scaffolds and trappings, allowing her beauty to radiate unobscured by decorous pretenses and posturings. Indeed, it is the Spotless Bride of Christ adorned only with her grace, truths, and morals (with all else now being but an obfuscation) that will draw the children of the third millennium to her and to Christ.

In this third millennium the papacy, having fulfilled its most essential charism of infallibly building up the Church, will now providentially be relegated to a relatively obscure, but still honored, place as the Church's foundational rock. This papacy that once increasingly acquired magnificent worldly encrustations and pretenses is now being stripped of these encrustations and pretenses. This papacy that became falsely equated with the very Church herself, at the same time and rate it acquired those worldly encrustations and pretenses, is now no longer being so falsely equated. As a result the papacy is to be most properly understood as the office of the *"servant of the servants of God,"* and not as equivalent to, but underneath the Church; yes, still foundational but nonetheless humbly subordinate to the Church and the Faith.[1]

But nor is there a crisis in third millennium Catholicism that has anything to do with rights, power struggles, or any form of identity politics: be these rights, powers, or identities papal, clerical, lay, or what have you. For these issues are issues of the predominant secular order, an order with which Christianity is intrinsically and increasingly at odds. Rather, the Christian crisis of the third millennium concerns the essential and common existence of all the faithful. As such, this crisis has as its remedy the purification, intensification, simplification, and remanding of the locus of authority, agency, militancy, and ecclesial existence to the most essential and ultimate human and Christian form: that of the individual Christian and his familial and communal milieu. The Christian crisis in the third millennium is then not one of discerning the truth but of living the truth. It is a crisis of living every day in the complete and certain truth, a crisis of choosing the integral good, which is to say, a crisis of Christian ethos.[2]

AN ETHOS THEOLOGY

An "ethos theology" (or theological ethos) is herein presented as a religion's truths and morals intentionally and integrally lived out in a believer's current milieu. Specifically presented herein is a Christian ethos theology that, because of the all-pervasive and absolute nature of the Christian faith, is lived out in personal, domestic, and communal life without compartmentalization or compromise. Due to the all-pervasive and absolute nature of the Christian religion, an uncompromised Christian theological ethos necessarily entails as well an ideological and moral orientation toward the world and the dominant culture. Adherence to this ideological and moral orientation necessarily results in an interactive attitude and bearing toward the dominant culture, which entails an increasingly remarkable (i.e., countercultural and militant) dynamic as per the degree that the dominant culture is antithetical to the Faith.

As per the requirements of orthodoxy, if a Christian ethos theology is to be truly Catholic, it will not present new truths, but rather rediscover, renew, and, as needed, re-prioritize and reapply essential truths. As a lived out theological ethos, these truths are so accentuated as to invigorate the faithful in their present vocational exigencies and properly reorient them in response to the present dominant culture. While an orthodox Christian ethos theology must be dogmatically rooted in the ancient and immutable Deposit of Faith, as an applied ethos it is not strictly speaking catechetical. Rather, a Christian ethos theology's specific difference is its being a dynamic application of dogma as per the requirements of a Christian's current milieu. In that sense, it is akin to a moral theology. But here too, a Christian ethos theology differs from a casuistic manual of right and wrong, but aims to be exhortative to the intentional, intense, and courageous celebration of Christian life as called for by a Christian's time and place.

As an exhortative application of both truth and morals, an ethos theology may be most similar to a pastoral theology. Yet even here it differs from pastoral theology in that it is not a subject taught to teachers so they can in turn teach it to students, nor can it be implemented (though it can be facilitated) from the pulpit or the confessional. Rather, it is inherent to an adequate Christian theological ethos that its truths, disposition, character, and fundamental values be made the believer's own in both intellectual assent and volitional embrace; that is, this ethos must be directly lived out by the choice of the individual Christian, who in doing so takes full responsibility for how it is lived out.

CHRISTIAN CRUCIALISM

As per requirements, the following work endeavors to formulate a theological ethos keyed to the essentials. Specifically, the essentials presented herein are uncompromisable Christian truths, morals, and values; so designated as such by the Holy Catholic Church and by both divine and natural law. As an endeavor to demarcate and apply the most essential principals of the Holy Faith, the following work entails nothing (may God forbid!) new or innovative. Rather, it seeks only to go beyond those accidentals and human inventions that may obscure the true countenance of the Church, impede the preaching of the Gospel, and distract from the militant embrace of Christian essentials.

These essential and uncompromisable truths, morals, and values are further prioritized and highlighted in so far as they intersectively collide with the contemporary, contradictory, and indeed anti-Christic third millennium secular culture. It is this very collision of the sacred and profane, in all its traumatic and yet miraculous reality, that determines the saliency of the theological ethos herein dubbed *crucialism*. As per *"isms,"* note well that "crucialism" is an *-ism* in that it indicates "an action, process, and result" of Catholicism; and it is "Catholicism" that is an *-ism* indicating "a doctrine, system, or body of principles and practices." Catholicism is thus the source of crucialism, and crucialism is but an application of Catholicism.

Serendipitously enough, crucial means both "of vital importance" and "cross-conformed." These two definitions are synergistically combined in the term *crucialism*, which, as a theological ethos, advances that the Gospel's most *vitally important* principle is to *conform to the Holy Cross*.

Jesus said to his disciples: If any man will come after

me, let him deny himself, and take up his cross, and follow me. MT 16:24

The following ethos theology aims to highlight those essentials of the Gospel that will most insistently mandate the Christian's embrace of the Holy Cross in the third millennium, and it advances that this embrace most adequately ensures the perseverance in and the promulgation of the Holy Catholic Faith. Thus, the truths and values of the Faith (and of unaided reason, too) highlighted and designated as most essential in the following pages are those deemed to be the most challenging for third millennium Christians to implement; that is, they entail counterculturality and thus persecution, indeed crucifixion. But in spite of the daunting challenges of the times, the perseverance in and the promulgation of the Holy Faith, and much more besides, can be assured by this very crucialism; for in the Christian dispensation victories and miracles readily happen, and they happen through the Holy Cross.

To effectively promote a crucial Christianity, where the vitally important truths of the Faith are ordered to Christ Crucified, not only must the third millennium culture be fully acknowledged as anti-Christic, but the subjective disposition of this culture's population as ill-disposed to those truths and to that Cross must as well be taken into account. For the population of the third millennium is enmeshed in a confusing maze of relativism and escapism, all of which is enabled and enhanced by material abundance and technological advances. So while the third millennium's anti-Christic culture insures intimate union with the Holy Cross by all who will uncompromisingly live out the Faith, at the same time, and counteractively, the population of this culture is inured from the cross.

But the third millennium populace is inured not only from the Cross of Christ but from the cross of mere reality as well. Indeed, it is the West's very apostasy from the Holy Faith and the Holy Cross that has likewise led to its inevitable turning away from the cross of reality and the truths of natural law. As such, crucialism aims at advancing not only essential and relevant *revealed* truths but essential and relevant *natural* truths as well. Grace builds upon nature, and thus grace is most efficaciously placed upon a firm foundation of nature. But in the third millennium there is a severe disconnection from, and vicious rejection of, both nature and natural law.

As a Christian ethos theology, crucialism is an exhortation to deep personal responsibility and commitment. For the Christian ideal goes beyond the bare minimum, entailing at its apex the love of God rather than the mere fearing of his just punishment. In accord with advancing personal responsibility and commitment, and in keeping with the Christian principle of subsidiarity,[3] the locus of inspiration, action, and holiness must occur at the most fundamental level: within the heart of the individual believer. Indeed, it is the individual believer who is called to the heights of sanctification via his baptism. In keeping with these principles of personal responsibility, commitment, and subsidiarity, it is the most fundamental social unit of the family as well that must be the locus and focal point of Christian life. And while all the faithful—lay, vowed evangelical,[4] and ordained—are called to singularly heed the call to holiness that is the crucial Baptismal Vocation (and to which all particular Christian vocations are ordered), it is Christian families that find themselves on the very cutting-edge of the third millennium's Christian crisis. It is then Christian families that now must take the lead and initiative in the inception of holiness. This means, too, that the advent of any possible new Christendom is likewise dependent on the initiative and holiness of these Christian families: of these marriages, fathers, and mothers.

PSYCHOMORAL FOUNDATION

The following theological Christian ethos of crucialism is premised on the conviction that the Church does have the answers (be they theological, philosophical, or psychomoral) to the ills, disorders, upheavals, and sins of third millennium humanity. But for these answers to be fully efficacious they must indeed be uncompartmentalized, and fully integrated. Therefore, an efficacious Christian theological ethos must advance both the crucial truths of Faith and nature. In doing so, such a crucial ethos will address the urgent need of the third millennium populace, a populace that must undergo a cultivation of the natural soil of their souls so as to render these souls' hotbeds of reality and thus fertile ground for the seeds of the Gospel.

> Hear ye: Behold, the sower went out to sow. And whilst he sowed, some fell by the way side, and the birds of the air came and ate it up. And other some fell upon stony ground, where it had not much earth; and it shot up immediately, because it had no depth of earth. And when the sun was risen, it was scorched; and because it had no root, it withered away. And some fell among thorns; and the thorns grew up, and choked it, and it yielded no fruit. And some fell upon good ground; and brought forth fruit that grew up, and increased and yielded, one thirty, another sixty, and another a hundred. MK 4:3–8

It is the psychomoralitic process[5] that prepares the soil of the soul so that spiritual seeds of reality—both natural and revealed—can germinate, take root, and flourish. This is done by the cultivation of the soul so that it is hospitable to reality and cleansed of those egoistic elements that would impede the flourishing of reality within it. The psychomoralitic process then is often a necessary remedial prerequisite for efficacious spiritual direction, for it weeds the soil of the soul and prunes and nurtures the now sprung psychomoral sprout of essential human well-being.

As philosophy is the handmaid of theology, psychomoralitics as a clinical application of Thomism is the handmaid of the applied ethos theology of crucialism. The need for this psychomoralitic foundational prerequisite for the crucial Christian ethos is due to the contemporary person's non-fulfillment of the natural Psychomoral (rational-volitional) Vocation.[6] This non-fulfillment of the Psychomoral Vocation stems from third millennium *technarcistic*[7] disconnect from natural law, and thus reality. The misuse of technology, with its subsequent soul-deadening effects and concomitant narcissism, makes the populace of the third millennium ill prepared for, indeed inured to, the seeds of reality and thus much more so unreceptive to the seeds of the Gospel.

Psychomoralitics essentially entails purgative abnegation of the pride and self-love so that the Psychomoral Vocation can be answered in an increasing openness to reality (*viz.*, receiving-the-real, assenting-to-truth, and choosing-the-good). The psychomoralitic process successfully entered into, be it via natural maturation or clinical intervention, is salubrious for the *imago Dei* in its rational-volitional nature and thus increases essential human well-being.

INTEGRATION OF
NATURE & GRACE

Such an uncompartmentalized crucial integration of nature and grace includes the harmonious nexus of the psychomoral and the sacramental; of the familial and the ecclesial; of the secular and the sacred; of praxis and prayer; and of doing and doctrine. For nature is built upon by grace; reason is integral with faith; philosophy is the handmaid of theology; the cross of reality is fully embraced in Christ Crucified; existential awareness becomes complete in transcendence; and the image of God through sanctifying grace becomes the indwelling of God.

The following pages will advance that in order to remedially apply the answers to the ills, disorders, and sins of third millennium humanity it is most urgent to promote an intentional Christian discipleship deeply rooted in the embrace of reality. Being rooted in reality has as its ultimate end Supreme Reality; and the salient fact of reality is the cross of existence. It is this Supreme Reality and its manifestation in the cross of reality that the third millennial technarcistic person must be made intentionally aware of and receptive to; for only then can this person mature according to nature and then further still be sanctified by grace. It is by embracing the cross of reality that the image of God within a person is made maturely manifest. Once reality is so embraced a person is poised, indeed eagerly impelled, to embrace the Cross of Christ that is found at the very heart of reality.

G.C. Dilsaver, P/M, Psy.D, M.T.S.
Holy Cross Farm
Northwest Montana
Epiphany, January 6, 2020

Prelude: The Inception of Crucialism

The following **ethos theology** of crucialism had its inception during this author's graduate theological studies of the Ecumenical Council of Vatican II, and the theological writings that led up to and followed it. In sum, during these studies it became apparent that though Vatican II (and its subsequent reforms) was all about the Mass, it wasn't at all about the Holy Cross. More emblematically, the following ethos theology has as its catalyst an encounter with a participant at Vatican II and future pope, the then Prefect of the Congregation for the Doctrine of the Faith, Joseph Cardinal Ratzinger. The Cardinal Prefect had just delivered a scholarly lecture entitled *Jesus Christ—Yesterday, Today, and Forever*[8] to prelates, ecclesial dignitaries, academic presidents, and deans; Knights of Columbus executive officers; and the faculty, friars, and graduate students of both the Dominican House of Studies and the *Pontifical Institute on* Marriage and Family. In the academic conference that followed, I was the first afforded the opportunity to dialogue with the Cardinal Prefect, the gist being:

Your Eminence, in your lecture you spoke of contemporary man's unwillingness to suffer and the many means available today to escape that suffering, implying that this was impeding the spread of the Gospel. If that is the case, and I agree that it is, what is to be made then of Vatican II's glaring failure to mention the Cross and the need to embrace it?

Cardinal Ratzinger replied in his ever so gentle and professorial manner:

Well, there is some mention in Gaudium et Spes *of the "paschal Mystery."*

Then he briefly paraphrased that passage, which reads:

Undergoing death itself for all of us sinners, He taught us by example that we too must shoulder that cross which the world and the flesh inflict upon those who search after peace and justice.[9]

My somewhat impertinent follow-up was:

That isn't much, your Eminence, especially considering that Vatican II was a pastoral council that advocated an openness to the world, an openness that would surely render the faithful quite vulnerable and with no other option but to either embrace that Cross or abandon their faith.

Cardinal Ratzinger admitted the deficiency of the documents in this regard, but seemingly defended this deficiency by stating:

The Council was not meant to present a complete ecclesiology.

At this point I refrained from imprudently remarking that the Cardinal did indeed once call the council "a complete ecclesiology" in his account of his *peritus* participation during the Vatican II,[10] and relinquished the floor. My refraining from challenging the Cardinal (though I had in my possession his very account) was warranted considering Cardinal Ratzinger's post-Vatican II return to sobriety:

We started out boldly and full of confidence in ourselves . . . we barricaded the door of a time that was past and proclaimed the abrogation and annihilation of all that lay behind it. . . . Gradually we have stopped laughing.[11]

Indeed, even then as we spoke, Cardinal Ratzinger, as prefect of the Congregation for the Doctrine of the Faith, was involved in the ongoing censoring of increasingly heterodox intellectuals,[12] actions that were for him personally very painful.

Dominican House of Studies, Washington, D.C., January 20, 1990

Josef Ratzinger and Karl Rahner as periti at Vatican II.

The passage of Cardinal Ratzinger's lecture that was referenced in my question is this challenging statement:

> There are no longer any elements [today] to protect spiritual immunity. Positive thinking offers the spiritual organism no spiritual resources to maintaining immunity; it is rather the ruination of the spiritual defense system. . . . It is at this point [in history] that the realism of the Christian has to reveal itself anew; Jesus Christ has to be discovered in today. A fresh understanding is needed by what is meant by: I am the Way, the Truth, and the Life. . . . [For today's man] to accept and endure life as a hardship becomes unthinkable. . . . Life is supposed to give itself to man without his giving himself. We could also say, therefore, that the essential feature of the whole proceeding is the denial of love which brings one to escape into deception. Behind this, however, stands a mistaken image of God, which is really a denial of God and worship of an idol.

But while Cardinal Ratzinger in his lecture succinctly diagnosed the illness, he was characteristically gentle, if somewhat sparse like the documents of Vatican II themselves, in prescribing the antidote:

> Conversion implies a dying. It is a cross which bears Easter within it but which nonetheless has to hurt.

So even the Cardinal's own lecture was strikingly deficient in the mention of the Cross of Christ.

As per Ratzinger's "realism of the Christian," it is certainly third millennium man's deficiency in realism, in philosophy and natural theology, that prevents him from knowing and accepting reality and from knowing and accepting the God of that reality. But even Christians of the third millennium, like superstitious shamans, often invoke God only to mitigate reality, thus showing their own deficient understanding of the God of reality and thus of that self-same God of revelation. This deficiency, as the Cardinal Prefect pointed out, is caused by man's desire to escape suffering and his subsequent use of the third millennium's myriad of readily accessible, but still superficial, anesthetizing means to so escape it. The following crucial theological ethos prescribes the antidote for this deficiency in realism is the embrace of the cross both natural and supernatural, the avoidance of which verily causes that deficiency. It is herein advanced that the zealous, charity impelled embrace of both the cross of reality and the Cross of Christ is not only the singular crucial exhortation of Christianity, but that the emphatic and intentional preaching of Christ Crucified is the only Gospel that will truly resonate with the ever so anesthetized and enslaved person of the *technarcistic*[13] third-millennium.

CRUCIAL CONFLUENCE

While the following theological ethos with its emphasis on the Holy Cross had its inception in graduate theological studies, it would come to a holistic and integrative completion in the subsequent study and practice of clinical psychology. Indeed, the following theological ethos as a specific third millennium application and integration of Christian doctrine and practice would be spurred on and melded together by this author's intense immersion in the post-Christian West's unique pressure-cooker of psychotherapy. To this clinical pressure-cooker, however, was added the detoxifying and rectifying ingredients of Thomistic philosophy. Psychomoralitics[14] is the result of this confluence of clinical psychotherapeutics and Thomistic philosophy. Psychomoralitics is a term and science necessarily distinguished from that of the secular mental health system's (*viz.*, State, professional, pharmaceutical, and insurance entities) definition and statutorily designated "psychology."

Simultaneous to the development of psychomoralitics, the gaining of degrees, certifications, and thousands upon thousands of session hours as a clinical psychologist, psychotherapist, and psychomoralist, I was able to witness firsthand the glaring falsehood of the mental health profession's conceptualization of the human person and its subsequent clinical inefficacy and inducing of grave harm. But by simply remaining recalcitrantly faithful to the Church, I was able to skirt these errors by positing my clinical practice (though surreptitiously to be sure) under Catholicism's illuminating truths and most directly within the anthropological truths of the perennial Thomistic philosophy she had validated. Blessed by the Church (and so due to no merit of mine) I was thus able to practice a clinical intervention that not only alleviated the symptomology of so-called "mental disorder," but also advanced therapants upon the path of human maturation and even Christian conversion.

During this time of ostensible participation in the mental health profession, I not only witnessed the very obvious and fully expected falsehoods and failures of that profession but also, in a striking *in vivo* clinical confluence, the apparent failure of Catholicism to remedy or even mitigate grave ego-reactive symptomology (a.k.a., "mental disorders"). I witnessed on the periphery of my practice many good Catholics (families, bishops, priests, nuns, and monks) that, though steeped in the wisdom, practices, prayers, and sacraments of the Church, were nonetheless falling into and unable to escape so-called "mental disorder." These Catholics were often scandalized and asked, "Why doesn't the Church have the answers? Why aren't the sacraments enough? Why can't Christ heal me?"

Though never from those who were fully engaged in psychomoralitics, I still heard constant and increasing accounts of hapless Catholics stumbling into the unbridgeable divide that exists between the mental health conceptualization and traditional Christian spirituality. Some would fearfully scamper back to one side or the other of this divide. On one side there where those that rejected not only the erroneous mental health field, but everything save a supernatural solution. These Catholics would often have recourse to deliverance and exorcistic interventions. On the other side, there were those who would come to hold the mental health conceptualization as paramount and definitive and Catholicism as ultimately subordinate to that conceptualization (as does the mental health field).

But most Catholics caught in the unbridgeable divide between traditional Christian spirituality and the mental health conceptualization would either gloss over the inherent contradictions or just falsely compartmentalize the spiritual issues from the ego-reactive issues. In both cases and in practice, these Catholics would fall into the material heresy of seeking the answers to the ills of the soul in medical or mental health treatments. Thus, the common contemporary heresy they inadvertently embraced was a material heresy, and in more ways than one. It is *material* as in an inadvertent, informal heresy, and it is *material* as in the heresy of materialism (and all those heresies that do not properly integrate the material and spiritual). For when a person seeks physical remedies for ills of the soul he gives a working precedent to the body over the soul, which is a practical diminishment, even denial, of the soul and the spiritual essence of the human person. Eventually, practices that give the body precedent over the soul lead to the denial of the hylomorphic composite of the human person, and the supremacy of the soul hylomorphism entails, which is a definitive cardinal truth of natural law and the Christian faith.

Again, as per crises, there is not in the third millennium a crisis of so-called "mental disorder" or of the Christian remedying of such disorder; rather, the crisis is rooted in the invalid and failed mental health conceptualization itself and this conceptualization's influence and confluence with a deficient and even false Christian piety. That is, there is a real world crisis of science and theology; of the natural and the supernatural; of philosophy and theology; of humanistic intervention and philosophical anthropology; of body and spirit; of nature and grace; of reason and faith; and yes, of reality and God. In sum, it is a crisis of compartmentalization; that is, of not integrating the above essential pairings. It is then, once again, a crisis of ethos: of worldview, values, and faith and the integral living out of that worldview, values, and faith.

A PRIVILEGED TIME
AND POSITION

The Catholic-based and wide-ranging clinical practice I have engaged in as a psychologist, psychomoralist, and spiritual director has afforded the unique opportunity to hear countless intimate autobiographical accounts from generations of Catholics whose lives span a most critical century in the Church and Western civilization. I garnered the experiences of older adults who had grown up before World War II and who ushered in Vatican II; and I worked with their children who were raised in both the pre- and post-Vatican II Church; and I worked as well with their children's children, unto even now the fifth generation.

With an objective clinical and scientific perspective being so afforded, the cultural and social patterns over multiple generations of Catholics were discernible. Discerned was the impact of post-World War II prosperity on those raised in the depression years of the 1930s. Discerned was the ensuing staunch conservative Catholicism of the 1940s and 50s. Discerned specifically was the effect of a triumphant and hyper-prospering America that corresponded with a similarly triumphing and prospering American Catholicism. But this apparently prosperous American Catholicism was likewise discerned to be incipiently schizophrenic, for despite its religious conservatism that had one leg in a rules-based and evermore superficial morality, its other leg was firmly planted in the popular and evermore materialistic and hedonistic culture. Discerned as well was that materialism and hedonism became explosive in the late 1960s; and that subsequently lead to the complete confusion of the 70s; that lead to the deep malaise of the 80s; that lead to the false hopes of the 90s; that ultimately lead to the total implosion of both the structural Church and the traditional family in the dawning third millennium.

As a doctor of the soul, but so too as a fellow believer, I heard the intimate firsthand accounts of generations-upon-generations of confounded Catholics. I heard from those Catholics whose well-intended but compartmentalized piety had failed mightily. I heard from those whose optimistic religiosity had ended in depressive sadness. I heard from those whose triumphant faith had ended in a tragic failure of faith. I heard from those who came from families with an ancient and staunchly Catholic lineage that had succumbed to apostasy when assaulted by the apostate Twentieth Century's materialism, hedonism, and profanity. I heard the firsthand accounts of those who were raised by fathers or mothers who were considered nothing less than pillars of the Catholic community; a father or mother who would *never* miss a daily Mass, but who nonetheless, nay even because of this, were gravely remiss in their parental affection and duties.

I heard of villages and towns that as per Church attendance, vocations, and parish activities were apparently thriving in an idyllic Catholicity, yet underneath—that is, in the recesses of the family and the person—were rotting with sin. I heard from liberal priests, who for all intents and purposes had lost their pre-Vatican II faith along the post-Vatican II way, but who nonetheless remained to function as mock priests, indeed as mock Catholics. I heard from conservative priests in cassocks who preached the pure Gospel from the pulpit but who outside the sanctuary and underneath it all lived a life of putrid impurity. I heard from the cloistered nun who under the auspices of a traditional spirituality was reduced to an infantilism and was thus sinfully manipulated by her superiors. I heard from the middle-aged woman who had entered a still Catholic monastery as a girl but left betrayed and bereft, her youth and hope squandered, as the monastery became infused with secular psychology and new ageism. I heard from the mother who in her faithfulness and generosity courageously bore many children but who then over a post-Vatican II night was considered a fool by even those in the Church. I heard from the mere vestige of a man who had since his boyhood wallowed in the toxins of pornography; and I heard from this man's sons who were steeped in even greater perversities.

While the Church remains the Spotless Bride of Christ, the practice of the Holy Faith by men does not; and the corrupt and festering underbelly of cultural Catholicism, such as it is, is a reality. Admittedly, the above clinical snippets are excessively gloomy, for it is the infected and diseased that come to doctors. As such, the unique insight that has been afforded clinically is not indicative of those concurrent areas of relative health. Nonetheless, this dark underbelly of cultural Catholicism must be taken into account so as to excise it and thus prevent it from infecting those very areas that are more salubrious. As always, the remedy is found in the Holy Cross of Christ, which turned even the ultimate sin of an attempted deicide into the act of an irrefutable redemption.

I. CRUCIAL CHRISTIANITY

If anyone will come after me,
let him deny himself, and take up his cross,
and follow me. MT 16:24

Religion **may either bind man to God** and the divine objective good, or attempt to bind God to man and the egoistic subjective good. With *religio*[15] (Lt.) construed as "binding to," true religion must necessarily bind man to God; for if God is bound to man, then it is really God who exists for man, and then really man who is the god. Man-made religion would be expected to attempt to bind God, indeed reality, to man. And man-made religions abound, be they religions of delayed gratification or religions of opiatic effect. But all man-made religions are but coping mechanisms that either seek to blunt and/or control reality and the God of that reality. That is, man-made religions seek to conform reality to human desires, rather than, as is the dynamics of true religion, to increasingly conform the human person to an ever more overwhelming and piercing reality.

A prime example of a delayed gratification man-made religion—indeed a *man qua male* made religion—is Islam. Islam, in return for a life of devotion to Allah, promises sensual reward after this life, which includes its male devotee's acquiring of numerous female conjugal relations. Another prominent example of a delayed gratification man-made religion—again another *man qua male* made religion—is Mormonism. Mormonism also promises its male devotees multiple female conjugal relations, but in addition offers as the procreative fruit of these relations the megalomaniacal reward of populating one's own planet with these offspring, and ruling over that planet as its god.

Religion as a human invention would also be expected to come up with the opiatic religions as well, religions such as Buddhism, with its dismissal of earthly reality and hence "blissful transcendence" of suffering. Indeed, even much of non-Catholic Christianity is in accord with this expected human invention. Maybe these opiatic religions, as opposed to the male delayed gratification religions, are more appealing to the feminine with their offering of peace and prosperity. A striking and very popular third millennium example of both delayed gratification and opiatic religiosity is that of so-called Evangelical Christianity, with its mantra of assertive positive thinking, "I am saved and I am going to be blessed and prosper," a mentality that certainly can take the edge off this vale of tears.

TRUE RELIGION

But there is one religion that is not at all man-made: the religion of ancient Christianity.[16] For what mere man, that is, a man in his right or even wrong mind, would make up such a religion? From the worship of its God who is a criminal being tortured to death, to the worship of what appears to be a piece of bread, this Christianity is not a human invention. Human invention would devise a worldly victorious savior as the Jews clamored for, or at least a golden calf as they had once devised. But God's ways are not men's ways.

> For my thoughts are not your thoughts: nor your ways my ways, saith the Lord. For as the heavens are exalted above the earth, so are my ways exalted above your ways, and my thoughts above your thoughts. IS 55:8–9

No person in their right mind would ever expect a religion such as Catholicism to sell. Imagine a committee meeting to cobble together this religion. *"Okay, so our God will come to earth under the cloud of shameful illegitimacy, be born in the squalor of an animal stable, and then, threatened with mortal danger, will flee into a dismal exile. Our God will then reappear publicly some thirty-years later for a brief three-years that will conclude with his being rejected by his people and the religious authorities, who will then work in league with the State to sentence him to the most gruesome and degrading capital punishment. Indeed, our very corporate trademark and brand will be the image of our God being executed in his torturous death upon the Cross. We will then place at the center of our corporate worship the reenactment of this torturous death by means of worshiping what appears to be a piece of bread. In keeping with this incipient corporate branding and culture, all of our founding CEOs will be executives in more ways than one—for they too will actually be executed! In fact, all members of our religion will be asked to follow this same way of the Cross as did our God. We will exhort our members to hasten their crucifixion by giving up not only bad things but even the best of things, be they material goods or even the great good of marriage. Sure, our God will rise from the dead and promise such resurrection to his followers, but this promise will be ordered towards these followers willfully embracing their own crosses, their own martyrdoms. Indeed, the persecution and execution of this religion's adherents will be our kickoff campaign to promulgate this religion. Yes, this religion should sell like hotcakes!"*

But that is Catholicism, truly the religion that takes the very greatest faith and that is the most paradoxical to human reasoning. As per faith, just as the Jews could not believe that that bloodied corpse hanging on a cross was the Christ and God Almighty, so too subsequent generations, nay even Christians, would not believe that an apparent piece of bread was that same Christ and God. Indeed, all the plethora of Christian paradoxes emanate from that same Cross and its principle paradox:

> Whosoever shall seek to save his life, shall lose it: and whosoever shall lose it, shall preserve it.
> LK 17:33

But the Catholic Faith is not a blind faith and its inherent paradoxes are not unreasonable. For while Catholicism calls for the greatest faith, it also admits of the fullness of reason. That is, Catholicism is at once and the same time the religion that both takes the most faith and is the most reasonable. From the beginning Catholicism was opened to reason, especially the superlative, searing reason of Greek philosophy. No separation of faith and reason here. Indeed, many stay or become Catholics—and this is the best reason—simply because it's true.

There has never been an institution, none even comes close, that has produced the scholarly works of the Catholic Church. This is true not only in the philosophical and theological works produced under the Church but in the scientific works produced as well; it is true in a myriad of other disciplines and arts, from the fine arts to the trades. By the Catholic Church's total openness to reason she necessarily makes herself totally *vulnerable* to reason. For the Church claims absolute certitude, a claim formalized in her assertion of nothing less than infallibility in regards to faith and morals. But with the Church's claim of absolute certitude all an adversary of Catholicism need find is but one formal teaching that is false, or even one that is contradictory, to another formal teaching, to debunk its claim. Catholicism's stupendous intellectual feat is to have woven the myriad of theological, philosophical, and moral truths into an immense and intricate tapestry that is a harmonious and integral whole, with nary a thread of discordance. But how often has the Catholic apologist answered, say for an adversarial Protestant interlocutor, a myriad of questions satisfactorily— and even more than satisfactorily with truths that go beyond even the scope of the question—only to hear but another question. The exasperated Catholic apologist might then ask his questioner, "But what about the 100 answers I just gave?" But those answers don't matter much to most, because in the third millennium truth has lost its mandate.

But Catholicism is true, whether one likes it or not! Which brings this back to the crucial element of the Cross. Complaints are waged against the Church because she is "so hard." But the Church is only as hard as she has to be. That is, though the Church calls and encourages all its members to heroic sanctity, it *requires* nothing more than merely doing good and avoiding evil. The Church is as hard as she must be in that she is as hard as reality demands. So blame not the Church in being true to reality. Blame reality. And, if you must, blame God. Yes, even that which a person doesn't like about the Church *qua* Spotless Spouse of Christ is due to her being indefectibly faithful to Christ and to reality.

Reality, whether we admit or like it or not, has in its essential composition crucifixion. This orientation to, and more so facilitation towards, the cross of reality is the necessary prerequisite of true religion; for the true is that which is in accord with reality. Reality, then, entails crucifixion and Catholicism is the only religion or worldview that leads a person deeper into that reality and crucifixion. Catholicism is the only religion or worldview that leads a person into the very heart of reality where is found Christ Crucified and redemption.

THIRD MILLENNIUM
TECHNARCISTIC MAN

In Jesus Christ's time, and through the vast span of human history, man did not need to be made aware of the cross of existence; of this he was painfully, truly unavoidably aware. Christ did not say to the Jews, "Look, the cross!" They knew the cross full well as the symbol of all that was oppressive, humiliating, degrading, and death-dealing. No, Christ said, "Pick up the cross." That is, intentionally embrace the most painful aspects of existence.

Third millennium's Technarcistic Man is mired in relativistic pride, a pride that leads him to expect, and even delusionally imagine, that reality conforms to his subjective desires. Whereas previous editions of man, though they may not necessarily have liked reality, nonetheless knew that they had to conform to that reality. Technological artifice and material abundance have afforded respites from reality and thus brought about Technarcistic Man and his many unique maladies.[17]

The technarcistic person has ample means to anesthetize himself to reality and affects an unawareness or certain blindness in regards to many aspects of reality and natural law, of basic right and wrong, of even the demands of basic logic; yes, even unto a blindness to something as obvious as God-given gender. But at the root of this technarcistic blindness is the nonrecognition, or at least depreciation, of a person's mortality and subsequently contingency, which are the most radical principles of creaturely human existence. The pathogenesis of this technarcistic unawareness or blindness is a person becoming myopically fixated on himself and his subjective good, and becoming addicted to his subjective pleasure and entertainment.

In addition to the material and technological abundance, third millennium technarcism has been brought about by the advancement of totalitarian ideological, political, and commercial agendas, authorities, and powers. These agendas, authorities, and powers—be their origins in secularism, materialism, capitalism, socialism, or communism—are essentially anti-God, and in the West, and its wide realm of influence, specifically anti-Christic. For a viable God limits these agendas, authorities, and powers. Being anti-God (and thus anti-human) these ideologies, in league with technarcism, end up denying even the most elementary truths of reality and creation; and necessarily so, since God is the author and source of reality. It is thus only the full assent to and lived-out Christian faith that is the efficacious means of liberation from such an enslaving totalitarianism; such a faith not only points the way to the Promised Land but gives the courage to embrace the cross along that way.

IDEOLOGICAL ATHEISM

The third millennium is not an age of faith as in the Holy Faith, but is an age of faith as in a blind, atheistic faith. For the atheistic position is premised on a blind faith that countermands logic and accepts the absurd. The third millennium's technarcistic blindness to reality necessarily entails a blindness to the reality of God, to the real nature of God, and to the real relationship of man to God. However, the rational creature's essential proper act and end is to give glory to God, and this must begin by saying *yes* to God being God and the creature not being God.

Adhering to and not rebelling against the essential reality that God is God, and the creature is not, is the crucial first principle of natural law. Contingency is the most radical principle of human existence because it is the principle of not having to exist. But contingency, even more radically, is also the principle of *having to exist for all eternity*, per God's enduring love of beings created in his immortal image.[18] When one's contingency is realized a person knows his existence has nothing to do with him; he knows that reality, his presence in reality, *indeed his own reality*, has nothing to do with his desires; he knows God is God and he is not. Thus, before the Gospel can be effectively preached to the technarcistic of the third millennium the principle of contingency must become known to them.

A person does not *believe* but *knows* that God exists. This is because the existence of God (or something totally Other that has as its essence existence) is mandated by the constructs of the human intellect and its incessant demands of logic. Conversely, a person believes but cannot know that God does not exist. Atheistic belief, being illogical, is visceral. In atheistic belief, the egoistic passions well up and bind the intellect, with a hateful denial rather than a logical reasoning forming the conclusion. This is not to say that religious belief cannot itself be a reality-denying "opiate," but that its basis in rational, non-faith assent means it need not be.

A close-minded atheism that rejects the possibility of a Supreme Being is untenable for the human intellect. Atheism specifically and necessarily does violence to human logic and leads to intellectual absurdity, as the modern existentialist's own conclusion of absurdity witnesses to. Even a mere agnostic non-entertainment of the question of a Supreme Being is restricting and stifling of the human intellect. For agnosticism is but a delaying tactic that ignores the most pressing issues of human existence and denies the crucial human vocation of seeking the truth at its most absolute.

To believe there is no God, nothing uncreated and thus Supremely Real, is illogical because commonsensically, as well as philosophically, the order of the universe, and even the existence of the universe, must emanate from principles not found in the universe itself. The universe's coming into being, its being set in motion, commonsensically requires another realm or cause that is *totally other* than that of this universe and the realm of empirical existence. To hold that there is such a realm is not a belief but a logical necessity. Human reason knows, *if it can know anything at all,* that this realm of existence has not within it the principles of eternity; that it could not have just always been. Logically there must needs be another realm that is totally Other, that does have as its nature the quality of having always been. Thus, the dictates of human logic require that there be a realm of being upon which the universe's very existence depends, otherwise human understanding necessarily falls into an inextricable web of absurdity.

Because for the human intellect an atheistic position entails a logical absurdity, and even an agnostic position entails the possibility of a logical absurdity, those that hold such positions necessarily do violence to the human reasoning process; and hence to the human concept of truth; and hence to the good and being itself; and hence to the human person as a truth seeker. Positing that God does not exist renders the crucial human vocation as a *seeker of truth, good, and beatitude* empty and tragic indeed. An atheistic life is an absolute absurdity that leaves nothing deeper within a person than a nihilistic void, nothing loftier outside a person than an insistent desire for an illusory divine chimera.

PRACTICAL ATHEISM

Like all men of all ages, Third Millennium Technarcistic Man knows—must know—that God exists. But the technarcistic person is reluctant to accept, indeed often rebels, against existence; against the real, the truth, and the good. To justify this rejection and rebellion a person must adopt either a blind atheistic faith or devise a false god, a god that is somehow separate from reality. While a blind atheistic faith is an illogical proposition for the human intellect and thus renders all absurd, a devised false god, be he the god of a technarcistic Christian or the superstitious pagan, is as well absurdly implored to mitigate reality and creation, a reality and creation that is of the true God. Somehow a believer in such a false god fools himself into thinking that reality can be changed or that God is somehow against the reality he authored. From this disconnect of the God of Reality and the God of Faith comes the nonrecognition or rejection of a myriad of existential realities, from those of the most mundane, such as biological gender, to those of the philosophical, such as natural law principles.

Again, even many Christians in the Third Millennium, instead of being oriented toward existing for God and his glory, deem, at least in practice, that God exists for them; that is, God exists to answer prayers, to make one happy, or to make life bearable. But this is tantamount to a practical atheism, for if God exists for man then God really isn't God but rather a genie in a bottle. Practical atheism can also lead to an ideological atheism. For when the genie in the bottle of one's own devising does not perform as expected a person may well rebel and rightly disbelieve in this false god. However, this doesn't lead to accepting the true God, but rather to the hating of the true God in the embrace of the blind faith of atheism. For the reality one has sought to escape is finally equated with its Divine Author. While unlike those with a false god, those with an atheistic faith at least recognize the relationship between God and reality; the violence done to their reason by this blind faith, in conjunction with their overweening egoistic passions and immorality, often enslaves them in this atheism. That is, a person with a blind, atheistic faith has no false gods save that of himself.

A RADICALLY ORTHODOX ETHOS

Third Millennium Technarcistic Man has heard the Good News but it just doesn't resonate. In fact, much of the Good News, its truths and sentiments, has been co-opted, distorted, and eviscerated by the ascendant anti-Christic culture. Searing truths have become stale pious platitudes that go in one ear and out the other of the technarcistic, yes even of technarcistic Catholics, bypassing both a jaded intellect and hardened heart. Therefore, the need in this Third Millennium to express in no uncertain terms the vitally important truths of the Faith and to dispose hearts to the reception of the cross is at the heart of both reality and the Gospel. A crucial theological ethos, then, is not aimed at presenting a comprehensive compendium of dogma but at presenting the compressed and compelling essence of all dogma, which is Christ Crucified, so as to penetrate the lethargy of the third millennium's technarcistic person.

When a Christian embraces the vitally important Gospel truths he will indeed be conformed to the Holy Cross, and as such, not be subject to scandalization but rather imbued with militant courage. Such a Christian will not, like the sedevacantists, expect too much from the imperfect crew and angrily mutiny; will not, like the conservatives, batten down the hatches and pretend all is well; will not, like the modernists, book passage on another ship destined for another land; will not, like the liberals, jump into the sea and drown in secularity; will not, like the Protestants, question the seaworthiness of the ship and willy-nilly abandon it; rather, such a Christian, intent upon the vitally important truths of the Faith and conforming to the Holy Cross, will heed the call for "all hands on deck," knowing both that the ship is on an unerring course and that it needs to be courageously manned to hasten that course. But, make no mistake, in this stormy, apostate age of malignant anti-Christic hostility and media-fed frenzies of scandal, the Faith is best buoyed by jettisoning overboard *all that is inessential.* For scandal only comes when the essentials of the Faith and that which is accidental or contrary to the Faith is not distinguished. This distinction is both doctrinal and practical, for doctrinally the Holy Cross is true north and, as a matter of practice, all that distracts that course must be jettisoned.[19]

A theological ethos of the essential will stay the course and neither veer to the right nor to the left; it will be neither exclusively traditionalist nor progressive. Nor is such an ethos either conservative or liberal, for it transcends the triteness of politics and repudiates group validation, identity politics, or being in the power curve as having any bearing on what is just, orthodox, and true. But such an essentialist Christian ethos is certainly radical, for it is "rooted" (Lt., *radix*) in the vitally important, timeless, and essential truths of the Faith and thus poised in the present to manifest the cutting-edge of that faith to a world that now denies essence and truth.

Unlike most of the in vogue secularized Christian theologies of the waning years of the second millennium, a crucial theological ethos seeks only to be radically Catholic; that is, it seeks to be radically ordered toward Christ Crucified. Again, such a crucial theological ethos is radical not in presenting newfangled truths but rather in applying the most essential ancient truths of the Gospel and nature in a manner that is most impactive on, and therefore most transformational and witnessing to, the people of the third millennium. As such, this crucial theological ethos is both radically conformed to the traditional truths of the Holy Faith and radically progressive in its implementation of those truths in the current hostile, anti-Christic milieu. A theological ethos is not so much a blueprint for living out the Faith, but an exhortation to do so; and one that is both radically traditional and radically progressive will lead inexorably to the Cross of Christ.

SEVEN CRUCIAL VOCATIONS

The third millennium person's disconnect with natural law and the ensuing prideful subjectivity and absurd intellectual orientation has resulted in a technarcistic ethos that distorts or destroys natural God-given charisms and vocations. As grace builds upon nature, this in turn gravely undermines Christian vocations. As such, a remedying Christian ethos must necessarily be most specific in the enunciation and most intentional in the inculcation of both natural and Christian vocations. Building upon the natural anthropological principles and clinical dynamics of psychomoralitics, the ethos theology of crucialism promotes seven essential human and Christian vocational states. Note well, all but the Electoral Vocation are givens and entail assent rather than election.

Natural	Supernatural
1. Psychomoral Vocation	4. Baptismal Vocation
2. Incarnational Vocation	5. Ecclesial Vocation
3. Familial Vocation	6. Electoral Vocation
7. Sociopolitical Vocation	

1) Psychomoral Vocation

The Psychomoral Vocation entails the human person's call as a rational-volitional being made in *imago Dei* (God's image). Here the psychomoral development of the human person occurs, that is, the ability to receive-the-real, assent-to-truth, and choose-the-good. This entails the acceptance of ego-abnegation for love of objective truth and good and the subsequent ordering of the ego to the intellect and will.

2) Incarnational Vocation

The Incarnational Vocation entails the human person's call as an *imago Dei enfleshed*. Here man's existential vocation as a mortal being in this "valley of tears" and his human incarnational status as either male or female is explicated and embraced in accord with philosophical truth and physiological givens.

3) Familial Vocation

The Familial Vocation is the fundamental locus of the natural human and supernatural Christian vocations. It is in the family that psychomoralitic formation fundamentally takes place. It is the family that is the basic unit of both secular and ecclesial societies. It is the good of the family that determines whether or not the sociopolitical order and the State is valid and righteous. It is in the family that the fullness of gender is expressed and comes to full fruition. It is the family that is the primary place of Christian formation. It is the family that the ecclesial ministries are ordered to serve. It is the family that is the ordinary means of sanctification in the lay State. It is from the family's poverty, chastity, and obedience that comes the blossoming of the evangelical (a.k.a., religious, that is, those in vows of poverty, chastity, and obedience) state. The familial vocation is based on God-given gender and its ensuing dynamics, especially as per wife-mother and husband-father. Via the Familial Vocation and in the familial realm both the preceding Psychomoral and Incarnational Vocations unfold essentially. So too, all subsequent vocational states are intrinsically linked properly to the familial realm by having either their inception in, or ordering to, the family— thus the importance of the family being given the primacy in the education and formation of the human person.

4) Baptismal Vocation

Correlating to and building upon the Psychomoral Vocation and its call to manifest the analogous imago of God, the

Baptismal Vocation is the call to holiness. Building upon the natural vocations and in accord with the traditional spirituality of the Church, the spiritual development of the Christian entails embracing the Cross, where he undergoes purgation and remission of sin, experiences grace and sanctification, and thus gives glory to God. The subsequent Christian vocations exist to facilitate the Baptismal Vocation.

5) Ecclesial Christian Vocation

The Ecclesial Christian Vocation entails the vivification of an informed Catholic conscience and the exercising of the absolute right to do one's duty to God as per that conscience so informed. Here the Church provides the truth and it is then incumbent upon the Christian to be true to that truth. Note well that here it is not the Church but the members of the Church that must be *reformed by being informed* by the Church herself. As grace builds upon nature, the Ecclesial Vocation as the call to incorporation into the Church as the Mystical Body of Christ correlates with and builds upon the Incarnational Vocation, which is the physical body of the person.

6) Electoral Christian Vocation

The Electoral Christian Vocation entails the specific and personal means in which the Christian achieves his crucial Baptismal Vocation (see above). Here the Christian is aided in discerning and living one of the three fundamental Christian vocational states: that of the Christian family, vowed evangelical life, or priestly orders. Each fundamental Christian vocational state has its particular means of self-abnegation (its specific cross) and charism as per the fulfillment of the Baptismal Vocation of sanctification and competency in the Ecclesial Vocation. Finally, the Electoral Christian Vocation also entails any unique, "special" charisms, competencies, or missions an individual Christian may be called to fulfill.

7) Sociopolitical Vocation

The Sociopolitical Vocation entails a person being a member of the community of families and the secular political body via personhood and family. The sociopolitical is properly ordered toward the well-being of the individual and the family. The sociopolitical order, according to the principles of subsidiarity, begins with the grassroots community of families and extends therefrom. It is here, too, that the Church Militant manifests itself by coming in contact with the secular and profane, and bringing about the Kingdom of God and Christendom, be that on the micro or macro level.

VOCATIONAL INTEGRATION

All the vocational states, be they natural or super-natural, build upon one another, are integral, one to the other, and reciprocally impact each other.

The natural Psychomoral Vocation, where the person fulfills his rational-volitional being in an analogous manner to God (that is similar in functionality but not sharing in the nature of God) is thus built upon in the supernatural Baptismal Vocation, where the person fulfills his sanctification (that is sharing in the very nature of God through divine indwelling).

The natural Incarnational Vocation, where the human person fulfills his vocation as a corporal body, is built upon by the supernatural Ecclesial Vocation, where the Christian fulfills his vocation in the Mystical Body of Christ.

The natural Familial Vocation, where the person fulfills his vocation as a member of the essential human society, is built upon in the supernatural Electoral Vocation, which entails the sacramental marital state, as well as the vowed evangelical state, which is a flowering of that marital state, and the ordained state, which is ordered toward the ministry to the faithful (the bulk of which is in the familial and marital state).

CRUCIAL CHRISTIAN EXISTENCE

In this third millennium a Christian must embrace a theological ethos that has a radical intentionality in regards to living out both the natural and the supernatural human vocations. In the past, the natural and most essential human vocations, specifically the human person as an incarnate being in the image of God, were givens that were not in need of an intentional embrace. But today they surely are. Today's Technarcistic Man does violence to his essential difference, and thus to his essential vocation as a rational-volitional being. He is not open to reality, is not receptive to the real, does not heed the mandate of truth, and determines subjectively and egoistically what is the good. Today's Technarcistic Man rejects the limitations of his incarnationality, of its obvious physical limitations and hence humiliations. He anesthetizes himself to its inexorable mortality, and even goes so far as to rebel against its equally inexorable, distinct, and unalterable delineation as male and female.

And today's Technarcistic Man has lost the very locus of the preceding vitally important natural human vocations, which is the family. He has lost not only the essential psychomoralitic formational dynamics that foundationally take place in the family, but again, stemming from his lack of incarnational acceptance, has lost his sense of its very core components, which are man and woman; that is, husband and wife; that is, father and mother. And finally, the third millennium's sociopolitical powers-that-be do violence unto the human person as a seeker of truth and doer of good; unto the person as a vulnerable, mortal, and contingent being; unto the family, which is the essential unit and good of any just sociopolitical dynamics; and unto the God-given gender upon which that family is comprised.

An ethos theology adequately responsive to the malignant anti-Christic third millennium must be stark, as stark as the purgation it prescribes and the crucial truths of nature and grace it pronounces. And it must be bold, as bold as the Holy Cross it exults and the Gospel truths it advances. Such a "crucialism" may seem too stark, too crushing; for it enunciates that the essence of human existence, and *still more* of essential Christian existence, is to be an annihilated burnt offering, a living sacrifice, unto the greater manifest glory of God.[20] But so too, it may seem too bold, too empowering; for it promotes an *imago Dei* individualism that holds as sacrosanct the gifts of reason and free will and the primordial primacy of informed conscience, and thus asserts the absolute right to defiantly do one's duty to God.

It is the very spirit of the Gospel itself that paradoxically, but intrinsically, unites both the stark and the bold, both the crushing and the empowering:

> My grace is sufficient for thee; for power is made perfect in infirmity. Gladly therefore will I glory in my infirmities, that the power of Christ may dwell in me. 2 COR 12:9

Grace is indeed sufficient, for it enkindles and provokes the love of God, which is the ultimate Christian, and thus supra-human, act. It is this charity that imparts both the courage to undergo the stark and crushing existential purgation of the Holy Cross and the boldness and power to lift high that same Holy Cross. Indeed, the embrace of the Holy Cross for love of God imparts peace and joy, which as the very fruits of loving God ease the yoke and lighten the burden along the purgative way unto salvation.

II. Heart of the Gospel

My God, my God,
why hast thou forsaken me?
MT 27:46

At **Jesus Christ's death on the Cross**, the colossal curtain of the temple of Israel was torn in half from *top to bottom*, that is, by the very hand of God. This curtain that shrouded the Holy of Holies was wrought in 72 squares, that gave it a height of 60 feet, a width of 30 feet, a thickness of four inches, and a weight of approximately four tons. The curtain was embroidered with blue, scarlet, and purple thread. It was designed with cherubim who represented the angelic guardians that shielded access to the thrice holy God.

With this rending of the magnificent temple curtain, the Chosen People of God would no longer have their locus in the Jewish people, the bulk of whom had rejected their Messiah and the Son of God, but now with a universal people and universal church. It was within this Universal Chosen People—in each and every sanctified believer—that would reside holiness. It was to this Universal Church that would be entrusted the sacred Deposit of Faith that would be infallibly explicated by her Magisterium until in the fullness of salvation history all was defined, preached, and taught. God, ever faithful to his covenant, would fulfill that covenant and remain present in his faithful people in the One Holy, Catholic, and Apostolic Church.

With the rending of the Temple curtain, the old and unsatisfactory sacrifice of animals would cease and the ever new and superlative sacrifice of the Spotless Lamb of God, Jesus Christ's death on the Cross, would perdure. As a wildly spendthrift gift, and as a gift non-essential and thus stupendously gracious, Christ would make his ceaseless and infinitely sufficient Sacrifice on the Cross immediately present and accessible to all men; the Lord would lavishly squander himself in the gift of his very Body and Blood as the staple spiritual food for his faithful. To administer this and other sacramental gifts, a special sacramental priesthood would pass from Christ to his apostles and their spiritual, ordained descendants. This sacramental priesthood would serve a people who were now themselves a priestly people, taking up to a superlative degree the priestly status of the genetically transmitted Levitical priesthood that no longer ran its course.

As prophesied, ancient Jerusalem would be destroyed and the people of Israel would be dispersed among the nations. Simultaneously, the Catholic Church would arise from the blood of martyrs, truly from the ashes of a razed Jerusalem herself, and this blood would seep into all nations. This was the *great purification/transformation of the Chosen People of God*, akin to the *great purification/ transformation of humanity* that occurred with the Flood, where initially in both cases most were lost, but nonetheless marked the beginning of a radically new order and dispensation.

THE PRELIMINARY GOSPEL

The Lord God always chastises his people. He purges them of that which is unclean and sinful by emptying them of that profane pride which is an unrightful claim. Likewise, he would also come to them by the very emptying of himself of his rightful claim. This *kenosis* (Gk: κένωσις, "the act of emptying") is the very essence of the Gospel, this kenosis is the very *sine qua non* and *raison d'etre* of the Second Person of the Holy Trinity's incarnation. Yes, to become man, Christ emptied himself of that which was rightfully his. This kenosis was the antithesis of man's (and the fallen angels') prideful rebellion. Whereas the Son of God, though God, did not hold equality with God something to be grasped at, man, though a mere contingent creature, *did* (and does) hold equality with God something to grasped at.

> For God doth know that in what day soever you shall eat thereof, your eyes shall be opened: and you shall be as gods, knowing good and evil. And the woman saw that the tree was good to eat, and fair to the eyes, and delightful to behold: and she took of the fruit thereof, and did eat, and gave to her husband who did eat. GN 3:5–6

But though Christ's human life began with kenosis, and was continually marked with the abnegating sign of the Cross, his ministry did not begin with his explicit preaching of the Cross, which in his day, as in all days, was a hard saying (and which in this day is especially so). Indeed, Jesus, in this period of introduction, early on in his ministry reached the height of his popularity. Though Our Lord would end his ministry by the turning of wine to blood that derived from imminent sacrificial spilling of that Blood, he would begin that ministry with the turning of water to wine to provide for the imminent celebratory spilling of that wine.

> And the third day, there was a marriage in Cana of Galilee: and the mother of Jesus was there. And Jesus also was invited, and his disciples, to the marriage. And the wine failing, the mother of Jesus saith to him: They have no wine. And Jesus saith to her: Woman, what is that to me and to thee? My hour is not yet come. His mother saith to the waiters: Whatsoever he shall say to you, do ye. JN 2:1–5

And he and she knew full well that this very first public miracle was not a mere miracle of conviviality, but the most solemn launching of their march to the hour of crucifixion. When he asked her, "What is that to us?" Mary saw in the depths of his eyes exactly what it was for them. Indeed, Jesus in his graciousness allowed his mother to begin his hour with her freely given "fiat," just as he had allowed her to freely choose to begin his very human existence.

This preaching of the introductory Gospel would commence with the casting out of evil spirits, the healing of the sick, and the feeding of the hungry. The fervid result being,

> Now those men, when they had seen what a miracle Jesus had done, said: This is of a truth the prophet, that is to come into the world. Jesus therefore, when he knew that they would come to take him by force, and make him king, fled again into the mountain himself alone. JN 6:14–15

THE HEART OF THE GOSPEL

Surely Our Lord Jesus Christ knew that as he healed the lame and fed the hungry he was appealing to the masses' self-interest and reaching a height of popularity based not on the essential Gospel message but on almost accidental ramifications of that Gospel.

But this preliminary Gospel was the door to the *heart of the Gospel*. Ultimately, why did Christ heal the lame? So that now enabled, these healed could pick up their cross and follow him.

> Then Jesus said to his disciples: If any man will come after me, let him deny himself, and take up his cross, and follow me. For he that will save his life, shall lose it: and he that shall lose his life for my sake, shall find it. MT 16:24–25

And why, ultimately, did Jesus feed the masses with the most delectable—and free!—fishes and loaves? So that once they were literally eating out of his sacred hands, he could proffer them the apparently and shockingly unkosher fruit of his crucifixion, his very Flesh and Blood,

> For my flesh is meat indeed: and my blood is drink indeed. He that eateth my flesh, and drinketh my blood, abideth in me, and I in him. As the living Father hath sent me, and I live by the Father; so he that eateth me, the same also shall live by me. This is the bread that came down from heaven. Not as your fathers did eat manna, and are dead. He that eateth this bread, shall live forever. These things he said, teaching in the synagogue, in Capharnaum. Many therefore of his disciples, hearing it, said: This saying is hard, and who can hear it? JN 6:56–61

Though the Blessed Virgin Mary, when allowed to hasten Our Lord's hour at the wedding feast, said to the servers,

"Do whatsoever he shall say to you," which they did, and subsequently freely partook of water turned to wine, the Lord would later be refused when he told them to "eat my flesh and drink my blood." Indeed, as Christ's ministry went to the heart of the Gospel, his increased preaching of crucifixion would *facilitate* his crucifixion. His popularity would wane, his conflict with religious authorities gain, and those very ones who would seek to force him to be king would end up forcing the State to "crucify him!" (LK 23:21)

The heart of the Gospel is the heart of crucifixion. No, though it gives heart, the Resurrection is not the heart of the Gospel. In fact, though the Resurrection is joyful and glorious beyond comprehension, it is not all that amazing. No, it is *not amazing* that God Almighty could raise himself, or anyone else for that matter, from the dead. Rather, the Resurrection shows that Jesus Christ is indeed God, that, dumbfoundingly, he who underwent a gruesome crucifixion and death was indeed God Almighty! Though Christ Resurrected is the joyful conclusion of the Gospel, it is *Christ Crucified* that is its crucial culmination. Our Lord did not come into the world to be resurrected but to die, "to give his life for the redemption of many." The glorious light of the Resurrection then reflects back onto the Crucifixion, which was the specific act of redemptive love. Conversely, man (at least man in touch with the reality of existence) expects to suffer and die, to be crucified. "For we know that every creature groaneth and travaileth in pain . . . ." It is man's partaking in the Crucifixion, of dying to himself and then partaking of the Resurrection and living divinely, that is mindbogglingly unexpected, for ". . . even till now for it is the redemption of creation and of man's own mortal flesh" (RM 8:22). And even until now we assert, "O God, Who by the Resurrection of Thy Son, Our Lord Jesus Christ, hast vouched safe to make glad the whole world . . . ."

Still the joy of Easter Sunday is inseparable from the sorrow of Good Friday. It is only to the degree that one accepts the purgation of mortal existence, of crucifixion, of suffering and death, of humiliation and sorrowful contrition, that one partakes in the divinization of new life, of resurrection, of healing and vivification, of sanctification and joyful transformation. This reciprocity of sorrow and joy, of purgation and sanctification, is completely proportional; for a person's degree of openness to reality necessarily entails both his openness to loss and gain. Indeed, sorrow heightens joy and joy sharpens the pain. But third millennium Technarcistic Man chooses not to know reality, his mortality, his sorrow; and thus he cannot know Christ Crucified, who is in the heart of that reality, the conqueror of that mortality, the giver of joy among that sorrow. Rather, and again as with all man-made religion, today's Technarcistic Man is even apt to misuse the Gospel itself to escape reality.

At the heart of reality is indeed Christ Crucified. And the reality, the nature, of Our Lord's passion, was that of the most extreme physical torture; a torture and death he underwent for man's sake. But there was a qualitatively and infinitely greater reality to Our Lord's Passion. Christ's Passion at its deepest was his experiencing in his human nature separation from God, the very experience of being forsaken and damned,[21]

> For our sake he made him to be sin who did not know sin, so that we might become the righteousness of God in him. 2 COR 5:21

THE CHRISTIAN IMAGE
IN THE GOSPEL

Could one surmise that the Good Thief St. Dismas, who was saved as he hung on the cross, not able to see the face of Christ due to being at the Crucified Christ's side, saw only the sorrowful countenance of the Blessed Mother? If so, St. Dismas saw Christ magnified in Mary's countenance, this being the truest sense of *Co-Redemptrix*,[22] as he was undergoing his agony and conversion. For it is the Blessed Virgin Mary, who being absolutely open to reality and its Author, entered into the full sorrows of Good Friday and the full joys, indeed glories, of Easter Sunday. It was the same Sorrowful Mary, who magnified in her soul Our Lord's Passion on the Cross, that magnified in her soul the glory of the Risen Lord on Easter morning. Indeed, as per holy tradition, the Lord verily rose unto his Mother Mary on Easter Sunday. And what else explains his initial absence, scripturally unaccounted for, that first Easter morning? Indeed, this event would need be an unaccounted mystery because it is too glorious for mortal men to comprehend. It may well be surmised that Our Lady beheld the beatific vision on earth! This Easter morning mystery correspondingly entails Mary being as gloriously one with Christ resurrected as she was sorrowfully one with him crucified.[23]

The Blessed Virgin Mary is a soul that magnified the Lord. She lived her human existence in the fullness of its sorrow, joy, and peace. She always responded *"yes"* to God, whether it was to the incomparable joy of his incarnation in her womb, or to the consummate sorrow of his sacrifice on the Cross, or to the supreme glory of his Resurrection. It was Mary alone who shared most intimately in the Passion of Good Friday;

hence it was Mary alone who rejoiced most fully in the triumph of Easter Sunday.

As God's Immaculate Mother, Mary lived a life most deeply, truly, and fully human. What unimaginable joys she experienced, holding and suckling her God and Savior! With what infinite and ever-expanding joy she was filled when her divine baby gazed into her eyes and smiled and cooed with all the love of he who is love! And what unfathomable, glorious joy was hers at the first moments of his Resurrection. Nor was there ever one who partook in Christ's suffering as she did. It was she whom Our Lord asked in response to her request for wine at the Wedding of Cana, *"What is it to thee and to me?"* that is, *"What is it to us?"* thus showing the intimate bond of his suffering and hers. Then, in honor of her motherhood and in consideration of the Passion she would suffer with him, he graciously submitted to her intercession that hastened his and her journey to Golgotha, though his hour had "not yet come." As mother and son, creature and Creator, silently gazed into each other's eyes and the depth of the coming passion was made known, she once again gave her "yes" to God's will, though it pierced her very heart:

"Whatsoever he shall say to you, do ye." (JN 2:5).

And so it came to pass that just as it was Our Lady's privilege to share in Our Lord's first steps toward his sacrificial death on the Cross, it was her privilege to receive him into her maternal arms after all had been accomplished. It is the Blessed Virgin Mary, full of peace and grace, who is united with God the Father as obedient daughter, with God the Holy Spirit as devoted spouse, and with God the Son as loving mother. By following holy Mary's example and availing oneself of her maternal embrace, one is able to say "yes" to the vicissitudes of existence and thus die to the self-love and pride that disfigures the image of God that is one's authentic self. In and through her Son, the Blessed Virgin Mary models for us the human image of God: for from her his humanity is singularly taken, and in her his divinity is pristinely partaken.

THE MAGISTERIAL IMAGE
IN THE GOSPEL

For man, including the men of the Magisterium, the heart of the Gospel, that is Christ Crucified, necessarily entails humiliation. The divine nature of the Magisterium and the papacy has nothing to do with human wisdom but with a charism given on high by election. It is the Cross and its humiliation that separates and defines the man from the office.

> And Jesus came into the quarters of Caesarea Philippi: and he asked his disciples, saying: Whom do men say that the Son of man is? But they said: Some John the Baptist, and other some Elias, and others Jeremias, or one of the prophets. Jesus saith to them: But whom do you say that I am?

> Simon Peter answered and said: Thou art Christ, the Son of the living God. And Jesus answering, said to him: Blessed art thou, Simon Bar-Jona: because flesh and blood hath not revealed it to thee, but my Father who is in heaven. And I say to thee: That thou art Peter; and upon this rock I will build my church, and the gates of hell shall not prevail against it. And I will give to thee the keys of the kingdom of heaven. And whatsoever thou shalt bind upon earth, it shall be bound also in heaven: and whatsoever thou shalt loose upon earth, it shall be loosed also in heaven. MT 16:13–19

But with the superlative divine charism must come superlative chastisement. If human nature would be the recipient of this charism it must needs be humiliated as well. Was Simon, now Peter, puffed up by this charism, commendation, and elevation? Is the Pope Catholic?

From that time Jesus began to show to his disciples,

> that he must go to Jerusalem, and suffer many things from the ancients and scribes and chief priests, and be put to death, and the third day rise again. And Peter taking him, began to rebuke him, saying: Lord, be it far from thee, this shall not be unto thee. Who turning, said to Peter: Go behind me, Satan, thou art a scandal unto me: because thou savourest not the things that are of God, but the things that are of men. MT 16:21–24

Peter was so full of himself that he actually rebuked Our Lord, and not in some minor detail but in Jesus Christ's very reason for being! This is always the great temptation: for men to avoid the cross and aggrandize the ego, and often it comes on the heels of divine grace and favor. But so too is chastisement and humiliation a divine grace and favor. Peter is the prototype of the papacy, both in his failures and in his charisms.

The man who fills the See of Peter was never so important as in the man Simon Peter. Here, as with the other eyewitness apostles, there was an equation of the man with the office, but still only so far as to demarcate that office's natural authority and limitations. Simon becomes Peter due to a pure gift of God,

> Blessed art thou, Simon Bar-Jona: because flesh and blood hath not revealed it to thee, but my Father who is in heaven. MT 16:17

But immediately, when left to his own devices, he is shown to be no wiser, much less holier, a man than others:

> Get behind me, Satan, thou art a scandal unto me: because thou savourest not the things that are of God, but the things that are of men. MT 16:23

There is the papal charism of Peter that is "of God," and there is the fallen nature of Peter that is "of men." This is the critical demarcation of all God-given charisms.

In short, the papacy and the Magisterium were at their peak importance in the apostolic Church and would proportionally become less important as the Deposit of Faith was excavated into dogma and doctrine. Indeed, all subsequent popes are but shadows of Peter, not only inadequate men, as was Peter, to be Christ's vicar, but inadequate men in regards to Peter himself. Subsequent popes would always be inadequate in their filling of "the shoes of the fisherman." Just as the servant, that is, the Christian, cannot be greater than his master, that is, Christ, so too, no pope, nor bishop, may deem to be or act greater than Peter and the Apostles.

Jesus Christ established magisterial authority, as encapsulated in the Petrine Office, as a primacy permeated with humility.

> That disciple therefore whom Jesus loved, said to Peter: It is the Lord. Simon Peter, when he heard that it was the Lord, girt his coat about him (for he was naked), and cast himself into the sea. But the other disciples came in the ship, (for they were not far from the land, but as it were two hundred cubits), dragging the net with fishes. JN 21:7–8

So Peter, being totally forgiven, was full of his old exuberance. Indeed, the conversation that followed between Peter and Jesus was their first private walk and talk since the Resurrection, and "the third time that Jesus was manifested to his disciples, after he was risen from the dead" (JN 21:14).

What would one expect, from a human perspective, this first conversation between Peter and Jesus to be? Words that only affirmed that all was forgiven, even forgotten, for "I am Risen!" But no, what Our Lord uttered to Peter were words most cruel, most cutting, most unrelenting:

> When therefore they had dined, Jesus saith to Simon Peter: Simon son of John, lovest thou me more than these? He saith to him: Yea, Lord, thou knowest that I love thee. He saith to him: Feed my lambs.
>
> He saith to him again: Simon, son of John, lovest thou me? He saith to him: Yea, Lord, thou knowest that I love thee. He saith to him: Feed my lambs. He said to him the third time: Simon, son of John, lovest thou me? Peter was grieved, because he had said to him

the third time: Lovest thou me? And he said to him: Lord, thou knowest all things: thou knowest that I love thee. He said to him: Feed my sheep. Amen, amen I say to thee, when thou wast younger, thou didst gird thyself, and didst walk where thou wouldst. But when thou shalt be old, thou shalt stretch forth thy hands, and another shall gird thee, and lead thee whither thou wouldst not. And this he said, signifying by what death he should glorify God. And when he had said this, he saith to him: Follow me. JN 21:15–19

Indicative enough, Christ offered no words of forgiveness, for Peter was already forgiven. Peter was already forgiven in his perfect and searing contrition experienced during the very hours of Christ's Passion,

And the Lord turning looked on Peter. And Peter remembered the word of the Lord, as he had said: Before the cock crow, thou shalt deny me thrice. And Peter going out, wept bitterly. LK 22:61–62

But even though Peter was forgiven, Christ deliberately and increasingly drove a dagger into his soul. Why this piercing chastisement, this just and exacting thrice recompense for the thrice betrayal? Because in this piercing Christ would bestow his final and greatest gift unto Peter, a gift that would ensure salvation. In this one and only intimate post-betrayal, post-Crucifixion, and post-Resurrection conversation between the Lord and his vicar, Christ gave unto Peter the gift of an enduring humiliation and sorrow (*read* compunction)[24], a gift that would continually nurture his sanctification, steadfastly ground his august office, and last to the end of his earthly life. Tradition tells us that this purgative compunction endured even unto Peter's death, where, when facing his own imminent crucifixion, all the condemned man could think of was his unworthiness to die as Christ had died; and thus he "was crucified at Rome with his head downwards, as he himself had desired to suffer."[25]

Christ firmly grounded his ecclesial hierarchy in humility

and sorrow. Note that Christ never connotes any monarchical qualities to the office of the apostles or the priesthood, quite the opposite.

> But Jesus called them to him, and said: You know that the princes of the Gentiles lord it over them; and they that are the greater, exercise power upon them. It shall not be so among you: but whosoever will be the greater among you, let him be your minister: And he that will be first among you, shall be your servant. Even as the Son of man is not come to be ministered unto, but to minister, and to give his life a redemption for many. MT 20:25–28

And Peter echoed this himself in his letters,

> Do not lord it over the group which is in your charge, but be an example for the flock. 1 PT 5:3

This humble spirit that Christ imbued Peter with was also meant to imbue the successors of Peter, but did so with less consistent results.

THE ARCH-HERESY OF EUDAEMONISM

Just as Peter's divinely revealed proclamation that Jesus is "Christ, the Son of the living God" is the arch-dogmatic truth of the Holy Faith, so too his very next demonically inspired words that Jesus need not "go to Jerusalem" entails the arch-heresy against the Holy Faith. Yes, all faith and morals can be judged by their relationship to the Holy Cross. Orthodoxy and holiness is always going toward and increasing the embrace of that Cross, and all heresy and sin is always a going away from and the rejection of that Cross. It is indeed satanic to assert that Our Lord, and thus his followers, need not "go to Jerusalem," need not pick up their cross to follow Christ, need not embrace the Holy Cross for redemption.

Though the heresy of eudaemonism is as old as the Shoes of the Fisherman, it is one particularly prevalent in this third millennium. Eudaemonism is the heresy that suffering is not willed by God, but is somehow due to sin, or curses, or just a lack of faith. This is in fact the quintessential Protestant heresy that holds when one is saved he is going to prosper, that if one but asks with enough earnestness he will receive that which he desires. But it is also a heresy prevalent among Catholics today, and even among those that would consider themselves conservative and orthodox Catholics. And again, it is the crucial heresy; that is, it is a heresy that rejects the Christian's need to be "cross-conformed," a conforming that is vital to salvation.

If God does not want us to suffer, then most, if not all, could say that their unregenerated wills are in perfect conformity to God's. And if God does not want us to suffer, so much for his omnipotence in this vale of tears. But God *does* want us to suffer. Indeed, he commands it:

> Then Jesus said to his disciples: If any man will come after me, let him deny himself, and take up his cross, and follow me. MT 16:24

Yes, God does will, even commands, our suffering. It is from this touchstone of Christ Crucified in the heart of the Gospel that the nature of Christianity, the spiritual life, the sacramental life, and all Christian theology, morality, and practice takes its bearings.

Some theologians seek to mitigate the idea that God wants us to suffer by making a distinction between his positive will and his permissive will. But God does positively will, for his greater manifest glory, the sufferings entailed in life and the very death of his creation, either in their absolute animal mortality or in their non-absolute human mortality. God does positively will that persons created in his image have the freedom to love and thus either serve him or sin. And though God does not positively, but permissively, allow sin, he knew from all eternity sin would happen. God thus positively wills that sin resolves in either purgative humiliation and sorrow, or punitive damnation and punishment.

SUFFERING IS NOT A MYSTERY

Though oft times it is said, "Suffering[H1] is a mystery," it is not. Suffering makes sense when it is recognized that all creation was created for God's greater manifest glory, that the human person was created to be a soul that magnifies the Lord. In short, the universe is an altar and all creation is a sacrificial offering unto God for his greater manifest glory. However, suffering does not make sense if a person thinks God created him for *one's own sake* as opposed to for God's sake. If God created the *imago Dei* person merely to be happy then suffering is a mystery, because maybe that person, and more and more often for the technarcistic, would rather not exist, would rather remain blissfully non-existent.

Suffering is inherent in being a creature and this inherent suffering is a necessary catalyst to achieve one's end as a creature created in God's image. Indeed, if a creature in God's image was without suffering, that is, without an awareness of his limitations (his contingency), without the awareness that God is God and he is not, then he would necessarily degrade into a demon in his delusion of self-sufficiency, that is, in his delusion of being a deity. Choosing the suffering of being a creature, in recognition of who God is, allows the *imago Dei* creature to ultimately manifest God and thus, in the process, achieve beatitude.[26]

Though suffering is not a mystery it is nonetheless confounding when one is in the throes of it. For it is the nature of the deepest suffering to not be able to cope with it, but to be overwhelmed by it. However, this calls for *suffering well for love of God*. Even though God's will confounds one, saying *yes* to his will for love of him makes perfect sense. Indeed, Jesus Christ in his human nature did exactly this as he hung confounded and forsaken on the Cross.[27]

Christians can trust in Divine Providence that all is for God's greater glory. So too, they can have faith that the vicissitudes of life, suffering, temptation, even the allowance of sin itself, is permitted as the best possible scenario to bring about this glory, which necessarily entails the best possible scenario for the bringing about of the Kingdom of God and man's sanctification as well. The good news is not that life is a bowl of opiatic cherries, but rather that life, being in reality crucifixion, can be courageously and fully entered into, totally embraced; and in its very center is found Christ Crucified, the sanctification of suffering, and the redemption of human existence.

III. Ecclesial Kenosis

For what doth it profit a man,
if he gain the whole world,
and suffer the loss of his own soul?
MT 16:26

There has always been a divine purification that separates the sheep from the goats. From the Great Flood and the purification of humanity, to the many defeats, exiles, and chastisements throughout the ancient history of Israel, unto the diasporic destruction of the Temple itself that brought forth the Catholic Church. Indeed, such a purification is the very hallmark of God's enduring presence with his chosen people. As such, this purification is the hallmark of the Holy Catholic Church; a Church that, in this apocalyp*esque*[H2] third millennium, is undergoing the culmination of a most pronounced *ecclesial kenosis*. This kenosis of the Church is in emulation of her Groom, Jesus Christ,

> Who, existing in the form of God, did not deem equality with God something to be grasped, but rather emptied Himself, taking the form of a slave . . . . PP 2:6–7

Ecclesial kenosis[28] entails a purification of the Church of not only that which is vicious and sinful, but even of that which she might rightly claim but nonetheless now encumbers her efficacy, impedes her mission, and obscures her true countenance. This ecclesial kenosis, if accepted, will produce a distillation of that which is crucial: it will separate the essentials from the accidentals that obscure them; it will free the divinely mandated from the human inventions that encumber them; it will purify the revealed truth from the extraneous ideologies that compromise them. As such, a God-ordained and humanly acquiesced to ecclesial kenosis empties the Church of that which are paltry prerogatives, ostentatious posturings, and worldly ways.

The following highly select red-letter salvation history isn't meant to be a condemnation of the policies and practices of Christendom I. For even the policies and practices that imposed influence and demanded allegiance through coercive political trappings and means can be praised for the great good accomplished, and not only in spite of these political trappings and means but through them. But the Church that forgoes such political trappings, its mundane means, and more so its machinations instills her influence in the individual conscience, evokes an allegiance unparalleled, and in doing so establishes a God-ordained, and thus absolute, monarchy. It is only such an allegiance and such a monarchy that will suffice for the thriving of a Christendom—be it in the heart, family, or society—in the third millennium.

SALVATION HISTORY

Salvation history is ensconced in secular history. But salvation history, like the Church herself, transcends the secular. Salvation history ever moves forward in the advancing of Christ's kingdom, even in, maybe especially in, secular defeat. Salvation history highlights the divine impetus as it pulsates through the Church in her specific mission to proclaim the Good News, promulgate truth and holiness, and inexorably advance the Kingdom of Christ. Salvation history is simplistic in comparison to other histories, for it deems all the accidentals of history, be they of political, social, or ecclesial relations, personality cults, cultural accouterments or encrustations, as only of import so as to identify them indeed as accidentals. In the following salvation history of ecclesial kenosis, these accidentals are noted as having served their purpose, for better or for worse, but in any case as purged or purgeable so as to manifest the Church in her essence as the Spotless Bride of Christ.

Salvation history has but one rhyme and reason: what God is bringing about through the triumphs and failures, the martyrdoms and betrayals, the miracles and scandals. And salvation history has but one given: that God's will, the advancing of his Kingdom, will not be thwarted, neither by the flesh, nor by the world, nor by the devil, nor by the very men of the Church herself. This truth is clear as per Catholic salvation history: the Church is pristinely indefectible despite the grave defectiveness of her people and churchmen.

From Peter to the present, popes have betrayed Christ; from the apostles to the present, prelates have been cowardly; from the beginning to now, there have been Judas priests; from the Jews to the Catholics, the masses have screamed, "Crucify him!" And in betrayal, and in cowardice, and in crucifixion, Our Lord Jesus Christ and his Holy Church advance steadily through time, with his and her countenances miraculously made evermore clear as the Kingdom advances. This is the miracle of the Catholic Church, this is the irrefutable proof of her divine nature and of her being sustained by the Holy Spirit: that she has survived the scoundrels who have made up too great a portion of her faithful: her people, priesthood, prelature, and papacy.

The following select snippets of salvation history pertains to the purification of accidentals that besmirched the Church in order to facilitate the taking of one's bearings in today's third millennium age of the laity and subsequent institutional decentralization. The following may be characterized as negative, but such a negativity at leastwise purges any rose-colored triumphalistic views from the history, and this negativity only turns to pessimism if the reader loses sight of the superlative good that comes out of repentance and purgation.

Whereas the following is a macro view of Christendom's first 2,000 years of salvation history as it pertains to ecclesial kenosis, the micro view of salvation history would be the story of each individual soul. Both of these macro and micro salvation histories differ from common histories that recount settings and relations that are almost accidental to a salvation history. What is deemed most important in salvation history is what is deemed most important in a Christian's salvation. So just as the essence of the Christian life is the purgation and sanctification of the person—the purification of all that besmirches the natural image of God and the decreasing of his egoistic self so as to facilitate the sanctifying increase of Christ—so too this dynamic is the essence of salvation history, of the Church, of the Christian people, indeed, of the world itself.

APOSTOLIC CHURCH

Contrary to the narrative of the progressive aggiornamento[29] and ressourcement[30] theology, and even a reductionistic and/or Protestant theology, that has been dominant in conjunction with Vatican II, the call for a more egalitarian Church does not find its justification in the model of the early Church. While there was indeed holistic lay communities of families that were the precursors of monasticism itself, the early Church was at the peak of its apostolic authoritativeness. Both this lay familial locus and apostolic authoritativeness coexisted:

> And they were persevering in the doctrine of the apostles, and in the communication of the breaking of bread, and in prayers. And fear came upon every soul: many wonders also and signs were done by the apostles in Jerusalem, and there was great fear in all. And all they that believed, were together, and had all things common. Their possessions and goods they sold, and divided them to all, according as every one had need. And continuing daily with one accord in the temple, and breaking bread from house to house, they took their meat with gladness and simplicity of heart; praising God, and having favor with all the people. And the Lord increased daily together such as should be saved. ACTS 2:42–47

The early Church was the apostolic *qua* apostles' Church. As such, it depended and respected not only the episcopal office, but the very persons of the apostles. These apostles were the eyewitnesses, and from them came the enunciation of public revelation, as the Church teaches that all such revelation ended with the death of the last apostle. Peter was not only the Vicar of Christ but worked the greatest of miracles, second only to Christ.

And they all being put forth, Peter kneeling down prayed, and turning to the body, he said: Tabitha, arise. And she opened her eyes; and seeing Peter, she sat up. And giving her his hand, he lifted her up. And when he had called the saints and the widows, he presented her alive. ACTS 9:40–41

But even at this ontological apex of the authority of the persons who were the apostles there were no monarchical trappings. Worldly and monarchical power would be claimed to such a degree as to be scandalous, though in directly *opposite* proportion to the decreasing importance of who that bishop or pope was. Indeed, as a baseline ideal, Peter's humility was legendary, even excessive. As per the final legend of his life, that of his death, attests he was quite unable to bear the thought that he should die as did the Lord Jesus Christ, and so asked to be crucified upside down.

POST-APOSTOLIC CHURCH

The curses and blessings of the State were catalysts for the early Church. Yes, it is proverbial that the blood of the holy martyrs, all victims of the State, established the Church in the very soil that it seeped into. But so too did the benevolence of the State, though not in such a crucial and indelible way as the blood of the martyrs, influence salvation history. So as the blood of martyrs' dries, Christianization is complete politically, but incomplete culturally,

> The year 538 A.D. became the turning point in the history of the Roman Empire since so many aspects on political, administrative and economical levels were already switched off that when Justinian declared himself to be a theologian from this year and no longer a soldier, he crossed the barrier of his mandate between what is purely civil obligation and what is religious obligation, similarly to Constantine before, and entered in competition with the papal function and this role is evidence of Justinian's ongoing caesaro-papism. The quest for unification of the empire by unification of the church, the fever for church-building projects with his wife Theodora, the persecution of enemies of the church and heretics, his disdain with the Sabbath although his second name was Sabbatini, his support for suppressing any eschatological fever in line with the church fathers and Oecumenius and yet trying to build the 'Kingdom of God' on earth, all this indicated the problem was for the Roman Empire and the Catholic Church.[31]

The threat of a "friendly" State that, through welfare, sought to co-opt the Church via a voracious caesaropapism was to be met by that Church with an equally voracious papal-caesarism. This may well have been necessary pastorally and politically to protect the Church's divine prerogatives, but was not necessary to her mission or even her orthodoxy. It is papal-caesarism that endured in an ultramontanism of overreaching papal prerogatives and the Church still suffers from it to this day.

But the alternative model of the Eastern Churches was even more inadequate and, truly, fatal. For the Eastern Churches are not really autocephalous but rather encephalous; that is, beyond appearances and posturing they have no earthly head save Caesar. Regional patriarchs cannot provide universal nor ultimate headship. In the Eastern Church this deficiency is intrinsic and its void is filled by the political powers that be. Though the Catholic Church has no such intrinsic deficiency, she is nonetheless vulnerable to the viciousness of her members. In her inherent autocephalic state, the Catholic Church may also, and has, fallen into an ultramontanism. Ultramontanism, at best, in an overreaction to encroaching secular power or caesaro-papism, claims for the papacy and Magisterium powers beyond their competency. The spirit of ultramontanism manifests itself all the way down to priestly orders as clericalism. The result being, that after the truly nourishing blood of martyrs dried, Catholicism grew in a union with monarchical power: first with Catholicism being supported, and to some extent usurped, by that power; then with the Church heavily influencing that monarchical power; and finally by a fusion of the papacy and monarchies. This fusion entailed both individual monarchies becoming united with the papacy and the papacy itself assuming an, even supreme, monarchical status. (See below, § *Three Crowns*.)

FIRST MILLENNIUM
CHURCH COUNCILS

Each antecedent council of the Church, of each antecedent millennium, paved the way for subsequent councils. Thus, in the first millennium Christology had to be defined first and foremost, before other dogma, such as sacraments, was defined in the second millennium. These dogmatic definitions of Christ purified an emerging Christendom of heretical, indeed essentially non-Christian, elements. It was the Holy Catholic Church's defining of Christ's nature that determined who was Christian or not, even if they be non-Catholic Christians.

The First Council of Nicaea (325) affirmed that Jesus is truly God and equal to the Father, repudiated Arianism, and adopted the Nicene Creed. In the subsequent 100 years, follow-up councils would reaffirm and define this Christology. The First Council of Constantinople (381) affirmed that Jesus was perfectly man; the Council of Ephesus (431) affirmed that Jesus is both true God and true man in one person and, thus necessarily, proclaimed the Virgin Mary as the "Mother of God"; the Council of Chalcedon (451) further defined the dogma of the Council of Ephesus and affirmed that in Jesus there are two distinct natures in one person that are hypostatically united "without confusion, change, division or separation." The Third Council of Constantinople (680–681) affirmed that Jesus had both a divine and human will. The essential work of the Christological councils complete, the Council of Trent would, for all intents and purposes, wrap up and set in stone its predecessors' dogmatic definitions.

Necessarily, the living Magisterium was working itself

out of its most urgent and essential job as it unpacked and defined the Deposit of Faith entrusted to it. Peter, as the foundational slab of the Church, was destined from the beginning to become obscured under the fully erected edifice he facilitated. Thus, in the third millennium, and providentially so, due to totalitarity and personality being empowered by technology, the living magisterial office holders are less important than ever, taking a backseat to the Church it made clearly and definitively manifest. But paradoxically, apparently as a compensation, the less dogmatically important the living office holders of the Magisterium became the more ecclesial, political, worldly importance they claimed. But while it would be hard to argue that there was not some need for papal political posturing, the fact remains that political leaders like Charles Martel (688–22 October 741), or Charlemagne (2 April 742–28 January 814), or El Cid (Rodrigo Díaz de Vivar (1043–10 July 1099) each did more individually to preserve the Christian West than all the political popes combined. Indeed, it was these men that brought about Christendom, the leadership of which would subsequently be greatly usurped by the papacy.

PORTENTOUS PAPAL PRETENSES

While the scholarly, religious, financial, and cultural achievements of the Catholic High Middle Ages cannot be overly commended, the magisterial overreach and hubris cannot be roundly enough condemned. During this time popes were eagerly carving out their worldly kingdom. Gregory VII (1073–1085) declared that popes have the right to depose kings and to make and revoke secular laws; Innocent III (1198–1216) proclaimed that he was ruler of the world; and Boniface VIII (1294–1303) summed it all up by voraciously proclaiming, "I am Caesar, I am the Emperor," and wore a crown covered with over 200 rubies, emeralds, sapphires, and large pearls.[32]

It is this infamous Pope Boniface VIII (Benedetto Caetani, 1230–11 October 1303) who brought the magisterial power grab to its crescendo. Knowing he had inherited a papal office that had acquired an immense worldly power adequate to make himself king of that world, he issued *Unam Sanctam*. In this his Bull of 1302 Boniface VIII stated that since the Church is one, since the Church is necessary for salvation, and since Christ appointed Peter to lead it, it is "absolutely necessary for salvation that every human creature be subject to the Roman pontiff." Or, as J. Nabuco states in his *Ius Pontificalium*:

> Being exempt from all human authority, The Apostolic Lord [the Pope] is crowned with a Tiara and uses it vested with the Sacred Royal Vestments as a sign of his supreme dignity in temporal as well as in spiritual matters.[33]

Or as per the Vatican:

> The Triregnum or the Papal Tiara formed by three crowns symbolizes the triple power of the Pope: father of kings, governor of the world, and Vicar of Christ.[34]

The Catholic triple crown debacle was even more scandalous than the ancient Jews demanding that Samuel and God give them a king, for the papal audacity was akin to Samuel himself seeking to be king!

> "Look," they said, "you are old, and your sons do not walk in your ways. Now appoint a king to judge us like all the other nations." But when they said, "Give us a king to judge us," their demand was evil in the sight of Samuel; so he prayed to the Lord. And the Lord said to Samuel, "Listen to the voice of the people in all that they say to you. For it is not you they have rejected, but they have rejected Me as their king." 1 SA 8:5–7

Rather, the papacy is to heed the Lord's example and flee from worldly honor,

> Jesus therefore, when he knew that they would come to take him by force, and make him king, fled again into the mountain himself alone. JN 6:15

But still, as per any ecclesial kenosis, the *Unam Sanctam* and similar debacles now do the Church a great service by inadvertently demarcating the limitations of papal infallibility and competency. The Magisterium has only moral and religious power, thus it has no coercive power. Yes, its moral and religious exhortation can influence the laity and the laity can, rightly or wrongly, implement politics and warfare in accord with that influence, but the Magisterium cannot do so directly. But the ecclesial kenosis of salvation history was responsive not only in retrospect to the ungodly magisterial hubris of the High Middle Ages. For, with the issuance and subsequent promulgation of *Unam Sanctam* and the apex of papal pretenses to worldly power, soon came the chastising emergence and proliferation of the Black Death, not to mention the ultimate failure of the Crusades and the mutilation of the Body of Christ in the Eastern Schism.

BLACK DEATH

It is hard to argue against the assertion that God chastised medieval Christendom for its magisterial hubris, its new oppressive aristocracy of bishops and cardinals, and in particular the Pope's pridefully grasping at totalitarian authority. The Black Death, which would kill more than half of the population of European Christendom, reached Sicily in October of 1347, in the very wake of Boniface VIII's foreboding papacy. But while the monstrous Boniface was mainly concerned with waging crusades against his own proximate Christian political opponents, overseas the warfare of the Crusades was ongoing through multiple papacies. Tragically, the crusades, though thwarting Muslim aggression to some extent, also sealed the Eastern schism,[35] and in forcefully opening up trades routes also opened the ports of Sicily to the Black Plague. In less than a year the plague spread from Sicily to Italy and across northwestern Europe, infecting France, Spain, Portugal and England. It then would rapidly spread east through Germany and Scandinavia.

The Black Plague was a tragic chastisement of unequal proportions for Christendom. God Almighty's allowance of this devastation should have been a sobering lesson for Catholicism. Most obviously and painfully, the plague was a call to embrace Christ Crucified; to return to the pure, simple, and stark doctrine of the Holy Cross. But this call, as jarring as it was, was not heeded by the ecclesial powers-that-be. While the Black Death brought Christendom to its knees and tested its faith, that faith, at least the magisterial manifestation of it, was found to be wanting. Instead of a reorientation of Christendom to God and Christ Crucified there was a turning from God and the Cross to man and the flesh.

Girolamo Savonarola (21 September 1452—23 May 1498) was the most prominent Catholic voice to denounce the increased worldliness and neo-paganism of post-plague ecclesial and sociopolitical authorities. As per Orestes Brownson,[36]

> The passion for heathen literature and art in the time of Savonarola involved in no slight degree the introduction of heathen morals and manners. It exalted Gentile antiquity above Christian antiquity, and threatened through literature and art, and the licentiousness of manners, to corrupt the faith of Christians.[37]

But the aristocratic churchmen and the Church-endorsed aristocrats put Savonarola to death as they continued to increase their worldliness and obstinately rebuff the chastisement of the Black Death. There would be no renewal of spirituality or an emphasis on inner conversion. Instead, there was the renewal of pre-Christian pagan culture and an emphasis on the material. In the architecture and building of churches, instead of promoting the austerity of the modest, maternal and simple Romanesque and its earthy rootedness in natural law and the vicissitudes of human existence, there was instead an increase in the gaudiness and ethereal of the Gothic that sought sky-high escape from the humiliation of this vale of tears, sickness, and death. In the composition and commission of art, the straight and narrow forms of robed saints and angels that ascetically subjected the body were replaced by ever so fleshy and curvaceous renditions that sought to obliterate the memory of the plague's wastings and festerings.

In St. Peter's itself, renditions of partially clad women now became acceptable religious art because they had wings attached. Similarly, but less lasciviously, the powerful guardians of God's glory, the angelic cherubim, were now depicted as corpulent baby *putti.* Indeed, St. Peter's itself would be raised to be the biggest possible and most lavish Church, built with the most magnificent structure and adorned with invaluable artwork. But in order to raise funds for St. Peter's the acquiring of indulgences would become the world's first corporate marketing effort and produce the first superstars of sales. It would also produce, or least provide an excuse, for Luther.

PROTESTATION

The horrendous wake-up call of the plague went unheeded; there was no repentance preached by the magisterium but rather a new and increasingly hedonistic humanism was preached and patronized. Following in the very path of the Black Death, the Renaissance would begin in Italy and then spread to the rest of Christian Europe. Because Christendom did not repent, because it did not embrace the lessons of the Black Death (nor even the lessons of the Crusades and Eastern Schism), it would now lose, not human life to a physical plague but spiritual life to the Protestant plague. In their egoistic carnal turn to Renaissance neo-paganism, the men of the magisterium provided an ample, though not justified, excuse for Protestantism.

Protestantism found its catalyst not in the realm of speculative theology but rather in that of manifest morality. Protestantism does not have its origins above the collar but below the belt. It was Luther's inability to live up to his vows of chastity and Henry VIII's inability to live up to his vows of exclusivity that drove their rebellion. However, it was the rampant immorality of Christendom, and especially as it was countenanced in ecclesial circles of power and priesthood, that produced both Luther and Henry VIII. Indeed, all of the immorality can be said to be found initially only in the Catholics, for initially all were Catholic.

The immoral manifestations of Catholic churchmen, especially the prelacy, provided scandal and the opportunity for unwarranted justification from the protesters. The opulent lifestyle of churchmen who flitted around episcopal palaces like spoiled aristocrats or intrigued in political machinations like worldly plenipotentiaries was indeed scandalous, being so much a mockery of the apostolic commission of Christ. It is not that immorality was rampant that was so scandalous, for it is always present here below, but rather that it had become not only acceptable, but part and parcel of a worldview or ethos that was supposedly Catholic. But it wasn't Catholic; and thus the Protestants were right, for if it wasn't Catholic it wasn't Christian. But the truth that the truly Catholic is the truly Christian was lost on the reformers, who threw out the proverbial baby with the bath water. There may be a fine line between courageous prophecy and recalcitrant rebellion, between the orthodox application of the spirit of the law and the protesting heresy of lawlessness. But still confusion is no excuse, for no matter how fine the lines they go in opposite directions: the orthodox one always toward the Holy Cross, the heretical always away.

Luther took seriously his sins of impurity, more seriously than many other priests and prelates, and so needed to separate nature from grace so he could continue to sin with a clear conscience. Henry took seriously his faith, and the propagation of a "Catholic" monarchy, and so he needed to separate that faith from ecclesial authority. But this Protestantism began the de-Christianizing of the West, a process that took only some five hundred years to undo 1500 years of Christianization. This Protestantism, instead of freeing man from the brute dominance of human power structures, rather fueled an authoritarian nationalism that has given rise to today's either existent or incipient totalitarianism. It is only a true Catholicism based in *imago Dei* individualism, the sacrosanct family, and the adherence to one's absolute right to do one's duty to God that can bring about a new Christendom and break the fetters of that enslaving totalitarianism.

COUNTER-REFORMATION

The Church's response to the Protestant rebellion was vigorous. The Council of Trent defined or reinforced all that Protestantism questioned or repudiated, especially the sacramental system, and most especially the doctrine of the Holy Mass and Eucharist. The same council also tightened up morality among the clergy, whose scandalous ranks gave an unjustified excuse to the dissenting Protestants. So too, missionary efforts to regain lost or compromised Catholic populations were enacted and were heroically spearheaded by the newly formed Society of Jesus.[38]

The Counter-Reformation, as the name denotes, was an intense reaction to the overwhelming tidal wave of heresy and rebellion that was Protestantism. With Protestantism also came political rebellion revolution. But in its reactive intensity to both religious and political upheaval, instead of a deepening implementation of the spirit of the law, the Counter-Reformation in most cases doubled down on the letter of the law by reinforcing truths that were under attack, that nonetheless still allowed, and even accentuated, deficiencies and improprieties of the past. This deficient letter of the law implementation led to an over-reactive and disproportional Catholicism that ultimately failed.

The most glaring and grave mistakes not to be rectified, but that were rather exacerbated, during the Counter-reformation were those of false dichotomies. Be the dichotomy of a supposedly inseparable union of the Church and the Crown (*read* state) versus "the people/laity," or the dichotomy of the Papacy versus the Crown, they were equally false dichotomies. In fact, the great bulk of the Counter-Reformation missionary efforts were aimed at bringing about an ecclesial-societal union of a monarchical pope and a papist monarch and opposing all powers that would balk at such a union. Instead of being concerned with the conversion of peoples, that is, the person, the efforts of the Counter-Reformation were concerned about the political conversion of nations to an ecclesial-societal homeostasis.

This misguided and truly soul-sapping cause of an inseparable Church and Crown would ultimately backfire, leading to the downfall of France's *ancien régime* and the resultant and lasting waywardness of the Church's "eldest daughter," to the complete loss of Britain and its extensive empire, and to the loss of much of the Germanic lands. Nay, even the Spanish brand of Catholicism that passed relatively unscathed through the Reformation and various revolutions was in the long run, and even short term (see *Armada* below), not favored by the God of Salvation History. And from France, to England, to Germany, and to Spain, et al., an erstwhile Christendom has in the third millennium become a dystopic, anti-Christic, and socialistic body politic.

In the France of erstwhile Christendom the *ancien régime* consisted of three social estates: the first being the clergy(!), the second the nobility, and the third the commoners. Prelates were normally aristocracy by birth, and parish clergy were normally commoners by birth. However, when a commoner was ordained he was automatically elevated to non-hereditary aristocracy.

The uprising of Vendée (March to December 1793) was for France the emblematic Catholic response to the Revolution, indeed there were little other responses. As blazingly heroic as the uprising was, it ultimately ended in the tragic genocide of the people of Vendée due to it being hijacked by Royalists of the ancien régime. Again, this *ancien régime* falsely equated Catholicism with the magisterial hierarchy and then inextricably linked this hierarchy with the monarchy, which produced the erroneous dichotomy of a Church and Crown united against all political comers and thus any popular uprisings.

At their inception, the insurrectionists of Vendée concisely called themselves "The Catholic Army." The Catholic Army's insignia was simply that of the Sacred Heart of Jesus, accompanied by the motto "God is the King." This statement, "God is the King," indicated that the Catholic Army's cause was definitely not the cause of the French monarchy and the ancien régime, which was a most significant point to make in light of the general uprising being against a decadent monarchy and aristocracy. Under such a pure cause, Vendée's army of Catholic laity was initially nothing less than miraculously successful (much like the much later efforts of the Mexican Cristeros) in their righteous defense of their Faith and families.

But soon the Catholic Army's leadership was usurped by opportunistic Royalists, most especially princely prelates, who upon seeing the miraculous success of that army came out of hiding. Thus the ever so righteous and victorious Vendée uprising for the defense of Faith and family was misappropriated[39] for the ungodly and doomed cause of the *ancien régime*. Sorrowfully duped, as per their conditioning for centuries,[40] the lay leadership of the uprising, that is, the leadership of Catholic family men, abdicated their office and acquiesced to princes and prelates; thus allowing their cause to be fatally hijacked.

The Royalists subsequently changed the name of "the Catholic Army" to "The Catholic and Royal Army." The flag with its simple image of the Sacred Heart of Jesus had added to it the profane crown of the King of France. The pure motto "God is the King" (*Dieu Le Roi*) was polluted to "God and the King" (*Dieu et Le Roi*). And with these changes came changes in fortune (indeed God's favor) as well. The miraculous victories where now replaced with devastating defeats. So too, any possible recruitment from the at-large French population, or any supportive sentiment or tolerance from revolutionary forces, was effectively eliminated by this Royalist hijacking.

Once taken over for the cause of the *ancien régime*, the army of Vendée would be routed, and not only the soldiers but the populace of Vendée itself would be either killed or forced to flee. The fleeing people of Vendée had their hopes for survival fueled by the expectation that the *ancien régimes* of other countries might soon come to their aid. But help never came, and the people of Vendée were slaughtered in a savage genocide; and nary a priest, much less a prelate, was there to minister unto them in their death agonies.

The false equation of the Church with its priests, prelates, and pope and then the further ungodly union of this "church" with the abusive totalitarian *ancien régime* prevented Catholicism from righteously influencing both French revolutionary ideology and implementation, which assured its atheistic and murderous turn. This false dichotomy of the Church and royalty united against the people would remain in place even after the Revolution and no pure party of Catholic Frenchmen would ever rise up again in the singular and holy defense of Faith and family.

The only truly Catholic answer to the French Revolution would have been to place the French commoner, that is, the common Catholic faithful, as the first estate; with both clergy and state authorities properly serving that estate. But alas, the Catholic cause in France continues to be identified with the integrist cause of the *ancien régime*,[41] and thus the overall lasting waywardness of the Church's "eldest daughter."

In the England of Christendom I there existed two estates, the first being the "lords," which consisted of the nobility and clergy, the second being the "commoners." The State's eventual Anglican involvement in doctrine and the liturgy was preceded by the Catholic Church's involvement in diplomacy and politics. Therefore, in England the Magisterium paved the way for a King who was head of the Church by its obliterating of the lines between Church and State, specifically papacy and crown, nobility and clergy.

Here it will be useful to briefly examine the Counter-Reformation's strategy for the re-Catholicization of a heretical and schismatic England. Though the Counter-Reformation was a heroic effort, it was a misguided and dismally failed effort. In this Jesuit spearheaded movement, the emphasis was exclusively on the Holy Mass and as such entailed the promulgation of priestly influence as well. In this effort, the laity, and most especially the lords and gentry, were relegated to shuttling around and providing hiding places for priests.

The belief of the Counter-Reformation was that if the gentry and their commoner constituents were dedicated enough to the cause of the priest and the promulgation of the Holy Mass then the country would be regained for Catholicism. The Jesuits thus sought, and have always sought, to influence the highest levels of society to achieve such dedication. As such, the Jesuits final objective in England was to say Mass in Windsor Castle itself, thus "capturing" the king and the nation. To achieve their ends, and because they ardently espoused the papacy-crown model, the Jesuits bent over backwards to show support for the now Anglican aristocracy and royalty of England.

But had the Counter-Reformation been ordered toward empowering the faithful, and had the Jesuits' efforts been ordered to ministering unto these faithful, a grace-emboldened Catholic populace would have at least been poised to do their God-given duty to speak truth to power and wage good against evil. Instead, as the infamous Guy Fawkes[42] incident is an example of, Church authorities did not want to rock the sociopolitical boat and so sold out the lay faithful, as they had done in previous monarchies, and as they would in the future do successively in Ireland, Mexico, pre-World War II Germany, Communist China, and numerous less prominent instances.

The Faith was lost in England despite the Jesuit's heroic efforts. In the misguided effort to re-Catholicize England, the few remaining recusant laity ended up existing for the priests, almost as if to say, "So long as we have a Mass, the rest can go to the devil." An effective English Counter-Reformation, or at least a more organically Catholic one, would have had the priests existing for the succor of the laity, ministering unto them as they go into battle. Though in England the laity did get into trouble for harboring priests, they should have instead gotten in trouble by directly rebelling against a totalitarian and evil State, and the priests should have morally abetted and sacramentally succored the laity in their tribulations.

Meanwhile, in erstwhile Germany's Christendom there were three estates: the first being that of the nobility, that is, of princes and prelates. Again, this enmeshment and total identification of the Church with worldly and often enslaving political power was not only foolish, but materially heretical as well. In 1530 Rhineland princes either chose Protestantism or Catholicism, which legally meant that every person in their principality either remained Catholic or became a heretical Protestant.[43] So much for individual informed God-given conscience; but it mustn't be glossed over that the German populace that acquiesced to such an abomination had been Catholic for centuries, and thus so much for their informed, rather deformed, Catholic conscience.

One may be tempted to opine that at least with Catholic Spain there was an adequate compensation for the grave losses that occurred in the widespread Protestantization of Christendom. However, the Spanish Catholicism that colonized the New World does not in retrospect seem particularly favored by the Lord of Salvation History. Here a brief evaluation of the defeat of the Spanish Armada is indicative.

Even Spaniards at the time of the Armada's annihilation recognized the will of God, as confounding and contrary as it was to their own sensibilities. The Spanish ambassador in Rome wrote to one of the Armada commanders that the defeat "was God's will" and thus attributed no "fault" to the commander. A Jesuit Spanish priest, and firm supporter of the conquest of England, Pedro de Ribadeneira, wrote:

> The judgments of God are most secret, so that we cannot know for certain the purpose of his Divine Majesty in the extraordinary fate He has decreed for the king's powerful fleet. Nevertheless, seeing that the cause was so much His, and was undertaken with such a holy intent, and was so much desired and assisted by the whole Catholic Church, the fact that He was not moved by the pious prayers and tears of so many and such great devotees makes us fearful that there are serious reasons why Our Lord has sent us this affliction... So that it is both necessary and advisable to seek and consider the causes that may have moved God to punish us in this way.[44]

But this quite manifest Divine disapproval of Spanish Catholicism did not mean there was Divine support for the heretical English. Indeed, immediately after the victory, the English fleet was smote with typhus, resulting in the death of thousands of English sailors. So no, it wasn't in support of murderous Elizabethan Protestantism, but rather the providential assertion that the advancement of Spain's brutal brand of inquisitional Catholicism was a greater evil than even a Protestant England; for such a Catholicism would have gravely besmirched the true countenance of the Church.

If not for the providential defeat of the Spanish brand of Catholicism, would the rise of a new and truer Christendom in the 21st century be possible? Spanish Catholicism was rife with arrogant elitism and a subsequent infantilism toward the lay commoner that translated into an ease with the enslaving of conquered indigenous peoples. Spanish Catholicism also had an ease with coercion and torture and, like the high priests in Christ's time, did not hesitate to use the totalitarian State to do its dirty inquisitional work.

In the end, no new Christendom arose in the new

world colonized and converted by Spain. Rather what did arise was a rule of autocratic military juntas that have subsequently given way to an equally autocratic, and even more murderous, socialism. The Jesuits again spearhead this colonization. The Jesuits, via liberation theology,[45] would also spearhead the subsequent socialism that was to come to the Hispanic regions of America.

CONTRA COUNTER-REFORMATION

Overall, the Counter-Reformation (and its long-lasting impetus) was unresponsive to the need to instill in the individual Christian an informed Catholic conscience and the zealous courage needed to heed that conscience, and thus it was doomed to fail. Sometimes this failure was immediate, as in all the Protestantized regions, but eventually it occurred in all the compromised or semi-Protestantized regions, and finally in all of Christendom. The Counter-Reformation issue was wrongly framed, and thus the battle wrongly waged. The Catholic issue was not papacy versus monarchy nor papacy-monarchy versus State. Rather it was, and always is, a question of Christ Crucified and his Spotless Bride arrayed in all her truth *versus* evil, worldly powers, and demonic principalities.

> For what doth it profit a man, if he gain the whole world, and suffer the loss of his own soul? MT 16:26

And, by divine providence, Catholicism did lose the world. Yes, the Church needs to be involved in the world and she used the world at times so as to find the freedom to grow without the coercion and stifling of a Caesaropapism. But all too soon the world began to use the Church, which beckoned her to forgo the realm of the world and seek instead the realm of the individual heart. The lesson to be learned and applied from Christendom I in this third millennium is that it is not about the crown and papacy but about faith and family; it is not about politics and intrigue but piety and holiness; it is not about priests, prelates, and popes but all about the faithful of God and their heroic witness and sanctification.

IV. Vatican I

My kingdom is not of this world. JN 18:36

The grandiose rise of the monarchical papacy began in the dawn of the second millennium and ignominiously ended in that millennium's twilight as the Papal States were conquered and the pope vanquished as a temporal leader.[46] In short, Christendom was lost, and with it the bulk of the Church's worldly kingdom. Schisms, plagues, nationalism, Protestantism, secularism, the *Kulturkampf*, et al., were the weapons employed against the Church in this defeat.

Much of these movements against the Church were given impetus and justification by the very worldliness of Catholics, especially of churchmen: of perfidious priests, princely prelates, and pompous popes. But as with the Cross of Christ itself, where miraculously the weight of sin crushes itself, the weight of worldly attacks against the Church crushes the very worldliness within the Church, thus manifesting to a greater degree her spotless nature.

Yes, persecution only purges away the egoistic dross of the Church's recalcitrant children, decreasing their pride and self-love so as to allow Christ to increase. This intrinsic ecclesial auto-immunity is of the essence of the Church's indefectibility. Through the miracle of the Cross, the very wounds of the Church's members make her ever more comely, their very shamefulness make her ever more glorious.

DETHRONEMENT

To the Church's loss of worldly power, one may say in ascetical hindsight "good-riddance" or, more appropriately, "God-riddance;" for if one is Catholic one must believe in the providence of salvation history, that is the indefectible unfolding of God's Kingdom and his Church throughout time, not only in spite of the vicissitudes but through them. However, God's ways are not man's ways, even if that man be the pope. Pius IX was confounded indeed by God's providence.

> 1. When We were defeated by Our enemies in accordance with the mysterious design of God, We observed the severely bitter fortunes of Our City and the downfall of the civil rule of the Apostolic See in the face of military invasion....Since that time the ills and disasters of this City and Ourselves, foreshadowed by those first unhappy experiences, have really exceeded all bounds in assailing Our Apostolic rank and authority, the sanctity of religion and morals, and Our dearest subjects. What is more, venerable brothers, since conditions worsen daily, We are compelled to repeat the words of St. Bernard: "this is the beginning of the evils; we fear worse evil." For wickedness advances on its path and promotes its designs. No longer does it take pains to conceal its worst deeds since they cannot remain hidden, but it is eager to carry off the last spoils from the overthrow of justice, honor, and religion. Our days are filled with bitterness.....

> 12. Since you and your faithful understand this well, you have all risen up for the sake of religion, justice, and tranquility, which are the foundation of all good things. You make the Church of God glorious with the worthy show of your faith, charity, constancy, and virtue; by your faithful efforts in the Church's defense, you fashion a new and wonderful example in

its history, which will be remembered by generations to come. But since the God of mercies is the source of those good things, We raise Our eyes, Our hearts, and Our hope to Him. We continually beseech Him to strengthen and increase the illustrious understanding of you and of the faithful, the piety you share, your love, and your zeal. We strongly exhort you and your people likewise to cry to the Lord with Us more strongly day by day, as the fighting grows more stern, that He may Himself deign to hasten the days of His propitiation.

13. The rulers of the earth do not want the usurpation which We are suffering to be established and to thrive to the ruin of all authority and order. May God unite all rulers in agreement of mind and will. By removing all discord, claiming the disturbance of rebellions, and rejecting the ruinous counsels of the sects, may these rulers join in a common effort to have the rights of the Holy See restored. Then tranquility will once again be restored to civil society.

14. Then request the divine clemency to dispel the blindness of impious minds and convert their hearts to penitence before the great and awful day of the Lord arrives, or to check their lawless plans and show them how foolish those men are who attempt to overthrow the rock founded by Christ and infringe its divine privileges. In these prayers may Our hope be set more strongly on God. "Do you think that God can turn His ear away from His dearest spouse when she cries while opposing those who straiten her? How shall He not acknowledge bone of His bones and flesh of His flesh and even in some manner spirit of His spirit? Now indeed is the hour of wickedness and the power of darkness. But it is the final hour and the power quickly passes away. Christ the strength of God and the wisdom of God is with us, and He is on our side. Have confidence: he has overcome the world." Meanwhile let Us follow with great courage and assured faith the voice of eternal truth which says: fight for justice with your life, and struggle for justice even to death, then God will conquer your enemies for you.[47]

Pius IX, to the end, pleaded with the "rulers of the world" to reinstate his temporal authority, but there was no Constantine or Charlemagne to save the Papal States. Yes, much to Pius IX's dismay, neither the rulers of the world, nor the faithful, nor Almighty God Himself, rose up to preserve the civil sovereignty of the Papacy.

> But the greed of the neighboring ruler coveted the regions of Our temporal realm, and he obstinately preferred the advice of the sects of perdition to Our repeated warning and summonses. Most recently, he has far outdone the shamelessness even of the Prodigal Son. He has stormed Our city by force and now even controls it. We are, of course, greatly upset at this lawless usurpation of which We are the victim. *We are utterly pained at the great wickedness of the plan to destroy Our civil rule, which at the same time would destroy Our spiritual power and the kingdom of Christ on earth.* We are pained at the sight of so many serious evils, especially of those which jeopardize the eternal salvation of Our people. In this bitterness, nothing is more saddening for Us than to be prevented by the state of Our defeated liberty from applying the necessary remedies to so many evils.[48] (*Emphasis added*).

Now here is a heretical statement: "We are utterly pained at the great wickedness of the plan to destroy Our civil rule, which at the same time would destroy Our spiritual power and the kingdom of Christ on earth."

So, "should [we] trust in horses and chariots?" (PS 20:17) Was not the Lord himself stripped and crucified triumphant thereby? Will the gates of hell prevail if the Church is stripped of all her temporal power? Of course not. As painful as the loss of the temporal glory and power of the Church was to Pope Pius IX, and indeed to any past, present, or future good son of the Church who has at least one foot still grounded in this prideful world, it is heretical hyperbole to despair of ultimate victory; that is, to the coming of God's Kingdom in all ways. For, as with all the vicissitudes of salvation history, indeed all the vicissitudes of human and Christian existence, it is all per God's Holy Providence.

THE CALLING OF THE COUNCIL

Unbeknownst at the time, Vatican I was to be the concluding statement of an already mortally wounded Christendom, the final all-out *salvo* in the eventually lost culture war of the West. This would subsequently leave Vatican II as the opening statement of the Church fully awakened to the defeat of Christendom, with the documents of Vatican II being the formal treaty with the New West of the post-Christian secular world.

Vatican I was a political council in that its catalyst was a political crisis. A response to the political crisis convulsing Christendom, Vatican I defined the Church's immunity from the rise and dominance of the all-powerful secular State and the pervasive popular and profane culture. Similarly, Vatican II, though deemed pastoral, was itself political, being an attempt to accommodate the now all-powerful secular State and to become relevant to the now completely dominant post-Christian culture. Vatican I was a council of aggression, a dogmatic assertion of essential magisterial authority. Vatican II was a council of reconstruction, an adaption to the postbellum, post-Christian, more aptly anti-Christic, West.

The pronouncements of Vatican Council I (opened 8 December 1869, adjourned on 20 October 1870) may be deemed to be the frantic grasps and final gasps of an unseemly ultramontanism, or hyper-papalism, in its death throes. But it can also be seen as a re-consolidation of the papal perimeter back to its essential boundaries. Against the encroaching secular powers that be, Vatican I aggressively manned the inner ramparts in its dogmatic assertions of essential magisterial authority. This re-consolidation was impenetrable for its core was immutable dogma and its perimeter was absolute certitude.

At the center of this Vatican I reconsolidation was the pronouncement of essential papal authority as infallible, an assurance that no matter the worldly status of the Church, no matter the vicissitudes of her popular persuasion or political power, her authority in faith and morals remained absolute. As such, Vatican I was a purifying council of rock solid reconsolidation. It wasn't what Vatican I declared about the papacy that would be most important, but what it didn't claim. Vatican I was a re-consolidation that defined the papacy in its bare essentials. Gone was any mention of monarchy and other accidental accouterments, encrustations, or artifices of worldly and political power. Gone in spirit was the *triple crown*, though it was the world that had resolutely knocked it off, and though not until the Pope of Vatican II was the *tiara* actually surrendered.[49] Rather the papacy was defined in accord with its *triple charge* to feed and serve Christ's faithful flock. As per Vatican I,

> And it was to Peter alone that Jesus, after his resurrection, confided the jurisdiction of supreme pastor and ruler of his whole fold, saying: Feed my lambs, feed my sheep.[50]

But Vatican I's doctrinal *salvos* were impactive not so much on the world, which remained recalcitrantly unaffected by such dogmatic statements, but on the faithful themselves. Vatican I made clear that though the papacy be stripped of all its inessential worldly,[51] political, and monarchical powers and pretenses, though the pope himself be a prisoner of the State, the papacy still maintained its essential power in faith and morals. That is, and thus avoiding scandalizing the faithful, Vatican I defined the papacy in its essential ministerial nature, and as a spiritual-moral power only. Yes, a spiritual-moral power only, but therefore as an absolute and indefectible power.

INFALLIBILITY'S LIMITS
ON THE PAPACY

Vatican I declared that the Petrine primacy came even before the Church. This is biblically irrefutable, for again,

> That thou art Peter; and upon this rock I will build my church . . . . And I will give to thee the keys of the kingdom of heaven." MT 16:18—19

This Petrine primacy was bestowed for the service of building the Church. But it was not given for the building of a brick and mortar church, for Peter was a fisherman not a carpenter; much less a political and worldly church, for Peter was to be "the servant of the servants of God," not a despotic king. The edifice built integrally upon the Rock of Peter is of doctrinal mortar and dogmatic stones. And this edifice, which for all intents and purposes is complete, cannot be undone, not even by Peter himself.

Indeed, Peter's role over 2,000 years has become less and less that of builder and more and more that of caretaker of the dogmatic edifice that has been erected. And with the dogmatic edifice now built, the person who is pope has become less and less important and is now properly obscured under the Church as its foundation. This lessening of importance of the person who is pope made a qualitative leap even with the very first successor of St. Peter, who was the historically obscure St. Linus. Peter's successors were destined to become obedient unto the very Church erected upon the rock of their papal office, and thus more and more constrained by that Church whose dogmatic truth weighed greater and greater upon them. Verily, the Petrine ministry's most vital role, the reason for its very authority, is to establish the paramount authority of the Church. The gift and assertion of Petrine primacy is rightly ordered only unto the manifestation of the Church's paramount authority. It is necessary then for Peter to be subservient unto the Church built upon him. The papacy is not an end in itself, but a means to an end, and a papacy not so ordered would be capricious, temporary, and subjective, and thus contrary to authority, much less infallibility, in any form.

So finally stripped of the bulk of its worldly power that had accumulated over nearly two millennia, the See of Peter at Vatican I was left to assert its essential and singular charism. Because dogma was for all intents and purposes completely defined, Pius IX issued what might appear to be an almost moot point concerning his infallibility to define such dogma. Yes, the ultimate infallible papal statement was a declaration on the infallibility of papal *ex cathedra* statements. This urgent need to empathize papal supremacy so as to prove the rock solid foundation of the Church would also allow that Church in the future to stand in truth and grace, unencumbered by accidentals that would become a liability in the coming third millennium.

Vatican I's reaffirmation of the infallibility of the magisterium on faith and morals set in stone past magisterial pronouncements, and thus paradoxically did more to limit future papal and magisterial authority than to empower it. By declaring the infallible dogmatic nature of the past magisterium the future magisterium would be bound and limited by that past. Again, such is the providence of salvation history,

> If anyone [e.g., popes and/or councils] says that it is possible that at some time, given the advancement of knowledge, a sense may be assigned to the dogmas propounded by the church which is different from that which the church has understood and understands: let him be anathema.[52]

WORLD WARS

The interim between the twin Vatican Councils was taken up by the twin World Wars, and their unleashing of the most extensive and horrific warfare ever visited upon mankind. These World Wars moved Christendom's ancient boundaries, displacing political powers and enthroned new powers. But more tellingly, it was the suffering and death these wars perpetrated upon humanity—upon men, women, and children, and upon their composite communities of families—that manifested the monstrous and hideous evil that had metastasized within decaying Christian civilizations. And finally, the most enduring results of these World Wars was the purging of those pockets of Christendom that had still survived, and indeed even thrived,[53] before the wars, leaving the secularized nations of a *post-bella* West without so much as a Christian leaven.

World War I introduced the machine gun, the meat-grinder of the common soldier, as well as mustard gas, the ethereal strangler of that same soldier and non-combatants as well.[54] Symbolically enough in salvation and secular history, "the Great War" would begin with the assassination of the heir apparent (or *Thronfolger*) of what remained of the Holy Roman Empire, an empire that had begun over a millennium before with the Pope's coronation of Charlemagne. Catholic Archduke Franz Ferdinand's death would begin the Great War and the Great War would end the kingdom of Austria-Hungary and the last vestige of the Holy Roman Empire. The end of World War I would subsequently usher in the decadent *Roaring 20's* and with it deal death blows to the West's adherence to core moral laws, especially in regards to sexuality, gender, and marriage and family;[55] a morality that had been enthroned even longer than the dynasty of the Holy Roman Empire.

Again, symbolically enough, World War II would begin with the blitzkrieg of the most vibrant and unified nation left of an erstwhile Christendom: Catholic Poland. Like the assassination that began World War I, the battle that opened World War II would pit the secular Satanic State against the ancient regimes of Christendom.[56] Caught between ideologies in which it had no affinity, Poland would be crushed in the vice of totalitarianism, both fascist and communist, and be subsequently sold out and enslaved to the latter by the Western democracies. Like Poland, the other Catholic nations such as Hungary, Austria, and Czechoslovakia, would likewise be handed over after World War II to the USSR, the most murderous regime in the history of the world.

And yes, in keeping with the anti-Christic dynamics, the final act of World War II would be the mass-murdering atomic bombing of Catholic Nagasaki.[57] The Catholics of Nagasaki were Catholic indeed, for the Shogun had persecuted them for centuries. These Japanese Catholics practiced their faith underground, baptized their children and converts, and preached and lived the Holy Gospel, unto very martyrdom. This Japanese Catholicism, and all with nary a priest nor Mass, produced saints in glorious abundance.

Once the shogun's persecution ended, the faithful of Nagasaki built the magnificent Immaculate Conception Cathedral, the first and largest Cathedral in all of East Asia. It was the soaring spires of this cathedral that were to become the designated target points, ground zero, for the crew that dropped the second atomic bomb. More Japanese Christians were killed in that moment than in all the previous shogunate persecutions of Christians combined. This horrendous act of murder against the civilians of the vibrant Catholic stronghold of Japan, would likewise mark the beginning of the end of a rapidly ascending Catholicism in the United States, the nation that perpetrated this most horrendous of crimes.

The World Wars were indeed the convulsing death-throes of Christendom. What would result from this death was not a mere post-Christian culture, but an anti-Christic one. This was because one cannot merely be indifferent to the Gospel, especially when that Gospel formed your very civilization. The new West necessarily rejected and built up anti-bodies against the Gospel, becoming not only immune to that Gospel but antithetical to that Gospel: that is, truly *anti-Christic*. As such, the new Western culture, unlike the ancient pagan cultures who were steeped in natural law and most receptive to the Gospel, is irredeemable.[58]

PARISHISM & CATHOLIC ACTION

With the 20th Century's no longer deniable collapse of Christendom there was an ecclesial scramble to realign politically. The magisterium[59] was forced to turn its centuries-long preoccupation with the secular powers-that-be—with kings and nobility—to their remaining popular base in the common laity. Indeed, the previous magisterial focus on the powers-that-be—both their own ecclesial power, as well as an alliance with secular powers—was the very reason for the fall of Christendom. For while in Christendom I the magisterium was focused on powers and principalities, the Church's lay-familial foundation—which the ministering unto is the magisterium's very *raison d'etre*—had laid-fallow and eventually began to decay.

To compensate for the breakup of the magisterial-monarchical alliance on the macro-level of the State, the magisterium would now seek to exert its political power through the micro-level of the parish. But alas, once again, these magisterial power-plays resulted in a form of Christian life that was against both nature and grace, for it centralized the parish and marginalized the family. Thus, under this *parishism*, the family, and hence the faithful, would continue to languish.

However, appearances would belie this languishing of the laity. Magnificent new churches, rectories, and schools, and the swelling of priestly and vowed evangelical ranks, would, especially in America, continue an upward trajectory all the way through Vatican II. However, these statistically good Catholic indicators would only disguise, and thus leave untreated, the underlying decay of the lay faithful and the domestic church of the family. With that decay of the domestic church, its fruits of priestly and evangelical vocations would also be less than sound. Thus, the way was paved for the Great Apostasy of the setting second millennia of Christianity.

So this first magisterial attempt to respond to the 20th Century crisis in Catholicism was still in essence political, albeit with an emphasis on the recruitment of the common lay faithful. To compensate for the loss of Christendom an all-out effort was made to restructure the Church's dynamics of influence through parishism and its programs of "Catholic Action." Parishism was an attempt to make the parish the all-inclusive center of the faithful's life and was built upon the still prevalent and solid pockets of lay faithful in the old world and upon an existing ethnicity based Catholic ghettoism in the new world.

In parishism nearly all aspects of human existence— from the educational to the recreational, from the social to the political—would be under the auspices of the Church hierarchy via the direct influence of the parish priest. An exception to this would be how a man made a living, which necessarily would not fall under the umbrella of parishism since an independent income stream was necessary to keep the parish and all its activities well-funded. But otherwise —be it devotions, education, entertainment, athletics, or politics—the parish would be the very center of a Catholic's life. In the fully developed parish one could have a drink at its bar, or bowl in its alleys, or dance in its hall, or play ball on its fields and in its Catholic league. And yes, if one wanted to pray in what was presented as the best possible way one would go to parish devotionals. In parishism, the better Catholic you were depended on how much time and energy (and/or money) you spent at the parish.

In parishism all was under the authority of the pastor and his priestly lieutenants; who themselves would be under the authority of the local ordinary; who in turn would be under the authority of the Holy See. In lockstep with this parishism, the Vatican orchestrated the Catholic

Action Movement,[60] which called upon all Catholics to sign up as foot soldiers in the causes of the hierarchy. The commanding officers of the Catholic Action Movement were the priests, prelates and pope, and the faithful were the troops. Pius XI had no qualms in defining Catholic Action as "the collaboration of the laity in the apostolate of the hierarchy."[61]

In parishism and Catholic Action it wasn't family life that would be advanced and sanctified; it wasn't Christian fatherhood that would be empowered and inaugurated; and it wasn't motherhood that would be supported and raised high. Rather, fathers, mothers, and children would be called away from the family and domestic church to enlist in whatever sociopolitical action the magisterium deemed to be expedient for the advancement of its influence and power.

Both parishism and Catholic Action had a gravely deficient ecclesiology that did not sufficiently recognize that there are multiple integrated manifestations of the Catholic "church." There is *Ecclesia Catholica*, or universal church, which is not to be equated with the magisterium, as it completely was in Christendom I. Nor conversely is *Ecclesia Catholica* to be equated with the faithful in general,[62] as it is done by current lay movements of identity-politics. Rather, *Ecclesia Catholica* is that to which all Christians (from peons to popes) must submit. The only other "church" that shares the same sense of meaning as *Ecclesia Catholica* is that of the *ecclesia domestica*, or the domestic church. Finally, though not in the same sense as *Ecclesia Catholica* or *ecclesia domestica*, there are physical churches, chapels or parishes, used for worship. The physical "church" is not a church in the spiritual and ontological sense, as are the Universal and domestic churches, but rather derives its name from its association and service to these two churches.

Parishism and Catholic Action lost sight of the fact that the parish and its physical buildings essentially exist only for the Universal Church and the domestic church. Lost sight of was the two-fold purpose of the parish, which was to derive from the *Ecclesia Catholica's* deposit of faith and treasury of grace so as to provide religious education and liturgy and sacraments. In this two-fold purpose the parish church functions only as a medium between Holy Mother Church and the domestic church. The ramifications being, that no parishes may validly dissent or go contrary to Holy Mother Church and all parishes must exist to minister unto the domestic church. Essentially then, the parish is where a community of families,[63] or collection of domestic churches, gather together for corporate liturgical worship, to partake in the sacraments, and for religious instruction as per the needs of these domestic churches.

Because of its disorientation away from the domestic church, the Catholic Action Movement and its coefficient of parishism, despite their Vatican-directed, highly concerted, and intensely vigorous efforts, failed spectacularly. These initial post-Christendom efforts were doomed to fail due to their intrinsic errors; specifically their lack of appreciation of the family as the faithful's foundational matrix; and the subsequent failure to see that the essential duties of the parish, clergy, and magisterium were to serve the family and the lay faithful versus the lay faithful serving the parish, clergy, and magisterium. Not only did parishism and Catholic Action fail to appreciate the domestic church, but in fact sought to supplant the domestic church, the family, the father and the mother. In this goal of supplantation can be seen the error implicit in these movements. And despite its attempts to remedy the subtle heresy of equating the Church with its hierarchy, these errors would be little rectified with the subsequent reforms of Vatican II.

V. VATICAN II

Every one that exalteth himself
shall be humbled
and he that humbleth himself
shall be exalted.
LK 18:10-14

Vatican I and Vatican II, as the names imply, are twin councils. Though their arrival was separated by nearly a century and two world wars, these councils were born in response to the same cataclysmic sociopolitical upheaval. The World Wars that separated these ecumenical councils were themselves twin manifestations of this same global cataclysm. Vatican II (1962—1965), then, was to bring Vatican I (1869—1870) to its final conclusion by being the initial statement of a Church now irrefutably ensconced in a post-Christian world. Indeed, while Vatican I in praxis ended with Rome being occupied and the papacy being divested of any sociopolitical power, it was not formally closed until 1960 as a preamble to the opening of Vatican II.

The long drawn out death agony of Christendom was certainly of the essence of the two global wars that wreaked havoc in the world and specifically the West. As the post-bellum smoke of the World Wars dissipated, as a shell-shocked Catholicism regained its bearings, it became increasingly clear that there would be no return to a sociopolitical order in which Christian values were dominant. With the nations of erstwhile Christendom racked with total war, the post-bellum and pre-conciliar Church of the 20th Century, and thus the young men who would be the future participants of Vatican II, could not help but recognize that there was a cataclysmic societal upheaval.

The prelates and theologians of Vatican II rightly intuited that there was a Catholic crisis, and they rightly sensed it had something to do with the laity and a needed recalibration as per subsidiarity of a dysfunctional top-heavy ecclesial structure. Nevertheless, the clericalization of Christian life had been so thorough since the Counter-Reformation that it had been seared into the mindset of even the most progressive of Vatican II participants. As such, the prelates and *periti* of Vatican II ironically ended up promoting the laity by promoting lay clericalization, that is, the involvement of the laity in priestly ministry. They also ended up promoting a subsidiarity that only increased bureaucracy by implementing all-powerful national episcopal conferences. Contrary to prevalent opinion that it was a watershed break with continuity, Vatican II was but the pre-Vatican II Church unleashed.

OPTIMISM

Incongruously, but humanly enough, the explosive prosperity between post-World War II and Vatican II gave rise to an undue optimism. Vatican Council II was indeed initiated by a pope who had spent his entire life under the clouds of world wars, who had spent the lion-share of his episcopal ministry under an Italian fascist regime, and yet who came out of this trauma recalcitrantly jolly. The Council John XXIII called was eventually steered by men from the Rhineland who themselves had grown up under Nazism. These men couldn't help but think things had certainly taken a turn for the better, if not ecclesially and spiritually at least politically and materially, for no other reason that the war had ended and the nightmare of fascism was apparently vanquished.

John XXIII in his address that opened Vatican II to the worldwide assembly of bishops—an assembly where even the youngest bishops grew up in the ominous time between the World Wars—proclaimed, with his characteristic optimism,

> In the daily exercise of our pastoral office, we sometimes have to listen, much to our regret, to voices of persons who, though burning with zeal, are not endowed with too much sense of discretion or measure. In these modern times they can see nothing but prevarication and ruin... We feel we must disagree with those prophets of gloom... In the present order of things, Divine Providence is leading us to a new order of human relations which, by men's own efforts and even beyond their very expectations, are directed toward the fulfillment of God's superior and inscrutable designs. And everything, even human differences, leads to the greater good of the Church.[64]

Note John XXIII's stated desire for a new order of

human relations. Thus, the so-called pastoral council was not really pastorally motivated, but rather it was sociopolitically motivated. Here again is the recurring magisterial preoccupation with a sociopolitical agenda, but this time it was fueled by a foolish optimism. As Josef Ratzinger, the Vatican II *peritus* and future pope, would write in retrospect,

> We started out boldly and full of confidence in ourselves; there may have been, in thought and, perhaps, also in reality, many an auto-da-fé of scholarly books that seemed to us to be foolish novels of chivalry that led us only into the land of dreams and made us see dangerous giants in the beneficial effects of technology, in the vanes of its windmills. Boldly and certain of victory, we barricaded the door of a time that was past and proclaimed the abrogation and annihilation of all that lay behind it. In conciliar and postconciliar literature, there is abundant evidence of the ridicule with which, like pupils ready for graduation, we bade farewell to our outmoded schoolbooks. In the meantime, however, our ears and our souls have been pierced by a different kind of ridicule that mocks more than we had wanted or wished. Gradually we have stopped laughing.[65]

In optimistic reaction to the collapse of the old order that the Church had been so heavily invested in, the churchmen at Vatican II sought to find relevance in the new world order. This optimism failed to recognize that this new order was not merely of a different paradigm of the erstwhile Christendom, but was an order that arose out of the rejection of that paradigm; again, it was a new order not merely post-Christian but necessarily anti-Christic. Due to this unrealistic optimism, it was imagined that the Church could regain her relevance by merely forgoing the condemnation of the world in favor of its accommodation. As such, Vatican II would not issue anathemas but panegyrics, even if those panegyrics were platitudes; it would not stress differences but commonalities, even if those commonalities were banalities; it would stress how

God was good for man, even if the good of man supplanted the good of God.

Men who were raised directly in the path of the juggernaut that had its beginning and end in two brutal world wars, the Rhineland prelates and *periti* experienced a crisis of faith and nature that would impel them to be the intellects and movers of the Vatican II. These men from the devastated Rhineland et al.,[66] were especially disillusioned with the past and in both visceral and ideological reaction were especially liberal and optimistic about the future. These Rhineland fathers' counterparts in the Vatican were their countries' conquerors, the English speaking prelates and *periti* from America and their World War II allies. These English speaking churchmen's countries were flush with victories, had gained world political dominance, experienced exponential economic growth, and their Catholic populations were experiencing a post-war baby-boom. As such, the English speaking bloc of Vatican II was especially arrogant and clericalistic, and hence especially overconfident, even utopic. Thus, at Vatican II shell-shocked Rhineland ecclesial intellectuals medicated on a metaphysical optimism met naive American ecclesial politicians raised on promises and privileged elitism. It was a Rhineland metaphysical optimism and liberal disillusionment with the past that in confluence with a privileged and elitist American establishment that arrogantly looked toward the future that created the very spirit of Vatican II.

The Rhineland churchmen et al. erred on the side of heresy, throwing out the proverbial baby with the bath water, while the American churchmen et al. erred on the side of presumption and power; and both left the common faithful in the lurch. Neither parties realized that the West was no longer merely agnostically post-Christian but now virulently anti-Christic. The result was the faithful's exposure to the toxins of an anti-Christic culture and the ensuing great apostasy.

This "Spirit of Vatican II" would subsequently run roughshod over the traditional piety of the common faithful. These blue-collar Catholics had neither the luxury to revel in metaphysical musings nor the privilege of being ensconced in academic and ecclesial ivory towers. Pastorally, that is in the harshness of day to day reality, these common faithful, for whom the Council was supposedly called for, were left unarmed against an evermore virulently anti-Christic culture.

CLERICALISM REDUX

The ills of the pre-Vatican II Church stemmed from a compartmentalizing of the Faith. In the pre-Vatican II Church attendance at Mass was seen as the primary indicator of what it meant to be a good Catholic. This liturgical compartmentalization, and its closely related clericalism, was the major cause of the pre-Vatican II ills that Vatican II somehow sensed and sought to address. However, Vatican II ended up being in complete continuity with pre-Vatican II liturgical compartmentalization; for Vatican II was all about the Mass as well. Vatican II's very first and flag ship document, with all other subsequent works of the Council being somewhat anticlimactic, was on the reform of the Mass. The Vatican II bishops and their experts absolutely embraced liturgicalism, for they sought first and foremost the remedying of any ills in liturgical reform. However, it was this very liturgicalism that was itself one of the major plagues of the Church. And enduringly, it is the Mass that remains the focus of all things pro-Vatican II as well as all things anti-Vatican II.

And so too, the council bishops and expert theologians (*priests all!*) in an act of patronizing clericalism sought to rescue the laity, who were floundering in a sea of secularism, by a draconian imposition of their pastoral vision on the them. Alas! it was this very clericalism and the resultant infantilized laity that was a major contributor to the laity's floundering. While Vatican II was supposedly all about the laity, it wasn't at all about the priest or magisterium serving the laity; it wasn't about strengthening fathers, and mothers, and families in their vocations. But again Vatican II was all about the bishops, the priests, and the liturgy, and about how the laity could be involved in these clerical vocations!

In trying to take up where the Catholic Action Movement failed, Vatican II sought to enable the lay faithful. But like Catholic Action and parishism, Vatican II missed the mark in not addressing the specifically lay charisms; in not specifically promoting the lay faithful in their familial and gender charisms; in not specifically nourishing the domestic dynamics of children, mothers, and fathers; in not specifically bolstering familial patriarchy as per its God-given locus of the faith and authority. Even though the documents of Vatican II spoke of the essential Christian call to holiness that pertains to all the faithful, it nonetheless fell into the same old heretical presupposition that the pinnacle of Christian life, what it meant to be fully Catholic, was to be somehow involved in priestly or magisterial functions. As such, Vatican II, in a supposed show of largesse, brought the laity into the sanctuary and condescendingly allowed them the privilege of partaking in clerical ministry as the subordinates of the priest. In the same spirit, the priest himself now had his own person emphasized at the expense of his *persona Christi*. Both of these changes only exacerbated the enduring heresy of clericalism.

So too, in an attempt to decentralize a top-heavy ecclesial bureaucracy (that is, reduce the political and micromanaging powers of the historical, but non-essential, Roman Curia) Vatican II only facilitated more politicking and micromanagement by assigning these arbitrary powers to the newfangled parliamentarian "national conferences of bishops." These national conferences of bishops were themselves premised on the political and clericalistic concept that local ordinaries were somehow imbued with independent presidential power. Bishops, rather than the conduits of sacramental grace and Church teachings that is their essential charism, were now cast as presidential prelates or ecclesial C.E.O.'s that personified the very Catholicity of their dioceses. While Vatican II's Dogmatic Constitution on the Church, *Lumen Gentium*,[67] starts out by giving lip service to the ultimate reality of ecclesial existence as that of the faithful (be they lay or ordained) heeding their informed Catholic conscience as per the teaching of Holy Mother Church, it quickly falls into the same old errors of clericalism and liturgicalism by primarily quoting the last pre-Vatican II pope, Pius XII. It needn't be argued here that what *Lumen Gentium* says is deficient, much less materially heretical, but that in its deficiencies it is gravely misleading, for in the spirit of the Counter-Reformation it continues to fixate on the liturgy and the ordained and magisterial ministries and falsely equates these with the Church herself.

Vatican II's coloring of bishops and their national conferences as somehow presidential or democratic was itself a mischaracterization, for these bishops were not elected but appointed by Roman authorities and usually came from outside of a diocese. But just as the ancient pre-Vatican II bureaucratic intrigues of the Roman Curia and papal power-plays had no Catholic, that is Christ-ordained, origin, neither did the post-Vatican II parliamentary powers of episcopal conferences nor the presidential powers of a local ordinary have a Gospel basis. True decentralization will find its authority only in that which Christ ordained, and it will make this authority more definitive. Thus, true Catholic decentralization finds its locus of authority in Holy Mother Church and her definitive teaching, and only eliminates the vagaries and caprices of men, and providentially so in this most unstable of times. So too, true decentralization brings to the forefront the individual conscience, which when informed by Holy Mother Church and the Holy Spirit, is the primary vicar of Christ. Finally, true Catholic decentralization is in accord with subsidiarity and hence will find its social and ecclesial locus of logistical authority in the God-given authority of the domestic church, that is, the family.

AN OXYMORONIC
PASTORAL COUNCIL

Vatican II was held at a time when the magisterium still maintained a most powerful momentum from the past and, subsequently, a powerful influence over the faithful. Indeed, while other institutions where shaken to the core in the World Wars, the Vatican stood firm and seemed to emerge sociopolitically victorious through it all. Though this momentum and influence would begin to drastically wane even during the Council itself, being fueled by Vatican II's hallmark optimism it would suffice to produce the last hurrah in draconian magisterial fiats. Though colored as egalitarian and pastoral, Vatican II would be in fact the final grand magisterial exercise in authoritarianism and elitism.

Pastoral competency is local, indeed familial, both in accord with practicality, subsidiarity, and post-Christendom diversity. Under pastoral pretense Vatican II may have sought to open up some select windows, but ended up closing off many more rooms, indeed wings, of the Church. This was due to an overreaching bureaucratic micromanagement. Yes, there was a stated desire to decentralize, but it only proliferated bureaucracy on the national level. Yes, there was an emphasis on collegiality, but this only resulted in local ordinaries being imbued with the authority of national conferences and thus becoming less accountable; less accountable not only to Rome but to the faithful they were meant to serve.

In the late Middle Ages there was a power-curve model that improperly presented a dichotomy of prince versus pope, or conversely of an inseparable throne and Church, or as a consequence of this inseparability of royalty, aristocracy, and magisterium versus revolutionary politics. So too, Vatican II improperly framed the power-curve issue as a dichotomy between the Roman Pontiff and the bishops, or of the Roman Curia versus episcopal conferences. But the final issue of ecclesial power is rather the dichotomy between the Church's fully explicated deposit of faith, truth, and good versus man-made institutional encrustations. It is a question of the faithful's fulfillment of their own full potential to discern this truth and live this good versus a stifling, impeding, and even jealous ecclesial bureaucratic power. The mere exchanging of one ecclesial authority for another is but a superficial letter of the law half-measure. In the case of empowering national episcopal conferences, such a maneuvering only leads to a greater tyranny of prelates who are vying for power via politburo politicking.

While there is manifestly no essential ecclesial reality to either the Roman Curia or national conferences of bishops, there is an essential ecclesial reality in the principle of dogmatic teachings, informed Catholic conscience, and to the principle of subsidiarity. The full and integral implementation of these ecclesial realities requires a true decentralization of authority, not a mere moving around of authoritarian power from the Pope to the local ordinary or from the Roman curia to national conferences of bishops. As such, true Catholic reform of political structures of power must aim to remand ecclesial authority to its inmost essential locus, that of the individual Christian's conscience informed by Church teachings. In other words, the fullness of the spirit of the law as per reforming ecclesial power structures stems from a recognition of and obedience to the absolute authority of *both* the Church and the human conscience.[68]

Indeed, the term *pastoral ecumenical council* is oxymoronic. This is nowhere more evident than in the imposed from on-high reforms of Vatican II. Vatican II academic elites empowered by the top echelons of ecclesial power pontificated from their ivory towers as to what was best on the pastoral, that is, grassroots, level. Not only was the out-of-touch formulation of pastoral practice contrary to common sense, efficacy, and the principles of subsidiarity, but it was an atrocious act of clericalism, and its implementation nothing less than dictatorial. Yes, there was a crisis in Catholicism, but the prelates and their *periti* only exacerbated it. As such, in the wake of Vatican II, there would be *the Great Apostasy*.

VATICAN I DEMILITARIZATION

The overall hue of the reforms of Vatican II were colored as a repudiation and abdication of triumphalism. And surely the triumphalism that so characterizes an erstwhile Christendom was out of place and time, even to the point of satire, in the new anti-Christic West. An update was thus not merely called for but mandated, since the Church had not triumphed but rather had been soundly defeated in the geopolitical realm. However, as Vatican II mothballed old-style triumphalism it muted the Church's militancy as well. This is a sure sign that that militancy had been misplaced, had been too worldly in the past, had been too tied to trust in chariots and horses, had depended upon the power of princes and popes, rather than it being grassroots, where the faithful, trusting in "the name of the Lord our God"[69] and the power of Jesus Christ Crucified, promulgated both Faith and family.

The Church's true militancy is to *speak truth to power*, not to be a power. Yes, go ahead and let down, as per the prescription of Vatican II, those worldly, bureaucratic, and monarchical barricades not yet breached, but defend unto death the sacred deposit of faith and truth. Yes, open the Church up to the winds of change but only so as to preach the Gospel more purely, more militantly, and more vigorously, unobscured by the walls and windows of accidentals, defenses, and fears. And yes, become as vulnerable as Our Venerable Lord, but then surely expect to be hated and crucified as was he.

True Christian militancy is that which extends God's kingdom. But the extension of God's kingdom, most especially in the anti-Christic third millennium, is not to be done under the auspices of princes and popes, or through the machinations of monarchies or magisteriums, or from political or ecclesial decrees from on high, rather the extension of God's kingdom in this anti-Christic third millennium is to be accomplished at the grassroots level, that is, the familial and individual level. Indeed, any new Christendom will not be spread kingdom by kingdom but family by family and soul by soul.

But the more things change the more they stay the same. For what puts-off course the Christian militancy needed for the Third Millennium is cut from the same sociopolitical fabric that in the past tied militancy to the worldly power curve. In the third millennium mainstream Church,[70] militancy has been co-opted on the left hand by the identity politics of social justice, and on the right by the compartmentalized quietism of a hidebound traditionalism.[71]

Social justice is a nebulous concept that contradictorily holds on principle that there can be no discriminatory principles of right and wrong.[72] Because it has no discriminatory borders, this social justice conceptualization claims to be akin to a seamless moral garment, but rather it is a garment ceaselessly unstitched and re-patched together as per the subjective dictates of the time. While social justice rights are subject to interpretation and human caprice, the law of God is not. Social justice lacks objectivity. It does not demarcate between that which is intrinsically evil and that which is not. As such, though it severely censures whoever it deems the enemy, it has not set commandments, but rather arbitrarily morphs according to subjective disposition and the sociopolitical milieu. On other hand, the compartmentalized quietism of traditionalism saps the conversional vigor of those who in this third millennium seek a deeper Catholicity and orders it all towards the same liturgicalism of old. This sort of traditionalism takes the militancy of masculine and patriarchal Christianity and emasculates it with clericalism. It takes the devotion to the feminine heart of the home and disingenuously stresses a compartmentalized devotion to a disembodied Queen of Heaven (with even a plaster pilgrim statue of her garnering more devotion within a home than the actual wife and mother) or a devotion to the Blessed Sacrament without a devotion to one's blessed family. Such a traditionalism seeks to build bigger churches but forgets that those churches exist solely for the families. Indeed, the very "charism" of the traditional orders of priests is the perfection of the priest and the liturgy, and thus they have the expectation that the lay faithful too must exist for the priest and the liturgy, however the exact opposite dynamic is the Catholic dynamic.

CHRISTIAN RIGHTS

Unlike subjective values of progressive social justice and the compartmentalization of traditional liturgicalism, the ecclesial principle of militancy is as objective as natural law and the ten commandments, and as integral as personal purgation and sanctification in the real life living out of the Faith. Militancy can be summed up succinctly as a Christian's *absolute right to do his duty to God*. As such, it is wrong to equate militancy with "the rights of the Church," meaning "the rights of the papacy and magisterium," for the Church and her priestly element have no rights in a world that is not of Christ's, and thus their, kingdom. The issue was wrongly framed both during Vatican I and Vatican II. Again, the pontiff of Vatican I, Pius IX, over-confidently proclaimed that:

> The rulers of the earth do not want the usurpation which We are suffering to be established .... May these rulers join in a common effort to have the rights of the Holy See restored.[73]

The issue of the sociopolitical dynamics of the Church is here wrongly framed, for it is neither about what "the rulers of the earth" want or do not want, nor about "the rights of the Holy See," but rather about the faithful's absolute right, as per both nature and grace, to do their duty to God, Faith, and family.

Nor did Vatican II succeed in correcting this error of equating the Church and her "rights" with the Holy See and its rights. Vatican II's sociopolitical document on Religious Liberty, *Dignitatis Humane*, speaks not of a Christian's rights but only of the rights of "the authorities of the Church":

> The freedom of the Church is the fundamental principle in what concerns the relations between the

> Church and governments and the whole civil order . . . . This independence is precisely what the authorities of the Church claim in society. At the same time, the Christian faithful, in common with all other men, possess the civil right not to be hindered in leading their lives in accordance with their consciences.[74]

Here, *Dignitatis Humane* is gravely deficient in the indication that Christians only have the rights afforded "all other men," that is the human rights that derive from the duty to abide by natural law. The only specific Christian rights claimed by *Dignitatis Humane* (and much proceeding theological comment on the subject) reside solely with the formal authorities—that is, the Magisterium, the Holy See, and the pope. Again, the root of this error can be found in falsely equating "the Church" only with the formal ecclesial authorities and structures. But "the Church" has no rights separate from the rights of the truth and the rights of the individual Christian. And more to the sociopolitical point, the State has no rights, no authority, and zero competency in regards to the Holy Faith.

There is no doubt that the State has no rights, authority, or competency over individual Christians in their informed Catholic consciences or over the Church in her divine teachings and practices. But nor does the Church in her divine nature have natural corporate rights, for she, unlike her members, is not at all of the Kingdom of this world. It is indeed in the Church's lack of natural rights that, due to her being not of this world, imbues the Church with a completely transcendent immunity from that world and its powers. Rather, it is the Christian who not only has natural civil rights to abide by natural law but the supernatural civil right to abide by divine law. In fact, not only does the Christian have the absolute inalienable right to do his duty as per the laws of nature and grace, he further has a mandate to follow divine inspirations that transcend the law. Such divine inspirations are not merely a question of not transgressing the law but about preaching and implementing the Gospel, about militantly bringing about the Kingdom of God. As per the specific issue of religious liberty, then, the Christian has the absolute right to prophetically speak truth to, and promulgate the good against, the powers-that-be; that is, to and against the State, corporation, culture, *etc.*

Dignitatis Humane fails to differentiate between natural *imago Dei* or human rights and Christian rights, nor recognizes that both are based only on individual rights. Natural *imago Dei* or human rights essentially emanate from the individual right to seek and assent to the truth, and to choose and do the good. [H3]So, contrary to *Dignitatis Humane's* position that individual Christians have only the same rights as all men, there are further and more extensive individual Christian rights that emanate beyond *imago Dei.* These additional and superlative rights of the individual Christian are derived from the unique *noblesse oblige* duties the individual Christian owes to the God of Revelation as per the mandates of divine law and the dictates of an informed Catholic conscience.

THE ANTHROPOLOGICAL TURN

John XXIII in his opening of the Council had this to say about its purpose and, indeed, competency:

> The greatest concern of the ecumenical council is this: that the sacred deposit of Christian doctrine be guarded and taught more effectively... The Lord has said: *'Seek first the kingdom of God and His justice.'* The word 'first' expresses the direction in which our thoughts and energies must move.[75] (*Emphasis* added).

But with John XXIII's untimely death the objective of seeking "first the kingdom of God" morphed into the seeking first to serve the kingdom of man. Paul VI, in his closing address of the Council, had this to say about its definitive course, interpretation, and desired outcome:

> But we cannot pass over one important consideration in our analysis of the religious meaning of the council: it has been deeply committed to the study of the modern world. Never before perhaps, so much as on this occasion, has the Church felt the *need to know, to draw near to, to understand, to penetrate, serve and evangelize the society in which she lives; and to get to grips with it, almost to run after it*, in its rapid and continuous change. This attitude, a response to the distances and divisions we have witnessed over recent centuries, in the last century and in our own especially, between the Church and secular society—this attitude has been strongly and unceasingly at work in the council...
>
> Yes, *the Church of the council* has been concerned, not just with herself and with her relationship of union with God, but with man...
>
> But one must realize that this council, which exposed itself to human judgment, insisted very much more

upon this pleasant side of man, rather than on his unpleasant one. Its attitude was very much and deliberately optimistic. A wave of affection and admiration flowed from the council over the modern world of humanity. Errors were condemned, indeed, because charity demanded this no less than did truth, but for the persons themselves there was only warning, respect and love. Instead of depressing diagnoses, encouraging remedies; instead of direful prognostics, messages of trust issued from the council to the present-day world. The modern world's values were not only respected but honored, its efforts approved, its aspirations purified and blessed...

We can now speak only too briefly on the very many and vast questions, relative to human welfare, with which the council dealt. It did not attempt to resolve all the urgent problems of modern life; some of these have been reserved for a further study which the Church intends to make of them, many of them were presented in very restricted and general terms, and for that reason are open to further investigation and various applications...

Another point we must stress is this: all this rich teaching is channeled in one direction, the service of mankind, of every condition, in every weakness and need. *The Church has, so to say, declared herself the servant of humanity, at the very time when her teaching role and her pastoral government have, by reason of the council's solemnity, assumed greater splendor and vigor*: the idea of service has been central... its concern is with man and with earth, but it rises to the kingdom of God...

The modern mind, accustomed to assess everything in terms of usefulness, will readily admit that the council's value is great if only because *everything has been referred to human usefulness*. Hence no one should ever say that a religion like the Catholic religion is without use, seeing that when it has its greatest self-awareness and effectiveness, as it has in council, it declares itself entirely on the side of man and in his service. In this way the Catholic religion and human life reaffirm their alliance with one another, the fact that they converge on one single human reality: the Catholic religion is for mankind...

And so this council can be summed up in its ultimate religious meaning, which is none other than a pressing and friendly invitation to mankind of today to rediscover in fraternal love the God "to turn away from whom is to fall, to turn to whom is to rise again, to remain in whom is to be secure...to return to whom is to be born again, in whom to dwell is to live" (St. Augustine, Solil. I, 1, 3; PL 32, 870)...

This is our hope at the conclusion of this Second Vatican Ecumenical Council and at the beginning of the human and religious renewal which the council proposed to study and promote; this is our hope for you, brothers and Fathers of the council; this is our hope for the whole of mankind which here we have learned to love more and to serve better.[76] (*Emphasis* added).

Paul VI's *"Church of the Council"* (which itself inadvertently implies discontinuity with the Church before the Council) erred in *"declar[ing] herself the servant of humanity"* rather than the servant of the faithful. This orientation toward man is known as "the anthropological turn," the council's value is great if only because *"everything has been referred to human usefulness."*

Paul VI also said in this concluding statement that,

"This council bequeaths to history an image of the Catholic Church symbolized by this hall, filled, as it is, with shepherds of souls . . . ."

Again this belies equating the Church with the Magisterium. In addition, Paul VI saw an even greater waxing in the grandeur of this Magisterium, as *"her teaching role and her pastoral government have, by reason of the council's solemnity, assumed greater splendor and vigor."* This Vatican II Magisterium, certainly did bequeath to history the false image that it was the Church, and indeed was so emboldened by its mass-media popularity and technologically enhanced bureaucratic efficiency as to see itself as of an even "greater splendor and vigor" of even past over-the-top monarchical magisteriums. But that splendor and vigor would wither in the high noon of societal decadence and that worldly adulation turn to condemnation in light of an ecclesial malfeasance brought on by that magisterial hubris.

Paul VI speaks for this magisterium, so freshly imbued with hubris and mass-media adulation, as ardent in their *"need to know, to draw near to, to understand, to penetrate, serve and evangelize the society in which she lives; and to get to grips with it, almost to run after it."* He speaks for a magisterium that is flush with a passion for the world, that thus seeks to woo and ingratiate itself to that world. These churchmen of Vatican II, seeing they had lost the world, ran after that world; but in doing so left the faithful, the common Catholic, in the lurch. As such, and paradoxically, the pastoral council of Vatican II was not truly pastoral but political: it was not the hierarchy's turning from power and clericalism to the service of the faithful but rather a turn that went right past the faithful to the ingratiating service of the world.

It certainly appears that the pope, prelates, and theologians of Vatican II were more concerned with worldly relevancy than priestly ministry. It seems that the same worldly mentality of an erstwhile triumphalism remained but had been "reformed" into a sociopolitical activism. But again, sociopolitical activism is not the job or competency of the magisterium *qua* Magisterium *qua* teaching authority of the Church. Be it concerned with alliances with royal houses or with the United Nations, with economics or ecology, with imperialism or immigration; these things are not the competency of the Magisterium, but of the Church *qua* faithful in their sociopolitical duties. The competency of the Magisterium is to simply feed Christ's sheep with the sacraments, and as John XXIII said (warned?) to guard and teach "the sacred deposit of Christian doctrine." But Vatican II saw prelates and theologians, following the Counter-

Reformation trend, arrogantly considering themselves as the select philosophers, poets, social workers, politicians, etc.; in sum, the experts and luminaries, etc., of the Church and indeed of the world. Vatican II in effect, for all its bloviations of democratization and egalitarianism, ended up being the last blast of the spirit of Christendom I and a monarchical, top-heavy authoritarianism. Again, Vatican II, in spite of itself, was an exercise in clericalism.

For the faithful of the Church, the "anthropological turn" of Vatican II was made symbolically manifest in the turning around of the altars. Though not mandated or even mentioned in the Council documents, this symbolical dis-orientation of the altar was bound to occur in the "spirit of Vatican II." For this spirit of Vatican II was definitively enunciated by its head legislator, the Pope, in his above closing address. Paul VI's finalizing statutory commentary made perfectly clear that the guiding spirit of Vatican II was indeed not only the anthropological turn but the worldly turn, truly from *ad orientem* to *versus populum.* This spirit in its most extreme misuse would entail a dynamics redolent of prideful apostasy itself, a turn from God and the Holy Cross towards not only man and the world but the flesh and devil as well.

TRUE REFORM

Christian life as a constant call to conversion is thus a constant call to reform. And as always, all Christian reform of externals is ordered toward an interior reform of the person. In addition to interiority, true Christian reform is necessarily radical. It is radical in that it goes towards the *radix* (Lt., root) of the Holy Faith; that is, towards the Holy Cross and Christ Crucified. True reform is radical in that it removes those letters of the law that obscure the essence of the Holy Faith; removes those oppressive fears that prevent the embrace of the Holy Cross; removes those obtuse archaisms that impede the piercing spirit of the law. True reform allows the waxing of a courageous freedom that comes from the love of Christ Crucified, pure and simple. As such, the aim of all true Christian *reform* is to *conform* to the Holy Cross.

In addition to interiority and radicality, true reform entails a greater integrity. Such an integrity means that there will be no inconsistent, contradictory, disproportionate, redundant, or hypocritical applications of the letter of the law, but rather that this letter is animated according to a deeper and all pervasive heeding of the spirit of the law. Again, true Christian reform is always a simplification; the deeper a Christian goes in the Faith the simpler it becomes, for the Faith becomes the pure assent to truth and embrace of the good which is found in the Savior Crucified.

The interiority, radicality, and integrity required for true reform are, to some extent, all entailed in the concept of propriety. Propriety, its understanding and implementation, is absolutely necessary for true Christian reform. Propriety is a most unique word in that its very divergent definitions are telling. Indeed, the term "propriety" has two diametrically opposed definitions. The dictionary's current, or post-

Christendom, definition of propriety is "that which conforms to current societal norms." This same dictionary lists as well what it deems the *obsolete*, or ancient Western and Christian, definition of propriety, as "that which conveys true essence." Significantly, these two definitions of propriety sum up the core philosophical difference of Christian and post-Christian cultures.

Rescued from the dustbin of lexicography, propriety's archaic definition as "conveying true essence" entails being true to the spirit of a thing, person, concept, or law. Again, both in the order of nature and grace, of philosophy and theology, the conveying of true essence is that which is most crucial, is that which is of "vital importance" and "cross [*read* reality] conformed." In regards to true reform, acquiring greater propriety requires the modification or elimination of certain letters of the law or cultural encrustations so as to manifest and implement the true essence of a law or charism. Thus, if there is to be justification for any reform it must always be proven to be a moving from a superficial letter of the law to a deeper spirit of the law; must facilitate a more interior conversion and conformity to the Holy Cross; must be a more radical rooting in the Holy Cross; and must be a more integral *embrace* of the Holy Cross. For the only true advance in the Faith goes from servile fear to sacrificial love, a sacrificial love that imbues the Christian with the requisite courage to intimately embrace Christ Crucified.

VATICAN I REFORM

In it being ordered toward interior personal conversion, true reform is not ordered toward changing the Church. For the Church, strictly and ontologically speaking, remains always the Spotless Bride of Christ. Any practical and tangible external reforms should always be ordered towards facilitating the interior reform of the Christian; that is, the way Christians live out their crucial Christian call to holiness and their subsequent particular vocations in conformity to Christ and his Spotless Bride. Thus there is always a need for the reform of Christian life, and this is especially urgent in the times of societal and cultural convulse.

The conveying of Vatican II and its agenda of reform was in response to the 20th Century's violent convulsing of civilizations and especially Western civilization. For when the smoke of the two world wars cleared mid-way through that cataclysmic century, the certain and irreparable collapse of Christendom I was undeniably revealed. But Vatican II got carried away in the externals and the call to interior conversion was muted. This external reform is most evident in Vatican II's flag-ship document: *Constitution on the Sacred Liturgy*.

Vatican II was all about reforming the Holy Mass but it was not at all about conforming to the Holy Cross. Vatican II, as was explicated in the preface, was highly deficient in its mention of the Holy Cross and thus not oriented towards that Cross in its call for reforms. So too, Vatican II's changing of the letter of the law often found its impetus in the spirit of the world rather than the spirit of Christ's law.

While there certainly was a disconnect between the pre-Vatican II Christian's external practices and his interior beliefs, instead of seeking an interior conversion that fulfilled the traditional externals, conciliar reforms sought to modify externals so as to make them relevant. This modification of relevancy entailed conforming to, and indeed hastening, the increasingly secular and compromised interior disposition of the faithful. But if conversely Vatican II, and in particular the reform of the liturgy, had been ordered toward conforming to Christ's Holy Cross, the "spirit of Vatican II" would not have been befouled by "the smoke of Satan,"[77] nor would there have been any possibility of liturgical abuses such as "clown Masses."

Whereas the men of the Church, inclusive of ecclesial administrative structures and other accidentals, are constantly in need of reform as per fallen human nature, the Church *qua* Spotless Bride of Christ is never in need of reform. Amidst the external upheavals of all too human power structures, amidst the sociopolitical struggles of her sons, the Church remains inviolate, serene, and constant.

While it is true that in the waning decades of the second millennium, and culminating with Vatican II, reform in a renewed universal call to holiness was emphasized, the proverbial "reforms of Vatican II" went astray as they focused on institutions and practices. The reforms of Vatican II focused on liturgy, bureaucratic structures, and ministries; on offices and rites; and on ecclesial, parish, social activism rather than on the Holy Cross, which is the source of all holiness. The call to holiness, that is, the call to personal spiritual reform, was skirted by Vatican II due to the all too human avoidance of the doctrine of the Cross, as well as by misdirecting the reform to institutions and practices that were still erroneous equated with the Church herself.

This is not to say there wasn't, or isn't, a need for reform of structures and ministries. However, such external reform is properly the fruit of a preeminent internal reform guided by the essence of the Church. When external reform is not preceded by such an interior reform, though the externals may change, things remain just more of the same.[78] But interior reform always inform externals. Even though externals may appear relatively unchanged, when there is an interior reform the external law and practice are informed and imbued with the spirit of that law and practice and thus achieve a purified focus and greater efficacy. And when such informed external reform does occur it is not from decrees on high but rather as an organic, that is grassroots, manifestation of the informing spirit of the law.

Though acquiescing to the call to holiness is an interior process, it is not an isolated process; indeed it is an all-permeating mystical process. Members of the mystical body of Christ, both those in heaven and purgatory, as well as those on earth, impact each other by their very purgation and sanctification. This is indeed a mystical dynamic that derives from the very dynamics of Our Lord's life itself. Jesus Christ's life was not about reforming institutions, but hearts. He came not to establish an earthly kingdom but a mystical one. He died apparently useless and ineffectual, his very hands and feet pinioned to a cross, and from there redeemed the world through his own Bleeding Heart.

ECCLESIAL KENOSIS
CONTINUED

True reform of the Church, then, always entails first the reform of the individual who is the source of the worldly elements that besmirch the true countenance of the Church. But manifesting the true countenance of the Church entails an ecclesial kenosis that goes beyond the basic requirements for the individual Christian, for it is a chastening and an emptying of even those things that rightfully belong to man or to sociopolitical entities. For these things of men[79] are not essential to the Kingdom of God, indeed, they can become a stumbling block to the coming of the Kingdom. Once again,

> Get behind Me, Satan! You are a stumbling block to Me. For you do not have in mind the things of God, but the things of men. MT 16:23

This ecclesial kenosis purifies the Church of that which is but paltry in comparison to her true and essential countenance as the Spotless Bride of Christ. As her accidental edifices crumble and cultural encrustations dissolve, the Church's true countenance as the Spotless Bride of the Spotless Lamb is only further revealed. The Church is not her bureaucracy, her buildings, much less her art and riches. The Church is her truth, and her only true possessions are her Deposit of Faith and her stores of grace. Nor is the Church to be equated with her official ministers. Indeed, the Church has most often, if not always, triumphed not because of but in spite of her ministers. This transcendence of bureaucracies, possessions, and the follies and sins of men is a mark of the Church's divine nature, a proof of her indefectibility.

In the wake of Vatican II, the Church is being purged of accidental encrustations and accouterments, of superfluous privileges and powers, so she may purely emerge in the third millennium in all her truth and grace as the Spotless Bride of Christ. Yes, the Church of feudal times that imposed her influence and demanded allegiance through monarchical trappings did great good, not only in spite of these trappings but even through them. But the Church that forgoes such trappings and instills her influence in the individual conscience evokes an allegiance unparalleled, and it is only such an allegiance that will suffice for the Third Millennium.

Yes, in the past the monarchical structures of the magisterium may have worked for the better, may have, for instance, impeded the take-over of the Church by exterior worldly powers; but so too for the worse. For though the Church in her indefectible immunity cannot be overtaken by worldly powers, the men in the Church can be and were so overtaken; and thus these churchmen were both manipulated by these powers and manipulated others under the false auspices of the Church. The danger is not of the Church misusing her power and purpose, but the danger is of men misusing the Church for their own power and purposes. An ecclesial kenosis, then, always entails a chastening of the human elements of the Church, indeed of the men themselves.

But time spent criticizing the past distracts from the task of purifying the present. The purification of the present entails not a condemnatory criticism of our forefathers but a contrite criticism of ourselves, and it is only such a contrite self-criticism that yields salubrious, yes miraculous, results. This contrite self-criticism entails a penitential call to conversion: to a turning away from the flesh, the world, and the devil and a metanoia of heart. For from the beginning, and in essence, any new Divine dispensation entailed a purification that separated the sheep from the goats. Indeed, this purification is the very hallmark of God's enduring presence with his people and is therefore a hallmark of Christ's Holy Catholic Church, that is now, in this third millennium, certainly undergoing a purifying ecclesial kenosis.

VI. Perversions of Power

*You know that the princes
of the Gentiles lord it over them.
It shall not be so among you.
He that will be first among you,
shall be your servant. MT 25-27*

Though **the Church was stripped** of a secular worldly power, the *libido dominandi*[80] of fallen human nature still remains. But the "desire to dominate," the lust for power, is diametrically opposed to the charisms of papacy, prelature, and priesthood. It is only by intentionally purifying these offices of that power—of monarchical manias, bureaucratic bulwarks, and prideful penchants—that their true charism of self-abnegating service is fully actualized.

Clericalism, be it at the papal, episcopal, or priestly level, is a mockery of Christ's high priesthood. For the Son of God became man and thus a priest by emptying himself of that which was justly his and "taking the form of a slave" (PP 2:7). But in clericalism, the man unjustly grasps equality with God and asserts a superiority over others. The slavery of Christ-the-Priest is perversely mocked by the bullying elitism of the clericalistic priest. But the priesthood is not about the man nor power, but the abnegation of the man so as to manifest Christ and him crucified.

No one exists for popes, prelates, or priests, rather the *sine qua non* charism of these ordained ministries is the converse; that is, popes, prelates, and priests exist *totally* for others, they exist to serve and minister unto the people of God and unto God himself. Thus, it is an abomination when an ordained office is used to exercise a bullying or manipulative power over the faithful. On a less malignant but more ubiquitous note, it is as well quite unseemly and contrary to their charism for priests or bishops to be condescending toward the faithful, for if these clerics are to avail themselves of the honorific "father" it is not as an adult to a child or as a superior to an inferior, but rather as someone solicitous for the welfare of another. Indeed, they are called to be sacrificially solicitous, placing themselves secondary to and always at the service of those they are dedicated to serve.

CHANCERY BUREAUCRACY

The predominant occupational hazard of being a pope or bishop has proven to be acting like a king. The Roman Curia, which is the mother bureaucracy that has formed over the ages around the papacy, means Roman Court, as in a royal court. This royal Roman Curia, while not necessarily preserving the patrimony of the Holy Faith all that well, has succeeded to some extent in preserving the ancient *Romanitas*,[81] that is, the palace intrigue and power plays surrounding the papacy.

But descending into the elaborate labyrinth of *Romanitas* is here forgone as it is now co-mingling with a new bureaucratic professionalism. It is this admixture of *Romanitas* and modern bureaucratic professionalism that is both most urgent to examine and *eradicate*, for it produces an especially virulent and unresponsive power structure, and it is a phenomenon being played out not only in the Vatican but in national episcopal conferences and diocesan chanceries across the world. In sum, the current functioning ecclesial power structure consists of bureaucracy—that is, a body of non-elective officials and administrative policy-making groups and departments—pervaded with clericalistic and aristocratic airs.

Some, especially non-believers, have attributed the Church's unprecedented 2,000 year old existence as a corporate entity to its administrative structure, rather than its divine indestructible nature. The famed Austrian economist L. Mises wrote,

> The Roman Church, under the Tridentine organization as it emerged from the Counter Reformation, is a perfect bureaucracy. It has successfully solved the most delicate problem of every non-Democratic

government, the selection of the top executives. To every boy access to the highest dignities of the Church is virtually open. The local priest is anxious to smooth the way to education of the most intelligent youths of his parish; they are trained in the Bishop's seminary; once ordained, their further career depends entirely upon their character, their zeal, and their intellect. There are among the prelates many scions of noble and wealthy families. But they do not owe their office to their ancestry. They have to compete, on almost equal terms, with the sons of poor peasants, workers and serfs. The princes of the Catholic Church, the abbots and teachers of the theological universities, are a body of eminent men. Even in the most advanced countries they are worthy rivals of the most brilliant scholars, philosophers, scientists, and statesmen.... No precedent of a perfect hierarchy could be found other than that presented by Catholicism....

The realm of Christianity which the Pope and the other Bishops administer is not subject to any change. It is built upon a perennial and immutable doctrine. The creed is fixed forever. There is no progress and no evolution. There is only obedience to law and the dogma. The methods of selection adopted by the Church are very efficient in the government of a body clinging to an undisputed, unchangeable set of rules and regulation. They are perfect in the choice of the guardians of an eternal treasure of doctrine....

Bureaucratization is necessarily rigid because it involves the observation of established rules and practices. But in social life rigidity amounts to petrification and death....In an all-round bureaucratic system neither the bureaucrats nor their subjects would any longer be real human beings."[82]

But of course the Church does not owe her existence to her bureaucratic structure, for she indeed existed for a millennium and a half before the Tridentine bureaucratic structuring, and even now is called to go beyond that structuring. The letter of the law that Mises above admires (not without some dissonance) is also that which eventually *killeth.* However, the spirit of the law gives life and transcends time and place. It is this spirit, indeed the Holy Spirit, not her bureaucracy, that keeps the ancient Catholic Church ever young and spotless.

It is clearly not the brilliance of the men, nor their moral rectitude that has kept the Church alive. And while scandalously some bishops, if of a more traditional bent, still prance around like aristocracy or, if of a more secular bent, pretend to be power-brokers and great CEOs, both in fact are only living off the incredible material and spiritual patrimony of Catholicism's past. Indeed, it is clear that the Church of the third millennium remains indefectible in spite of the men. According to truly Catholic sensibilities, those who would be "perfect [as] the choice of the guardians of an eternal treasure of doctrine" would not be the elite but the humble, not princes and scholars but fishermen and common men.

The past ecclesial bureaucratic structure is of the mundane, is of the deadest letter of the law, and must be so relegated. As decentralization occurs the priest and prelate will be seen as ministers for the people rather than as elite rulers. Most tellingly and unprecedentedly, the Holy Catholic Church miraculously survives in spite of its clericalism and all too human bureaucracy (a fact if recognized by Mises would have provoked his conversion).

If clericalism has subsided a bit at the parish level (though it is on the rise in traditional circles), it is still quite alive and thriving at the diocesan level; and this clericalism is present all along the ecclesial political spectrum, from liberal-progressive to conservative-traditional. The chancery has remained a last vestige of monarchical culture, inclusive of princes and palace intrigues. The proverbial "chancery rats" are those ensconced in a bureaucracy of the unelected and unresponsive. In the recesses of chancery environs *prima dona* priests prance around and chancery shenanigans are scandalously legendary for those in-the-know.

The business of the chancery is a business

indeed, with governmental corporate contracts[83] coming with compromise. Bishops play at being both pastoral and dictatorial. A magisterial Machiavellianism that employs duplicity and stonewalling characterizes chancery bureaucracies. But bishops shouldn't be so concerned with a show of power, but rather with a show of truth; rather than stonewalling the faithful, they should be unflinchingly obstinate in the face of the profane powers that be; rather than their tending to business, they should be tending to the flock.

Yes, the pure and pristine Holy Mother Church survives and thrives not due to her human element, but in spite of it. Truly, her indefectibility, while governed by quite defective men, is proof of her supernaturality. The authority of the Church resides in her teachings, and the power of the Church is in the truth itself. This authority and power then emanates not from top to bottom but wells up ever fresh and refreshing from deep within the recesses of the Deposit of Faith and from the conscience of each believer so informed by that Holy Depository. It is indeed the immutable and definite truth of the Church that must reign more and more supreme. Let the lowliest peasant rule, even in chanceries or the papal court itself, if he is invested with the truth of Holy Mother Church.

THE CANCER OF CLERICALISM

The beginnings of the third millennium of Christianity will be forever marked by the sordid scandals perpetrated by its priests. As such it is of most immediate import for the faithful, and as well for the renewal of the ministries of the priesthood, episcopacy and even papacy, to understanding the priestly charism.[84] It is also, unhappily, most necessary to understand what the perversion of the priesthood entails. This perversion of priesthood is specified as "clericalism," and clericalism is the fertile matrix from which scandalous sacerdotal sins spring.

Clericalism is not only a vicious behavior but a heretical ideological perversion of the priesthood. In the heresy of clericalism the person of the priest in his human nature is believed (by either the priest and/or other Christians) to be imbued with superiority through ordination, making the *man himself* superior to non-ordained Christians, who remain in a relatively degraded state.

The etiological dynamics of the progression of the heresy of clericalism and the subsequent sacerdotal scandals that have rocked Catholicism have been quite linear and precipitous. From the popular heights of a near deification of the priest in the latter part of the second millennium, the priest in the third millennium has now fallen to the status of a pariah. In fact, it is the very countries (*e.g.*, the United States, Ireland, and Quebec) where the priest was held in the highest esteem that the sins of priests would prove most scandalous. This is because clericalism makes scandal possible.

The very placing of the priest upon a pedestal made possible the sacerdotal scandals, and it was the ecclesial powers-that-be that not only infamously failed in addressing these scandals but who were instrumental in placing the priest upon a pedestal in the first place. For clericalism imbues the man who is a priest with an undue authority, prestige, and ensuing license which is the *sine qua non* of scandal. So too, when non-ordained Christians themselves embrace the heresy of clericalism and do not separate the man from his priestly office they make themselves susceptible to scandal; that is, they put themselves in an occasion of sin, namely, the occasion of being scandalized. In regards to sacerdotal scandals, the sin of the scandalized is the denigration or rejection of the priesthood, and subsequently the Church, because of the sins of the man. The dynamics of clericalism and its corollary scandal applies as well to those who fall into the akin heresies of ultramontanism and papolatry, who place themselves in an occasion to be scandalized by a papacy or "the Vatican," which may be unfit or not Catholic enough.

As such, in the course of the second millennium, the stage of sacerdotal scandal was set with clericalism. Like an enduring multi-generational curse, the magisterium's second millennial pact with worldly power continued to infect the ordained ministries even after the loss of worldly power and the fall of Christendom. With the sociopolitical fall of Christendom the king or State would no longer be the strong-arm of the magisterium. To compensate for this loss of high echelon political leverage, the magisterium sought local leverage by empowering and aggrandizing priests as their lieutenants and enforcers. As such, the priest would now claim to rule over his parish (*i.e.*, over the Catholic inhabitants of his local area) just as popes in the past laid claim to ruling over princes. It is this reallocation of illicit power that would eventually lead to the outbreaks of clerical perversion so sordidly manifested in the sexual abuse scandals.

CLERICAL HUBRIS

Again, as the Church lost political power she sought to gain grassroots power. This was done by aggrandizing the priest and the pastor. Popes Pius X and XII, and others, would continually promote the dignity of the priest and be haphazardly lavish in extending his authority. This would correlate with an unprecedented jump in vocations, but also with an increase of clerical hubris, pastoral bullying, priestly sexual perversion, and an episcopal stonewalling that will ever besmirch the 20th Century.

Clericalistic sins are specifically sins of hubris. It is hubris that caused the downfall of the angels and Adam. It is hubris that caused the Jews to apostatize time and again and to ultimately reject Christ. And yes, it is hubris that has led to the cancer of clericalism and its ungodly and ever so damaging fruit of scandal. The proverb "pride goeth before destruction, and a haughty spirit before a fall," sums up the perverse phenomenon of clericalistic hubris (PRV 16:18). The priestly hubris that resulted in scandal in the latter part of the second millennium entailed mainly sexual perversity, and most especially the sin of homosexuality. "In ancient Athens, hubris was defined as the use of violence to shame [a] victim," as is the case with sexual bullying and/or the rape of a person who is a subordinate.[85] As per the nature of homosexual perversion, the seduction of adolescent males is apical. For such a seduction of the young male entails a power differential that feeds the perpetrator's disordered egoistic need for aggrandizement. This aggrandizement is heightened by the shaming and humiliation of the victim. Such men as those that caused the priestly scandals had a gnawing egoistic need for high aggrandizement, yet were in themselves inadequate to achieve such an aggrandizement through their own efforts or excellence, and thus such men seek in ordination a means to be imbued themselves with a special and superior status.

A typical profile[86] of a man who becomes a clericalistic or narcissistic priest is that of a proverbial "beta male" who, though greatly desiring admiration and esteem, doesn't have the wherewithal to earn that admiration in the "free market." Such a man is drawn to Holy Orders so as to become a kind of aristocrat, that is, so as to gain a privileged rank above and beyond his ability to merit it. This phenomenon was quite prevalent in the past, what with admission to the ranks of the priesthood even in the latter part of the second millennium being tantamount to becoming royalty. It is no wonder that homosexuality was a concomitant vice of clericalism that bloomed unchecked in the lust-laden atmosphere of the late 1960's and the 1970's. This aristocratic lure of ordination and its accompanying clericalistic hubris is still quite prevalent with traditional and conservative priests, but present as well in the mainstream priesthood.[87]

The predacious homosexual abuse of minors (which, tellingly, the Church's prelatic bureaucracy was *forced* to respond to only because of the secular statutory illegality entailed therein) is but a perverse form of bullying. Indeed, even without predatory homosexuality, clericalistic hubris is always manifested in bullying. Note well, the degradation of others that is entailed in hubris is not necessarily enacted through physical or sexual abuse, and is more commonly manifest through the psychological and social degradation of others. Thus, clerical bullying, though not as overtly sinful and sensational as sexual abuse, is nonetheless a precursor to it. Clerical bullies can operate under the auspices of legitimate authority and even overt appearance of virtue; indeed, the most demonic of all appear to be holy men of God.

Aristotle defined hubris as "shaming the victim," merely for that bully's own gratification:

[Hubris] is to cause shame to the victim, not in

order that anything may happen to you, nor because anything has happened to you, but merely for your own gratification. Hubris is not the requital of past injuries; this is revenge. As for the pleasure in hubris, its cause is this: naive [read inadequate, emasculated] men think that by ill-treating others they make their own superiority the greater.[88]

Violations of the ancient Greek law against hubris included what today are termed assault and battery (i.e., violent bullying), sexual crimes (especially homosexuality), and the theft of public or sacred property. Therefore, along with bullying and homosexuality, the sins of greed and embezzlement, too, are intrinsic to hubris. Embezzlement from the Church has almost always been part and parcel of the clerical sexual perversion scandals. However, because this embezzlement by clerics involves theft from a parish or diocese it is without an identifiable victim who (along with his lawyers) can be recompensed, thus it has garnered little secular or legal interest.

Sexual perversity, greed, and bullying are but the fruits of prideful hubris. Clericalism derives from the same prideful hubris and has as concomitant the same aforementioned fruits. Again, in clericalism, the priest believes his person is imbued with superiority through ordination, that somehow holy orders makes him as a man superior to others, that is to the laity, who are seen as in a degraded state. The need to exercise superiority and continually degrade the laity, at least those that are not subservient enough, is a driving force of clericalism. This means, for example, that the conservative clericalistic pastor who is but a demigod and not a sexual pervert has already perverted the priesthood and paved the way for homosexual perversion itself. Yes, that means the authoritarian clericalism of pre-Vatican II priests produced (even before Vatican II) the sins of homosexuality[89] within the priestly ranks, sins that exploded once the moral strictures were loosened in the late 1960's and 1970's.

Even so, the mere absence or deficiency of normal

heterosexual desires should be considered, *in and of itself*, a bar to ordination. The first and most basic evaluation of applicants to the seminary should be their feelings toward marriage and family. If an applicant has a desire to marry, if he views giving up feminine marital companionship and the fathering of children as a sacrifice, then he may well have a vocation to the priesthood. When such is the case a possible future priest's intentions are validated by sacrifice; that is the subordination of self is present from the beginning. Such a man's motives are essentially pure, for his ascent of the Tabor of priestly ordination is not an enterprise of aggrandizement but an ascent of Golgotha as well unto sacrificial immolation.

THE CULPABILITY OF THE LAITY

At the end of the second millennium in Catholic culture priests were of the ruling class. When a young man but entered the seminary he and his family became part of the parish aristocracy. Indeed, the most pervasive and enduring monarchical culture that remained in the West was that of the popes, prelates, and priests of the Holy Catholic Church. But simply put, the ordained ministries, like all Christian ministries, are not about the priest, bishop, or pope, but rather the priest, bishop, and pope are about the faithful. Again, no one exists for the priest or prelate, rather they exists for others. Yes, they have some similarity to the familial father who in unsung sacrifice exists for his family. But the father has a devoted wife and doting children; not so the priest, nor should he seek this homage, much less usurp it, which rightly belongs to the familial father.

Thus, we see the need for the deep psychomoral rectitude, especially a lack of egoistic neediness, of the man who would advance to priesthood. His pride must be easily subsumed under the fires of humiliation. The need to distinguish between the ordained office and the man is crucial so that the man does not misuse and abuse the office. The man himself can only do this by being inculcated in a deep humility, thus making the distinction deep within his own person. While chastity, poverty, and obedience as evangelical counsels are appropriate to the ordained, *humility is crucial*. But since humility cannot be the subject of a vow, it must be enshrined as the paramount priestly ideal.

Christians should love the priesthood of Jesus Christ enough not to be occasions of sin to those who are ordained unto Christ. Clericalism and its attendants must not be tolerated by those who love the priesthood of Jesus Christ. It is a form of pride to kowtow and be a respecter of persons. It is Protestantism that respects the man, his preaching ability, his particular insights and wisdom. But Catholics are not respecters of persons, save the persons of the Holy Trinity. A man is a priest through no merits of his own. That is the point of ordination: the *sub*ordination of self.

Take for example, the presence of a priest at the deathbed of a loved one is a gift of God, even a sign of salvation with the bestowing of the Last Rights. But even after all the sacraments and blessings of the Church have been bestowed, the presence of the priest is still irreplaceable, and not dependent on any words of comfort or compassion he uttered. No, it is not anything the priest does, save drag himself out of bed in the middle of a dark night, but rather his mere presence that provides the sacerdotal succor of Christ the High Priest who resides indelibly in his soul.

And as per the despicable scandals that infected the priesthood and episcopacy, if the laity had been doing their job, if they had truly loved the priesthood of Jesus Christ, these scandals would have been nipped in the bud. As perverse bullying clericalistic priests were shuffled from parish to parish, one must ask the obvious question, "Where were the fathers of these boys who were abused?" Any abusive priest so shuffled should, as per the dictates of justice and fatherly duty, have arrived at his new parish at the very least with a broken nose! So too, any stonewalling autocratic bishop should have been called out and confronted in no uncertain terms and actions, and rode out of the diocese on a rail if need be by the faithful! Yes, it is rightly an excomunicable offense to strike a priest or prelate *qua* priest or prelate; that is, because they are a priest or prelate. But it may well be a solemn duty to strike a priest or prelate because they are profaning the priesthood, episcopacy, Holy Mother Church, the innocent and the sacred. For those men who have besmirched the holy priesthood, episcopal offices, and papal patrimonies with perversions of power have sinned first and foremost against the High Priest Jesus Christ Himself; they are nothing less than Judas priests.

Paradoxically, it often those most doctrinally conservative who in adhering to the letter of the law not only disallow its spirit, but actually allow a demonic spirit to reign. This was true in the past, but is still true today, especially in traditionalist circles. In such circles, one may hear sentiments such as, "Yes, we know Father X is wrong, but what can we do? If we confront or report him we will lose the traditional Mass." In short, these faithful are willing to acquiesce to evil so as to have the Mass! But the Mass is about Christ Crucified, and Christ Crucified is about the Spotless Lamb refusing to compromise one iota with, and thus defeating, all evil.

A HERETICAL
AUTHORITARIANISM

The heresy of clericalism is empowered by another heresy promulgated in the latter part of the second millennium. This is the heresy that promotes servile or blind obedience as the highest Christian act. This is heretical because it is contrary and does violence to the Christian freedom that emanates from God creating man in his image. The top-heavy and authoritarian monarchical structure that characterized the early part of the Catholic second millennium became quite draconian in the latter part of that millennium. Though the Counter-Reformation was proceeded by the blessings of the concise dogmatic definitions of Trent, it ended up facilitating a bureaucratic structure that demanded nothing less than a blind obedience to one's superiors.

The predominant Counter-Reformation organization, both for good and ill, were the Jesuits,[90] and the Ignatian idea of obedience was totalitarian indeed. Though St. Ignatius himself apparently did not in practice demand such obedience, his writing most certainly justified it in his successors.

> In the highest and most meritorious degree of obedience, the follower has no more will of his own in obeying than an inanimate object. 'Everyone of those who live under obedience ought to allow himself to be carried and directed by Divine Providence through the agency of the superior as if he were a lifeless body which allows itself to be carried to any place and to be treated in any manner desired, or as if he were an old man's staff which serves in any place and in any manner whatsoever in which the holder wishes to use

it.[91]

This unchristian, indeed heretical, notion of obedience was further promulgated in Alphonsus Rodriguez S.J.'s explication of Ignatian obedience in *Practice of Perfection and Christian Virtues*, which was published in 1609. From the Counter-Reformation on, *Practice of Perfection and Christian Virtues* was the go-to singular authoritative manual on Christian life and was promulgated throughout the Church, in her seminaries and religious institutions. Indeed, *Practice of Perfection and Christian Virtues* was the introductory manual for Jesuit novices through the Second Vatican Council.

> II. To obey in will and heart, having one and the same wish and will as the Superior.
>
> III. To obey also with the understanding and judgment, adopting the same view and sentiment as the Superior, not giving place to any judgments or reasonings to the contrary.
>
> IV. To take the voice of the Superior … as the voice of God, and obey the Superior, whoever he may be, as Christ our Lord, and the same for subordinate officials.
>
> V. To follow blind obedience, that is obedience without enquiry or examination, or any seeking of reasons for the why and wherefore, it being reason enough for me that it is obedience and the command of the Superior.[92]

Rodriguez goes on to further emphasize the most unchristian aspects of this heretical notion of obedience,

> One of the greatest comforts and consolations that we have in Religion is this, that we are safe in doing what obedience commands. The Superior it is that may be wrong in commanding this or that, but you are certain that you are not wrong in doing what is commanded, for the only account that God will ask of you is if you have done what they commanded you, and with that your account will be sufficiently discharged before God. It is not for you to render account whether the thing commanded was a good thing, or whether something else would not have been better; that does

not belong to you, but to the account of the Superior. When you act under obedience, God takes it off your books, and puts it on the books of the Superior.[93]

The Suplican[94] order, founded 100 years after the Jesuits and dominant in priestly and religious formation up to Vatican II, practiced and greatly advanced this heretical notion of obedience. John R. T. Lamont, in an essay on the episcopal sexual abuse scandal circa 2018, states:

> It became prevalent in the new institution of the Counter-Reformation seminary; the *Treatise on Obedience* of the Sulpician Louis Tronson gave St. Ignatius's teaching and writings as the summit of Catholic teaching on obedience. The Sulpician adoption of this conception was particularly important because of their central role in the training of priests in seminaries from the seventeenth century onwards. The servile conception of obedience remained the standard one into the twentieth century. Adolphe Tanquerey, in his widely read and translated (and in many ways excellent) work *Précis de théologie ascétique et mystique*, could write that perfect souls who have reached the highest degree of obedience submit their judgment to that of their superior, without even examining the reasons for which he commands them. The conception of religious authority and religious obedience that became dominant in the Church from the sixteenth century onwards was thus a fundamental innovation that departed from previous Catholic positions. It came to influence the Church through the training given in seminaries for diocesan priests, and the approach to discipline in religious congregations. The daily life of seminarians and religious was structured by a multitude of rules governing the minutiae of behavior, and activities that fell outside this routine could generally be pursued only with the permission of the superior. Such permission was arbitrarily refused from time to time in order to encourage submissiveness in subordinates. Reasons for orders were not provided, and questions about the reasons for orders were not answered.[95]

As Christendom I and the monarchical power of the Church waned political authoritarianism was replaced with a growing and much more draconian spiritual totalitarianism. Whereas political authoritarianism sought control through political and social structures, spiritual totalitarianism sought control over the very interiority of the person, of their very thoughts, volitions, and emotions. It is this spiritual totalitarianism, this rationally blind and volitionally slavish obedience, that created an overall ecclesial culture of both chancerism and clericalism and produced the monstrosities of bullying bishops and perverse predator priests.

Over a 400 hundred year period spiritual totalitarianism conditioned not only the clergy but the faithful themselves for the sexual abuse scandals of the 20th Century,

> Both superiors and subordinates in a tyrannical system are taught to worship power and those who hold it, and to despise inferiors, the weak, and victims. . . . The infantilization produced by this understanding of authority contributed to sexual abuse in several ways. An infantilized person cannot exercise independent judgment and is not able to stand up for himself or others. Infants are not able to comprehend evil, and they are not able to admit or even understand that their father figures are evil. Those priests who took the tyrannical understanding of authority seriously, rather than conforming to it in order to realize their ambitions and enjoy the pleasures of tyranny, were thus psychologically unable to speak out against sexual abuse and take risks to correct it. The ambitious did not do so because there was no percentage in it for them. As for the laity, the brutal truth is that much sexual abuse of children[[96]] by priests occurred with the collusion of the parents of these children. Without this collusion, the sexual abuse of children and adolescents by priests could never have taken on the dimensions that it did.[[97]]

Even into the third millennium, such notions of spiritual totalitarianism and of blind and slavish obedience are widely promulgated in traditional and conservative fraternities of priests and the evangelical (*a.k.a* religious) orders that these fraternities have sway over. Indeed, it is a tenant of the prominent fraternities of traditional priests to impose a total obedience upon the laity who are their spiritual directees, and even over the entirety of their parishioners if they can get away with it. Indeed, some lay directees have been ordered under the false threat of the pain of sin by their priest spiritual directors to enter evangelical life: that is, quite outrageously, ordered under obedience to take vows of obedience.[98]

THE SERVANTS OF THE SERVANTS OF GOD

God's grand gamble was to create beings in his image, being capable of divinization but as such also capable of damnation. This grand gamble can be further seen in God's having a chosen people, a people called to bring salvation to the world but capable of an equivalent apostasy as well. And maybe God's greatest and most gratuitous gamble of all is to have chosen men to take upon themselves his very person in Christ as portals of his grace; but as such, in this *persona Christi* intimacy, these men are also able to betray him unto death with a very kiss. As always in God's necessary economy of grace the chosen have both the potential for the greatest good and the greatest evil.

The horrendous scandals of perversion in the priesthood have made it clear that the cancer of clericalism must never be countenanced again. Yes, the precipitous toppling of Christendom I, falling like a house of cards, showed that a top-heavy structure ordered toward popes, prelates, and priests, no matter how apparently magnificent, could not stand while her very familial foundation, and thus the essential individual and Christian vocation, was rotting.

In the anti-Christic third millennium the Church's truth is fully explicated and available. Today the men of the magisterium and ordained ministers must take a supporting role and not obfuscate or impede that Church nor the living out of that truth by her faithful. If seen as shepherds at all, they are not to be seen as rulers of mindless sheep but as humble ministers tending to God's flock; they are to be seen as servants who exist solely to attend to the needs of the faithful, as per Christ's final injunction to Peter himself, "Feed my lambs." (JN 21:15)

Today, seen in a purely supportive role, priests and prelates are called to humbly eschew even their just privileges and be deaf even to warranted praise, all in keeping with the spirit of the High Priest Jesus Christ's kenosis, "who emptied himself and took the form of a slave," (PP 2:7), as well as the Church's divinely destined third millennium ecclesial kenosis.

VII. Imago Dei Individualism

But Jesus, calling them together, said:
Suffer children to come to me,
and forbid them not:
for of such is the kingdom of God.
LK 18:16

T**he drama of human existence**, and even more so the drama of Christian existence, is the drama of the individual. In fulfillment of the preeminent crucial human natural vocation (*viz.,* the Psychomoral Vocation) it is only the individual that can assent to truth and choose the good, for it is only the individual soul that manifests the analogous image of God. Infinitely more so, in fulfillment of the crucial Christian supernatural vocation, it is only the individual that can answer the call to holiness, for it is only the individual soul that can magnify the living Lord. Thus, individualism forms the basis for both the crucial human and crucial Christian vocations.

The human individual in his *imago Dei* nature analogously[99] manifests God's own being in his rational and volitional functions. This *imago Dei* nature entails man's specific difference, that is, the ability to assent to truth and choose the good. In the *imago Dei* is found the ultimate natural drama of free will, of reason and love, of human maturation. Here the *imago Dei* becomes more manifest in so far as the subjective and often irrational and enslaving egoistic self is diminished by the impact of reality. The essential drama of each person's life unfolds in this *imago Dei vs.* ego dynamic; in whether or not a person loves himself more or another more; in whether or not a person loves objective reality more or his own subjective desires more. Indeed, the drama of human existence comes down to whether or not a person chooses to love God and God's reality more than he loves himself, for God's ways are not man's ways.

ASSERTING IMAGO DEI INDIVIDUALISM

The human person's vocation, then, is not only the calling (Lt. *vocare*) to be a seeker of truth, but to assent to truth and choose it as the good. As such, the human person is called to witness to truth by doing the good. And yes, to be a witness to truth and a doer of good is much more so the vocation of the Christian, for the Christian has the fullness of the truth and the good. Furthermore, the Christian is called to be a prophetic witness to truth and militant doer of the good, especially unto the malevolent powers-that-be.

Each person, even on the natural level, is called to assent to the truth and choose the objective good; that is, to assent to and choose reality and the true God who is the Author of Reality. As grace builds upon nature and the crucial Christian vocation upon the crucial human vocation, each Christian is given the grace to assent to the truth and choose the objective good in a superlative way; that is, with a supernatural faith, hope, and love. As per God's greater glory, the Christian is called and enabled by grace to fully choose the good by loving Christ and him crucified, who is at the very heart of reality. To fulfill this Christian vocation, which is as well the means to the transcendent fulfillment of the natural human vocation, requires an intentionality from the individual; that is, a personal commitment that entails vigorous seeking, ascetical focusing, and courageous doing.

> Not every one that saith to me, Lord, Lord, shall enter into the kingdom of heaven: but he that doth the will of my Father who is in heaven, he shall enter into the kingdom of heaven. MT 7:21

The timelessly required intentionality to achieve the human and Christian vocation as a holder of truth and doer of good must be all that more intense in this third millennium of blinding pride and self-absorbed narcissism. If that intentionality is dependent on the individual, on his assent to truth and doing of the good, the antidote to Technarcistic Man's egoistic individualism is *imago Dei individualism*. For though both are an individualism,[100] they are diametrically opposed. Indeed, egoistic individualism with its pride and subjective desires is eradicated by *imago Dei* individualism which is based on the humility of the creature and the acquiescence to the mandate of truth to do the good.

As diametrically opposed to egoistic individualism, *imago Dei* individualism is the very *antidote* to egoistic individualism. The remedying of third millennium rampant egoistic individualism requires the specific and intentional embrace of *imago Dei* individualism to open woeful Technarcistic Man to reality. Opening a person to reality by the embrace of *imago Dei* individualism is a psychomoralitic[101] process that breaks the egoistic fetters that limit free will and render the person vulnerable to manipulation and various degrees of enslavement: be those manipulations and enslavements from other individuals, the mass-media, popular culture, the State, the demonic, or the myriad of other powers and principalities that be.

THE PRIMACY OF INFORMED CONSCIENCE

As per the mandate of truth, the Holy Catholic Church asserts that there is an absolute authority that requires an absolute obedience. No, it's not obedience to a pope, pastor, priest, superior, or even to parents or a husband. Rather, it is obedience to the innate, absolute, and supreme authority that resides naturally within each and every person created in God's image. This natural, innate, absolute, and supreme authority is a person's conscience.

> Deep within his conscience man discovers a law which he has not laid upon himself but which he must obey. Its voice, ever calling him to love and to do what is good and to avoid evil, sounds in his heart at the right moment.... For man has in his heart a law inscribed by God.... His conscience is man's most secret core and his sanctuary. There he is alone with God whose voice echoes in his depths. (CCC 1776)

For natural man an informed conscience and its mandate depend on natural law and its all-inclusive and guiding mandate to "do good and avoid evil." When the natural *imago Dei* is supernaturally recreated and vivified via baptism and the subsequent sources of grace, it gains the addition supernatural ability to become informed by revealed truth.

> Conscience is the aboriginal Vicar of Christ, a prophet in its informations, a monarch in its peremptoriness, a priest in its blessings and anathemas, and even though the eternal priesthood throughout the Church should cease to be, in it the sacerdotal principle would remain and would have a sway.[102]

God so ordains that each person made in his image take full responsibility for the serving of his Absolute Divine

Authority. Even if wrong in his choice, no man will be culpable if he in good will is heeding his informed natural and supernatural conscience. Therefore, the individual Christian has the primary duty to heed the promptings of his informed Catholic conscience, that is, to assent to and enact the mandate of truth to the best of his knowledge and abilities.

Thus, the natural human person in his secret core and inner sanctuary of his *imago Dei* individualism is properly ensconced in natural law and reality, and building upon this the Christian is properly ensconced not only in natural law and reality but superabundantly in Christ and his Church. Here, the natural man and the Christian is alone with God whose voice echoes in his depths. Here, the heeding of one's conscience informed by natural and divine law is not merely an exercise in scholarship but in piety.

Once again, as grace builds upon nature, natural law's all-inclusive and guiding mandate to "do good and avoid evil" is the foundation for the Christian law's all-inclusive and guiding mandate to "love God and do what you will."[103] For when a person is willing to love God more than himself he is also most likely to assent to and choose the objective truth and good over his own subjective good. Strictly speaking then, the road to hell is not paved with good intentions but rather with bad intentions (or at least with bad intentions that are more intentional than the good ones) and the volitional rejection of an informed Catholic conscience that entails natural law, divine commands, and Church teachings.

Informed Catholic conscience means that a Christian is tasked with following the Church and her definitive teaching first and foremost. While a mere external obedience to ecclesial authorities is at face value good, a deeper and more mature internal obedience to the Church is preeminently Catholic. To accept the Church's definitive teachings on the very primacy of informed Catholic conscience presupposes that one accepts the teaching that all

Catholics, even the Pope himself, are subject to the Church; that is, the Church and no man has absolute primacy. The Catholic Church then is both radically authoritative and radically egalitarian in her upholding of both an unyielding hierarchy of objective truths and the ultimate requirement for individual discernment of these truths.

A truly informed Catholic conscience will never bid a person to compromise or to be less Catholic, and it will never justify rejecting exhortations to be more Catholic. Thus, it cannot be emphasized too strongly that an informed Catholic conscience is not an informed *worldly* conscience. When the dissenters and heretics claim they are following their conscience, it is a conscience informed by profane falsehoods. Indeed, those that heed a conscience that goes against the Church have that conscience informed by either the world, the flesh, or the devil. In fact, heresiarchs, such as Luther, and other lesser heretics and apostates, generally do not reject the Church and her teachings due to qualms of conscience but rather to the urgencies of concupiscence. Here again, the problem is not above the collar but below the belt. These dissenters are unable to accept the Cross of Christ, or even that of reality, because they are enslaved by their immoral egoistic passions (often sexual), though they may subsequently seek an intellectual/theological excuse and rationalization for their egoistic-based dissent.

An authentic informed Catholic conscience is based on the principle that it is impossible for one to be too Catholic; that is, it is impossible to be too conformed to Christ and him crucified. No one, neither prince, nor pope, nor even parents, can justly ask a person to be less Catholic. Legitimate authorities can rightly exhort one to kneel down in God's presence but they have no authority to tell one to get off of one's knees, to be less *authentically* penitential, to be less adoring. Herein lies the true dynamic of an informed Catholic conscience: *one has the absolute right to do his duty to God*.

The effective bringing about of the ecclesial age of

the laity requires the bringing about as well of deeply formed Catholic consciences. Only those faithful with a deeply informed Catholic conscience will withstand the mass indoctrination and enslavement of the third millennium's powerful totalitarian forces. In the laity's formulating of a battle plan for the advancement of Faith, family, and a new Christendom, an informed Catholic conscience is an absolute necessity.

THE MANDATE OF TRUTH

The primacy of an upright conscience is based upon the primacy and mandate of truth. But in this third millennium, truth is equated with the mundanely quantifiable, the egotistically subjective, or the statutorily haphazard. So in the third millennium, where truth has no mandate, the individual human person, and much more so the Christian, must be intensely intent upon the truth.

For evangelizing to be effective in the surreal third millennium it must begin by asking, "What is truth?"[104] The definition of truth is found in ontology, that is, the science of being. Very simply, being is that which is real, be it spiritual or material. When that which is real is assented to cognitively then it is the truth. When that which is real and true is chosen volitionally it is the good. The important understanding here is that reality does not depend on a person's perception; reality—like the truth and the good—has an objective existence that may or may not be in accord with one's subjective egoistic desires. The fact that existence itself entails ego-abnegation is the crux of evangelizing Technarcistic Man in the truth of reality and of the Gospel.

How crucial is the truth? The human person can perform a moral act because he is capable of consciously assenting to truth and volitionally choosing it as a good or rejecting it for a lower good. But a person's ability to assent to the truth or choose the good can be impeded by his psychomoral mal-being, namely coping mechanisms and dominating ego passions, that hamper assent and choice. It is in the moral or fully psychomoral act, the *rational assent to truth and volitional choosing of the good*, that is found the specific difference that distinguishes the human person from animals. Thus, this moral ability that is the specific difference of the human person is also the key to psychomoral well-being. For when a person assents to the fullest truth and chooses the most integral good, a person is assenting to and choosing reality; and what is essential well-being for the human *qua* seeker-of-the-truth than living in accord with the truth and reality?

When truth loses its mandate all is lost and the father of lies, the great deceiver, has won. Truth has lost its mandate in the third millennium's world of legal positivism, personal subjectivism, egoistic primacy, and mundane empiricism. In militant response, the truth must be intentionally inculcated in an uncompromised and synthesized[105] manner as per *imago Dei* individualism. Truth must be held as an integral tapestry of all truths and find its source in the Truth and the Good; the Why and the Way; the Life and the Redemption; the Word and Son of God. The common contemporary occurrence of Christians compromising the truth and not passionately dedicated to its promulgation makes a mockery of all their vows, including those of baptism.

THE INDIVIDUAL'S
ABSOLUTE RIGHT

Once the sacrosanct status of the individual conscience informed by the mandate of truth is recognized and observed, an absolute and inalienable individual right to assert that conscience is established. The *imago Dei* individual has an absolute right that neither powers, nor principalities, nor even papal decrees can take away or infringe. The crucial and absolutely inalienable right that is intrinsic to the human person made in the image of God, and much more so to Christians transformed in the person of Christ, is to the right to do one's duty to God. This absolute right to do one's duty to God is dictated by a conscience informed by natural law and revealed truth. This absolute, essential, and God-given right to be true to the truth and do the good must be intentionally espoused, vigorously cultivated, and courageously asserted in this third millennium's atmosphere of totalitarianism and manipulation; an atmosphere that oppresses, eviscerates, and enslaves man in a truth-obfuscating and good-obscuring technological matrix of smoke and mirrors.

In this day and age, to exercise one's absolute right to do one's duty to God will take nothing less than a heroic courage. Such a courage will only find its impetus in the love of God and its focus in Christ Crucified. Such a charity-charged courage cannot be manipulated, for it is undeterred by humiliations and thus transcends a person's pride and self-love. Such a courage remains undaunted by failure for it seeks only faithfulness.

The absolute right to do one's duty to God is not meant to be a mere pious platitude or exercise in political theory but rather an urgent common practice. It is a duty to be exercised every day and in all interactions, big or small, with the secular, profane, and/or evil. This means no compromise and no compartmentalization. This means courageously applying truth, good, and faith to every aspect and moment of one's life. This means having a totally synthesized[106] crucial Christian ethos.

As per the fundamental human vocation, the heart of this absolute right and solemn duty is to be true to the truth and to champion the good. From the discounting of human respect, to the contempt of the world and its perverse popular culture, to the refusal to kowtow to the threats of the increasingly totalitarian State, both locally and nationally, to the proactive speaking of truth to malignant powers and principalities, the uncompromised exercising of the absolute right to do one's duty to God applies. And if it is not exercised but rather compromised, even for convenience sake, then this crucial right is slowly lost. It is slowly lost within the person as an *imago Dei* ability, and more so as a Christian charism, and it is hence slowly lost as well both in the body politic and within the Church herself as their members become more and more enslaved.

DEHUMANIZING OBEDIENCE

As previously discussed,[107] there has been a prevalent imperfect and even insidious obedience promulgated in the Church, especially during and after the Counter-Reformation. It was this non-Christian authoritarian obedience that led to the very scandals that have plagued Holy Mother Church since those times and especially in the dawn of the third millennium. But in the third millennium, more than ever, only a perfect obedience that finds it impetus in charity will suffice. This charity-infused obedience is an act of the free will, an informed consent that is ultimately rendered unto Christ alone. Indeed, true Christian obedience is more aptly conceived of as an act of love.

When one follows this path of perfect obedience for love of Christ, one will not be obedient or disobedient due to respect of persons, obedient or disobedient out of fear, or obedient or disobedient unto doing evil. All authority derives from God, but this does not mean that all those who claim authority must be obeyed. Quite the opposite, it means authority is only legitimate in so far as it is in accord with God. This automatically rules out any coercive or manipulative authority, and *any and all* acquiescence to evil.

The servile obedience prominent and promoted in the Church's past, be it familial, sociopolitical, or ecclesial obedience, is calculating and stultifying. A person calculates his suffering and pleasure here and now so as to avoid suffering and gain pleasure in the next life. Thus, the popular "indulgence spirituality" of the past not only was an excuse for Luther's rebellion but the cause of his debilitating and stultifying scruples as well. Nor does such a calculating and stultifying piety suffice for today, where Technarcistic Man is barely in touch with the reality of his here and now existence, of this earthly vale of tears, much less the next.

But servile obedience, as imperfect as it is, is not intrinsically sinful. Though based on pride and self-interest, it can be ordered to the good. However, it can also be ordered to the bad and it can be manipulated by those who are demanding obedience. Furthermore, such obedience is but a superficial manifestation of true Christian obedience which is an essential act of self-abnegating charity. Enabled by technology, the third millennium's ability for totalitarian manipulation and micromanagement of the human person urgently necessitates this charity-induced obedience and highlights the grave dangers of servile obedience.

The crucial human, and infinitely more so Christian, absolute right to do one's duty to God is the essence of human freedom, and thus of man made in God's image as a rational-volitional being. It is manifestly antithetical to the authoritarianism and infantilism that ended up being promulgated in the Church during the Counter-Reformation/ Pre-Vatican II period. Already cited was the imprudent Ignatian exhortation to "live under obedience . . . as if [one were] a lifeless body . . . ." This is justly deemed imprudent because in further extrapolations (be these extrapolations of an obsessive-compulsive casuistry or revelings in private revelation) have brought this imperfect sense of obedience to an absurd, indeed heretical, point. This is the case of those spiritualities[108] that seek, for all intents and purposes, to excise a person's will from his soul. Of course, this is an impossibility, and if so accomplished would render one no longer an image of God, but more akin to a mere animal, indeed a soulless body if not a "lifeless" one. Not only is it heretical, but it is a blatantly absurd proposition to *will* ones *will* away.

This attempt to diminish or excise one's will is nothing less than an abdication of one's crucial *imago Dei* duty and a retreat into infantilism. It is this very infantilism, which was standard in the later quarter of Christendom I, that was responsible for the collapse of Christendom I. For infantilism allowed the familial foundation to rot, even as the worldly power of the magisterial grew.[109] Infantilism, as the name denotes, keeps a Christian in, or reduces him to, an immature state. Namely, the very Christian *qua* Christian person's faith and ecclesial existence remains servile and motivated by egoistic fears and desires. But not only is such an infantilism motivated by egoistic fears and desires, it is also manipulated by these fears and desires. The end result is an infantilism that paradoxically feeds both the perpetrator and the victim, for the victim slavishly seeks to avoid responsibility and to be in the good graces of the powers-that-be. And here may enter the clericalistic priest or prelate, or the chauvinistic husband, or the scolding wife, or the abusive evangelical superior: bullies all.

The authentic and pre-Counter-Reformation understanding of obedience is given by St. Thomas Aquinas:

> In matters touching the internal movement of the will man is not bound to obey his fellow-man, but God alone.[110]

In a heretical inversion, this singular Catholic understanding of obedience was held to be inferior in the Ignatian and Sulpican informed spiritualities[111] dominant from Trent unto Vatican II. But the true Catholic and Thomistic understanding of obedience does not even recognize this Ignatian and Sulpican et al. version of obedience as a virtue; and in fact holds that the blinder the obedience is the more vicious it is. This is because the obedience promoted in the Ignatian and Sulpican et al. spirituality is a slavish obedience that appeals to the pride and self-love and because it does violence to man's *imago Dei* free will.

INDIVIDUALISM: AN ANTIDOTE
TO DEHUMANIZATION

Thus, all the dehumanizing spiritualities that preach the destruction of the individual will are intrinsically heretical, and are but versions of the past nominalism that so viciously and detrimentally infected the Church. William of Ockham (1287—1347) is the most infamous proponent of nominalism. Though St. Thomas Aquinas taught the contrary, nominalism still gained a firm foothold in the post-Trent Church. Nominalism (like Islam and most pagan religions) holds that what is deemed a good action is so as per an arbitrary decree of God. As such, God could reverse at least eight of the Ten Commandments and natural law itself. Here God is not the way, the truth and the life, but rather the shackle, the tyranny, and the fear. Where the Church was infected with this sort of heresy—and she was infected in the Counter-Reformation period and beyond universally and from top to bottom—ecclesial offices became tyrannical, bullying tyrants rose to positions of authority both in the Church and in the Catholic body politic, and blind obedience became the highest of virtues.

Insidiously, even apparently virtuous, religious behavior can be based on pride and self-love. Such are the pitfalls of nominalism, pharisaism, liturgicalism, clericalism, and any form of compartmentalization. This is because ordinary, or acquired, virtues are *apparently* rightly ordered. However, ordinary virtues can be rightly ordered on a superficial level, but wrongly ordered on a deeper level. An act ultimately ordered toward the aggrandizement of the pride may be superficially ordered, but it is ultimately disordered or, at the very least, imperfect. In so far as ordinary virtues are not built upon the primary psychomoralitic virtue of receptivity, they remain only superficial virtues. If ordinary virtues are ultimately means to defend or aggrandize the ego then they are false virtues. While true and habitually chosen avenues of approach may be conceptualized as ordinary virtues, and habitually chosen ego defenses may be conceptualized as ordinary vices, that which *appears* or is considered as "virtuous" or "vicious" may not be, respectively, actual avenues of ego abnegation or conversely defenses of ego preservation. Thus, apparent ordinary virtues are more aptly viewed as acquired disciplines rather than virtues when applying the psychomoralitic standard.

> A person...may be considered virtuous because he is not being challenged by, or is not open to, an urgent and intense impacting reality. Or a person may be considered virtuous due to the disciplined implementation of temporary ego-abnegation through an ego-motivated delayed gratification, which is surely disciplined but not necessarily ego-abnegating. Conversely, a person may be considered vicious because in heeding a higher good he harms a lower good, but that higher good is not recognized by others—due to viciousness, superficiality, or unawareness—but the lower good is.[112]

So even when properly ordered, and thus not sinful, acts motivated by the pride and self-love are imperfect.[113] And, again, all attempts to abdicate one's *imago Dei* responsibility to exercise one's absolute right to do one's duty to God out of love of God—even when done under the facade of humility—is an atypical[114] act of the pride. Blind obedience is of the pride and love of self. True obedience is of humility and love of God.

Erroneous concepts on obedience, usually exacerbated rehashes of errors prevalent in the 1950's and before, are still alive and well in the third millennium, especially among conservative and traditional Catholics. This rejection of freewill, this regressing to infantilism, dovetails perfectly with the renewed clericalism that is also part of the reactionary culture of many conservative, and almost all traditional, clergy.

INDIVIDUALISM & RELATIONAL COMMUNION

Individualism and relational communion were commonly seen in counter-reformational spirituality—or maybe more aptly in reaction to enlightenment individualism—as exclusive of each other. But individualism and relational communion can also be, indeed, need to be, synergistic when authentic. When individualism is based on egoistic pride and self-love it prevents authentic communion of persons (or souls); for pride and self-love disfigure a person's authentic self which is the *imago Dei*, thus impeding authentic communion with another person's *imago Dei*. However, when individualism is non-egoistic, that is when the *imago Dei* predominates, then true and deep communion between individuals is made possible.

The unawareness of the influence of the pride-based subjective ego versus the objective *imago Dei* led to not only the degradation of *imago Dei* individualism, but to the implementation of other dehumanizing, and thus unchristian, principals. In the counter-reformational Church, such dehumanizing principles included the muting of the passions. Human passions, which as Aquinas says are necessary for "human flourishing," were, on principle, to be inhibited without distinguishing between those that were from the ego and those that were from the *imago Dei*. Similarly, particular friendships were to be barred without distinguishing between inauthentic friendships of egoistic interplay and those of true *imago Dei* communion.

The idea that somehow God's image in the human person needs to be eviscerated, that the full use of reason and freewill are dangerous or even flaws, is heretical.

The spiritual perfection of the human person is not done by reducing the individuality of the person, but rather by actualizing that person in his *imago Dei* individuality and sanctifying that person in supernatural transformation of that individuality. So too, to see the passions and particular friendships as flaws, without any distinctions, is dehumanizing.

The effects of these dehumanizing principals prevalent in the counter-reformational period are best seen in those whom they could be fully imposed; that is, those in evangelical and priestly life. Religious formation tainted by these dehumanizing principals facilitated a standard of stoicism[115] and the inauthentic facade of the *pious persona*. This inauthenticity was further augmented by the promulgation of estrangement of members within a religious community as per the barring of all particular friendships. But, of course, all friendships are particular or they are not really friendships at all. Finally, and most impiously, these dehumanizing principles and practices facilitated the estrangement of those in evangelical and priestly life from their very families, who were to be seen as but distractions from the pursuit of evangelical and priestly perfection.

Authentic relational communion necessarily requires *imago Dei* individualism, for communion, by definition, requires at least two individuals in relationship. So too, authentic relational communion does no violence to familial or personal relationship, but only purifies them unto a deeper and more intimate union.

Again, the false counter-reformational blanket belief that individualism is not conducive to relational communion is due to a certain unawareness of the influence of the pride-based subjective ego versus the objective *imago Dei*. This unawareness is itself derived from the very incorporation of the pride-based ego into that period's dominant spirituality.[116] This dominant spirituality was very stoical and inauthentic in its putting a premium on external placidity and pious personas, such that a person who appeared holy was considered to be one of the elect. But such an emphasis on tangible degrees of holiness is necessarily egoistic, for it is a fixation on one's spiritual perfection.

INDIVIDUAL COURAGE

A false and dehumanizing obedience disallows a person from the essential human vocation of pursuing truth and good, for it is based on an egoistic servile fear. This fear inculcates cowardice and thus prevents the person from speaking the truth and doing the good. And make no mistake, as grace builds upon nature, without this natural ability to speak the truth and do the good the supernatural ability to prophesize as per the Holy Spirit's promptings is gravely inhibited and even prohibited. One cannot cowardly succumb to natural and egoistic fears and expect to have supernatural and divine courage.

In the third millennium, true Catholics will be known for their courage and conviction, for their freedom from coercion and their unflinching witness to truth in the face of both perverse peer pressure and totalitarian power. True Catholics in the third millennium will be known for their intellectual integrity and unbending adherence to a conscience informed by truth, both natural and revealed. True Catholics will be known for refusing to be cowed by bullying, be that bullying done by State jackboots and administrators, corporate minions and demigods, political correctness and pop culture, or even chancery bureaucrats and ecclesial opportunists. True Catholics will be known for their unflinching assertion of their absolute right to do their duty to Faith and family and the Holy Triune God. And, yes, this means true Catholics in the third millennium will ultimately be known for their love, for "perfect love casts out all fear." (1JN 4:18)

VIII. Human Maturation

And you shall know the truth,
and the truth shall make you free. JN 8:32

The **human person's specific difference** is being in *imago Dei*; that is, being a rational volitional incarnate creature. As such, the Psychomoral Vocation, which is rationally assenting to truth and volitionally choosing the good, is the crucial natural human vocation. The increasing manifestation of the image of God, that is, the progressing in unimpeded rationality and volition, is the essence of human development and maturation.

Specifically, human maturation and essential well-being entails the actualization of a person's *imago Dei* potential for receiving-the-real, assenting-to-truth, and choosing-the-good.[117] Human beings (along with angelic beings) in their rational and volitional nature share analogously in the being of God to the highest degree. Indeed, *imago Dei* can be seen as analogous to the very triune nature of the true God: with *receiving-the-real* analogous to the Father as I Am, *assenting-to-truth* is analogous to the Son as the *Word*, and *choosing-the-good* (or loving the good) analogous to the Holy Spirit as the *Love* between the Father and the Son.[118]

It is in the state of pristine *imago Dei* that both the angels and man were created before their falls. Not yet with the indwelling, for that would be the very creating of gods, these pre-fallen persons nonetheless manifested the perfect analogous being of God (the similar functionality of reason and volition), that is the ability for receiving-the-real, assenting-to-truth, and choosing-the-good. The pre-fallen

190

person as pristinely in the image of God was poised to receive the real, assent to the truth, and choose the good, specifically receive the ultimate reality of "I Am," assent to that "I Am" and that "I am not," and choose the good of that Creator/creature dynamics. It is this receiving, assent, and choice that would then allow the preternatural person to be transformed by the divine indwelling and move from mere analogous being to God to God's actual living within them. Conversely, and necessarily, the *imago Dei* persons can reject that real, truth, and good; that is, pridefully reject God and their own lowly state as creatures[H4]. It is this rejection, this rebellion, that not only disfigures the *imago Dei* but damns a person to the possibility of the indwelling. This dramatic choice is intrinsic to the person's definitive *imago Dei* ability to assent (or not) to truth and lovingly choose (or not) the good.

Essential human maturation, then, entails the increase of a person's image of God, his essential rational-volitional well-being, as that person is increasingly receptive to the real, assents to the truth, and chooses the good. Because this receptivity, assent, and choice includes within it all that is overwhelming and humiliating, it as well necessarily requires the diminishment of the egoistic self. Indeed, it is the egoistic self, with its subjective and often irrational passions and defenses, that disfigures and binds the *imago Dei* and thus hampers human maturation.

THE CRUCIAL NATURAL VOCATION

The Psychomoral Vocation is the first and most crucial natural vocation. Here the human person is called to fulfill his nature as an individual rational-volitional being made in God's image. While the Psychomoral Vocation is of the natural order, it is nonetheless spiritual. This is important to note, for even in Catholic circles there is a prevalent tendency to separate not just nature from grace (as per the Protestant heresy) but to equate nature purely with the material.[119] But the natural order entails not only the material but the spiritual as well, as per any Catholic vetted hylomorphic ontology.

In the Psychomoral Vocation a person is called to essential human well-being as per his spiritual ability to receive-the-real, assent-to-truth, and choose-the-good. To fulfill this Psychomoral Vocation a person must accept ego-abnegation in assent to objective truth and love of the subsequent good. This process orders the ego and its passions to the person's rational-volitional faculty and gives predominance to the psychic passions.[120] To the degree this is done one flourishes as a human person *qua* image of God.

All creation in its realness, truthfulness, and goodness emanates analogously from God, whose realness, truthfulness, and goodness is of his *I-Am* essence. At the most fundamental, existential level the receptive human intellect (and angelic beings as well), in its *rasa tabula* state, encounters the ultimate reality of God, and from there encounters being *qua* being also. This receptivity takes place at the first stage of receiving-the-real. The intellect then enters the stage of assent-to-truth.[121] Here, the intellect is called to assent to *God is God*, to *I Am*, to an Ultimate Being whose essence is existence and to volitionally choose this truth as the good. The necessary corollary to this assent is *and I am not*, that one is but a contingent and completely dependent being, as such choosing this truth as the good is necessarily choosing God over oneself. It is here that the holy angels, the non-incarnate images of God, submitted and rejoiced in this truth and lovingly chose it. It is here that the fallen angels rebelled and hated this truth and instead chose themselves over God. It is here that Adam and Eve fell from grace, and it is here that, for all persons, salvation or damnation weighs in the balance.[122]

Indeed, if a person does not know and accept the true God of reality (the acceptance of which can be done with unaided reason on the natural level), that person is not in a position to accept the true God of Revelation, nor the true God-Man, Jesus Christ. For the true God is indeed the God of reality, the God of existence, the God of one's particular existence. That is, the true God is the God of this vale of tears, of this meat-grinder world: in sum, he is the *God of crucifixion*. If a person rejects reality, he cannot know the true God. He may posit a god that is somehow compartmentalized from reality or is even (and quite commonly) invoked to somehow thwart or change reality. But again, such a god is more a genie in a bottle, a god that if manipulated rightly, rubbed the right way, does one's bidding. Such a god is no god at all, for it is the creature who manipulates it, and thus it is the creature that is more of the god.

So accepting, assenting to, and choosing the reality of existence is to accept, assent to, and choose the Author of Existence. And, again, this entails accepting that one is not God, but rather a vulnerable, weak, and contingent creature: a very humiliating, that is, ego-abnegating, reality. This reality entails a certain helplessness and the state of being overwhelmed.[123] It entails accepting suffering and death.

And that means accepting the fact, made manifest in a plethora of facts, that God's ways are not man's ways.

> For my thoughts are not your thoughts, neither are your ways my ways. IS 55:8

But still, since God's ways are reality—that is, they are true and good—a person is called to say *yes* to his ways. Thus, the Psychomoral Vocation entails a rational assent to the truth and subsequent choosing and promulgation of that truth in a volitional doing of the good.

THE TRUE & THE GOOD

As per the Psychomoral Vocation, the human person is called to assent to the truth and choose it as the good unto the abnegation of egoistic pride and self-love so as to manifest an unblemished image of God. But in this third millennium there is rarely even posited the question, "What is truth?" Rather, in this third millennium, truth is equated with the mundanely empirical, the egotistically subjective, or the statutorily haphazard. As such, in the third millennium where truth has no mandate the human person, and much more so the Christian, must be ardently intent upon the truth.

Truth forms a magnificent and ever-expansive tapestry. In this tapestry of truth all the threads are harmoniously integrated. Every truth is synthesized. There is no facet of life that cannot be so synthesized. One is called therefore to synthesize all concepts, all experiences, all things. The process of such a synthesization entails weighing all concepts and experiences in light of an already assented to anchor truth(s). Thus, the assented to truth is not stagnant, but ever expanding and integrating; where even the truth of those recognizing falsehoods is an expansion of truth. If a person allows unsynthesized concepts to reside in the mind they will manifest themselves in incongruous actions.

Truth can, and should, also deepen. This may happen when a new concept or experience seems incongruous to an anchor truth. Here, either the new concept[H5] or experience can be further examined to assure it is understood correctly, but so can the anchor truth be further contemplated to discern if it is known adequately. The inadequately known anchor truth is often the case when the letter of the law is known but the spirit of the law is not.

Thomistic ontology holds that the *real*, the *true*, and the *good* all signify *being* (Lt., *esse*), although from differing viewpoints. To understand the convertibility of being, the real, the true, and the good, is to ground existence firmly in an objective order that is independent of man's subjective thinking, cognitive grasp of it, or wishful desires. Such an objective order is also a unifying principle that integrates all aspects of human experience, from spiritual intuitions to mundane calculation.

In this existential objective order, all derives from and hinges on Supreme Being, being whose essence is existence and therefore is not caused but is the prime cause of all. This Supreme Being is thus the Ultimately Real, the Ultimately True, and the Ultimately Good. Inherent in this Thomistic understanding is the ramification that the human person's final end, the very reason for human existence, is to receive the Ultimate Real, assent to the Ultimate Truth, and to possess the real and the true as the Ultimate Good; all of which is consisted in Ultimate or Supreme Being.

Being, the real, the true, and the good refer to the same entity as its analogies because an Ultimate Supreme Being necessarily is the Ultimately Real, the Ultimately True, and the Ultimately Good. For purposes of moral application (or as per psychomoralitic intervention) these different aspects of being are conceptualized as:

> *Being*: When some objective being has been receptively encountered existentially in itself, it is the real. This is to apprehend[124] that being (things or a thing) exists without yet naming or defining what that being specifically is.
>
> *Truth*: As object of a mind knowing it to be as it is, a being is true. "Truth is the proclamation of being."[125]
>
> *Good*: As object of a will in positive regard toward it for some perfection it is or has, a being is called good. The good is that which is desirable.

NATURAL MATURATION

The Psychomoral Vocation of receiving-the-real, assenting-to-truth, and choosing-the-good is properly formed and developed in the realm of the third natural vocation: that of the family. For a child to begin the maturation process properly the presence of authentic parental love is required. Parental love is the prototypical *sacrificial* love. Sacrificial love derives from the psyche rather than the ego. A child will only have the courage to let go of his ego's subjective good, that is, to turn from his subjective self-love, if he experiences a parental love that is greater than his ego generated self-love. Because sacrificial parental love is of the objective truth and psyche, and may be willed even to the detriment of the parent's own ego, it necessarily transcends egocentric self-love. It is this true parental sacrificial love instilled in the child that is the *sine qua non* of proper childhood formation.

The maturation process begins in childhood and exactly requires that the child begin to let go of his egocentricity and open himself up to the greater reality. Again, a child that does not adequately experience a greater parental love will not have the courage to undergo a budding ego's abnegation or to open himself up to a greater reality.

So the more a person is open to reality, especially the reality of limitations and suffering, the more a person must be humbled. So the more a person is humbled the less a person is his egoistical self. The cross of reality, this purgative abnegation that is earthly existence, is crushing indeed. It is truly too much to endure. Thus, a person must choose either to try and escape that reality or to enter into its depths.

Escaping reality is the path of stultified maturation, of illusion and ego-aggrandizement, of myopic coping, of hardness of heart. Entering into its depths is the path of maturation, of increased openness to reality and ego-abnegation, of clear vision within and without, of one's decreasing. It is this maturation that leads one to the heart of reality wherein is found Christ Crucified, for the decrease of self is the precursor for the increase of Christ. It is this path of maturation—be it a gradual developmental maturation or a traumatic psychomoralitic maturation—that impels one who is in the depths of the crucifixion of reality to accept the gift of faith and redemption that is found infinitely deeper still in Christ Crucified.

RECEPTIVE VIRTUE

The first vocation in the natural realm, that is, the Psychomoral Vocation, has as its crucial virtue *receptivity to reality*. In the past there was not a general need to promulgate this volitional acceptance of reality as an intentional virtue, for such an acceptance was tantamount to a given in a person's life. To be receptive to reality is to be in touch with natural law. To be receptive to reality in its harshest and most absolute aspects is to be in touch with the most fundamental premise of natural law: a person's mortality and thus utter spiritual contingency. In the non-technological past a person's mortality was strikingly present from infancy on (indeed, infant mortality was especially and most poignantly high). But, as has been delineated,[126] third millennium's Technarcistic Man is not so in touch with the brutal impact of mortality and hence his utter spiritual contingency. As such, in this third millennium, receptivity, or the psychomoral acceptance of reality, must be an intentional, and even focal, virtue.

In that receptive virtue entails being open to impacting reality, its fulfillment can be considered as the natural powers perfected.[127] Receptive virtue entails the most fundamental act of the human intellect that was activated in its primordial *rasa tabula* state. Receptive virtue is present when receiving-the-real is followed by an assenting-to-truth, that is, receptive virtue is a simple *yes* to the truth of the real, and choosing-the-good. Receptive virtue is simply not exerting the will against the real and true. So receptive virtue uniquely[128] differs from acquired virtue in that it does not culminate in an exertion of the will unto habitual disposition, but in a moment-to-moment volitional non-exertion of the will against impacting reality. While this receptive non-exertion is indeed an act of the will, it does not end in volitional pro-activity but in volitional *docility*. Whereas acquired virtue is developed by exertion and characterized by a disciplined and steadfast intractability, receptive virtue is characterized by docility and a vulnerable and spontaneous malleability.

Furthermore, as per psychomoralitics, unlike acquired virtue with its many distinct virtues receptive virtue is singular. Receptive virtue is singular both as a single virtue and as a single act. As a single virtue, receptive virtue nonetheless entails all of the perfecting virtues and properly marshals all of the passions in its actualization. This is because receptive virtue comes from the love of reality, and thus of God. Love is always the chief passion[129] from which all passions flow. But love is not only a passion but a choice and virtue. As it is chief among the passions, so is love chief and all-inclusive of the virtues as well. In that love of God is the highest and chief virtue, and love of reality is due to its analogous being to God, receptive virtue, though singular, is all-inclusive.

So though a single act, receptive virtue is always a singular act of love issued anew. Acquired virtues become habitual and are therefore enduring and resilient, but like any habit, they can also be broken, become infrequently used, or be lost entirely. Unlike acquired virtues, receptive virtue (like infused theological virtue) can be lost moment-by-moment. But because it is a moment-by-moment choice, receptive virtue (again, like infused theological virtue) need never be lost; and if lost it can be regained, to even a superlative degree, in the aftermath by one being receptive to the humiliation (ego-abnegation) and sorrow of the loss.

Receptive virtue is more akin to infused theological virtue[130] than acquired virtue in its receptivity. Nonetheless, receptive virtue, though it may entail actual grace, does not entail sanctifying grace and remains, like acquired virtue, in the natural realm. Like the infused virtues, receptive virtue in its very lack of habituation does not have the durability of habituated acquired virtues and can be lost in the very psychomoralitic moment. But so too, receptive virtue need not ever be stressed to breaking point as can all acquired virtues. Receptive virtue, in its very lack of habituation, is spontaneous and thus never need not suffice, rather it can always take place in the moment by the choice not to exert the will in the issuance of a receptive *yes* to reality.

Whereas acquired virtue is habitual, receptive virtue never becomes habitual, for it does not entail a repeated, and thus habit-forming, exertion of the will, but the choice *not* to exert the will. That is, where acquired virtue is developed by repeated actions leading to dispositions and habits, receptive virtue is a singular and in-the-moment act. Receptive virtue could be said to be the non-habituation of exertions of the will against impacting reality. Thus, receptive virtue is always fully free and thus a fully human loving act of reason and volition.

So too, whereas common acquired virtue can be congruent with, and even based on pride, the receptive virtue is necessarily based on humiliation. In the ego-abnegation of the psychomoralitic process of receptive virtue a person cannot become habituated to the humiliation nor any ensuing sorrow; that is, this humiliation and sorrow always hurts; indeed it always pierces deeper; and it always goes contrary to the subjective ego or even the objective *imago Dei* psyche and its sense of loss.

EGO-ABNEGATING
RECEPTIVE VIRTUE

Receptive virtue occurs when a person chooses not to exert his will and implement egoistic defenses against an impacting reality.[131] Whereas natural acquired virtue can be a mere ordering of the ego in congruence with objective reality, the psychomoralitic virtue of receptivity is in essence not congruent with the ego. Whereas acquired virtue is ordered toward an objective good, it can still be motivated by pride and the motivation of delayed gratification. Thus, through acquired virtue the egoistic passions can be properly ordered so as to achieve the subjective good of the ego, thereby not decreasing but aggrandizing that ego. But receptive virtue as *the* psychomoralitic act is necessarily ego abnegating.

Whereas acquired virtue as per Aristotelian ethics[132] is a mean between two extremes, receptive virtue is ordered toward an unmodulated and radical openness to reality. Whereas in acquired virtue the egoistic passions may be at one with what virtue requires, in receptive virtue not only may the egoistic self be at odds with the reality to be received, but the psychic self (that is, the image of God, and more so even the Christic self) may be at odds with the reality to be received.[133]

Because it is not ego-generated or dependent on volitional exertion receptive virtue does not require that a person be what is commonly considered as "strong" or "disciplined;" that is, he need not be enabled with acquired virtue.[134] Indeed, a person's weakness, haplessness, and wretchedness becomes the very stuff of receptive virtue's psychomoralitic abnegation. In short, in receptive virtue that which has previously been a negative curse may now become a positive blessing. This is done by saying *yes* to the painful humiliation and sorrow that accompanies one's failures; both to saying *yes* to one's haunting failures of the past and to one's looming failures of the future. This is, in short, saying *yes* to feeling subjectively bad, which is humiliation, and objectively bad, which is sorrow. For it is receptivity to the humiliation and sorrow that is the very remedy to ego-reactivity and the very catalyst for growth in maturation and essential well-being.

LIVING THE TRUTH

As grace builds upon nature, it is the psychomoralitic process that facilitates the sanctification process. Psychomoralitics entails purgative abnegation of the pride and self-love so that the Psychomoral Vocation can be answered in an increasing openness to reality (*viz.*, receiving-the-real, assenting-to-truth, and choosing-the-good). The psychomoralitic process successfully entered into, be it via natural maturation or clinical intervention, is salubrious for the *imago Dei* in its rational-volitional nature and thus increases essential human well-being.

When a person not only assents to the truth but chooses it as the good, he can be said to be *living the truth*. The Christian vocation, which is examined next, is akin to the crucial human vocation, and indeed builds upon it as grace builds upon nature. For whereas the human vocation is to *assent* to the truth and *do* the good, the Christian vocation is to miraculously *become* the truth and the good.

IX. Christian Sanctification

If any man will come after me,
let him deny himself, take up his cross,
and follow me. MT 16:24

Holiness is the Christian vocation, for it is the call to absolute union with Christ that is the Christian's specific difference. So not only is a Christian called on the natural level to mature by decreasing the ego[135] and manifesting the *imago Dei*, but called on the supernatural level to eventually proclaim that "no longer I live, but Christ lives within me."(GA 2:20) Thus, a Christian is called to not only live the truth as per his crucial human vocation, but to become the Truth as per his crucial Christian vocation.

In the crucial Christian vocation, then, the call is not only to naturally manifest the analogous image of God but to have a soul indwelled by divinity that verily "magnifies the Lord."(LK 1:46) Here, natural maturation is infinitely enhanced by way of a supernatural purgation and a subsequent sanctification. For the Christian, then, the call to decrease the self is simultaneously accompanied by the call for Christ to increase. Going beyond the natural and contingent analogous being[136] of the crucial human vocation where a person is called as *imago Dei* to assent to truth and do the good, the Christian is called to be indwelled by supernatural, and non-contingent, Supreme Being, Supreme Truth, and Supreme Good. This fullness of Supreme Being is made singularly accessible in and through the Incarnate Second Person of the Blessed Trinity: Jesus Christ

Again, as grace builds upon nature, the natural Psychomoral Vocation and the supernatural Christian vocation form one integral vocation, with the human person's analogous image of God becoming indwelled by the person of God himself. Indeed, the natural crucial human call to assent to truth and choose the good is only fully achievable, in fact infinitely transcended, when supernaturalized in the Christian's crucial call to holiness. All other aspects of human and Christian existence, then, are properly secondary to the crucial human and crucial Christian vocations and must be ordered toward these vocations' fulfillment.

THE CHRISTIAN VOCATION

The dynamic of the Christian vocation is the decreasing of self so that Christ might increase. This decreasing of self takes place foundationally, but only partially as a prerequisite, in the fulfillment of the crucial human Psychomoral Vocation and its process of natural human maturation. As a person matures psychomorally he opens himself up more and more to reality. This maturation and increased openness to reality necessarily reduces egocentricity by ordering it to objective good. This natural ordering and decreasing of the egocentric self-manifests the analogous image of God,[137] that is, man's rational-volitional nature.

This psychomoral vocational maturation of natural decreasing of self is intensified supernaturally in the grace-filled purgation of the Christian vocation. This purgation simultaneously decreases the ego and allows the increasing of Jesus Christ. As grace builds upon nature, the natural dynamics of a maturing decrease of the ego fulfills the natural vocation of the human person to be *imago Dei*, which segues into the supernatural and superlative dynamics of a penitential purgation of the egoistic self for love of God. Reciprocally, once the natural *imago Dei* is indwelled with the supernatural *Verbum Dei* further egoistic decrease and maturation is facilitated. These dynamics of egoistic decrease and Christic increase fulfill the singular destiny of the Christian to be a soul that magnifies the Lord.

The dynamics of egoistic decrease and Christic increase can be seen in key New Testament personages. Penitential maturation in preparation for the grace of the Christian dispensation, that is, the bridging of the natural and supernatural crucial vocations, is personified in St. John the Baptist: "He must increase, but I must decrease." (JN 3:30)[138] St. John is calling his hearers to acquire a volitional repentance where they forcefully turn away from sin and enter the waters of baptism. Then there is St. Paul, already high in acquired virtue, even as a persecutor of Christians, who experienced the impacting reality of being knocked off his high horse. St. Paul's conversional receptivity to this humiliation and purgation begins the process that culminates in his declaring, "I have been crucified with Christ, and no longer I live, but Christ lives within me." (GA 2:20) And it is the Blessed Virgin Mary who—being in no need of conversion or acquired virtue but rather always perfectly receptive to nature and full of infused grace—is able to proclaim, "My soul doth magnify the Lord." (LK 1:46)

The dynamics of Christian spirituality highlighted in these three prototypical biblical personages admit of the simultaneous and fluctuating interplay in the spiritual life of most Christians. But some degree of categorization can be achieved by recognizing the dominant type of virtue, be it acquired, receptive, or infused. Again, acquired virtue is where, on the natural order, a person's pride, self-love, and egoistic passions are rightly ordered toward higher goods and receptive virtue is where natural reality is acquiesced[139] to and the natural maturation of egotistic abnegation and *imago Dei* manifestation occurs. The supernatural infused virtues come, as per God's beneficence, with the soul being in a state of grace, and indeed are an indwelling of sanctifying grace that culminates in a soul that magnifies the Lord.

> How narrow is the gate, and strait is the way that leadeth to life: and few there are that find it! MT 7:14

How narrow, for adhering to the mandate of truth entails humiliation. For even according to the Holy Faith imbued with the Good News, human existence is an "exile," where man is "mourning and weeping in a vale of tears."

And on the natural level, those who ardently seek the truth do so because of this exiled, sorrowful existence. For all philosophy is a philosophy of death, that is, it is man's contingent existence that is the catalyst for true philosophizing. It is death itself that is the most poignant aspect of reality, the reality that causes a person to seek meaning because confronted with meaninglessness. It can then be asserted without hyperbole that earthly existence is a meat-grinder, and reality a crucifixion; an existence and reality made all the more poignant by the joys and pleasures therein. Grace will always build upon nature, and grace and nature will always be integrated in the True Faith. For the True Faith does not turn away from reality, is not an opiate, but rather ventures ever deeper into reality. Herein, the Faith finds Christ Crucified. Here, in the very heart of reality, the Faith finds the pierced heart of Christ; it finds salvation in suffering and life in death.

CRUCIAL CHRISTIAN RECEPTIVITY

The acquired virtue alluded to above entails the dynamics of self-discipline, and self-mastery. One need not be a Christian to practice it, indeed one may practice and advance in it with a large degree of pride and self-interest involved. This acquired virtue path of human perfection was foundationally enunciated in Aristotelian ethics and was subsequently and exhaustively Christianized and explicated from the time of St. Thomas Aquinas unto the bulk of pre-Vatican II manuals on spiritual perfection. However, due to the unprecedented debilitation of third millennium Technarcistic Man, there comes an urgent and crucial need to explicate a path of perfection that can bypass the rigorous (and even semi-Pelagianistic[140]) school of acquired virtue. This path of receptive natural and supernatural virtue is specifically Christian.

As per the spirit of the law, which can be only a deepening of the letter, and as per the spirit of orthodox reform, which can only be a closer conforming to Christ Crucified, the only path that properly bypasses that of acquired virtue is that of receptive virtue.[141] The path of receptive virtue is most apt, and providentially so, for third millennium Technarcistic Man because of his very debilitation in acquired virtue. So while in this third millennium the populace can be seen as the last in acquired virtue, they can as such be seen as being called to be the first in receptive virtue. Or at least the second, for it is the Mary Magadalenes and the Good Thieves who in their lack of acquired virtue and abundance of receptive virtue are first found heart to heart with the Sorrowful Blessed Virgin Mary in her primacy at the foot of the Cross.

Receptive virtue is the specific Christian virtue for ultimately sanctification and salvation is not found in the acquired perfecting of self but in the receptive *purgation of self.* Unlike Adam's and Eve's grasping of the fruit of divine knowledge, or even some Christians' grasping at and claiming[142] of Jesus Christ as savior, salvation is not something a person can take by force of will, but rather it is a gift that is to be volitionally received. This voluntary reception of redemption most immediately entails a voluntary reception of repenting purgation. This repenting purgation is the only time any sort of grasping takes place, for it is where the cross is embraced. The process of redemption begins with the process of repenting purgation, and purgation is choosing to love God over self. Redemption, then, is not about self at all, but about loving God unto crucifixion of that self; the fruit of which is joy, sanctification, and salvation.

What is of essential vital importance to human existence, even on the natural and psychomoral level, is to be receptive to reality. This receptivity to reality calls a person to choose and be conformed to reality; *viz.*, to be cross-conformed in that reality indeed entails the cross of existence. On the supernatural Christian level to be cross-conformed means to enter *ever deeper into reality* by picking up the cross and following Christ, a process that culminates with the embrace of him crucified at the very heart of reality. In the anti-realistic and anti-Christic third millennium—what with all the ability to be removed and turned from, anesthetized and blinded to, the natural vicissitudes of life—there must not only be a most intentional embrace of the Cross of Christ, but a most intentional embrace of the cross of reality as well.

It is in the realm of receptive virtue that actual grace plays out.[143] And it is in the realm of infused virtue that sanctifying grace occurs. Receptive virtue can lead seamlessly, that is, without egoistic influence, to infused virtue. For receptive virtue necessarily is an acceptance of humiliation and sorrow for its own sake, and so necessarily it does not allow for egoistic motivation or at leastwise diminishes it to an inconsequential degree. In being accepted for its own sake, humiliation and sorrow is accepted because it is part and parcel of reality. Accepting this reality thus entails accepting the Author of Reality, the true God. This maturing acceptance of reality and God then lays the groundwork for the acceptance of the Gospel and Jesus Christ. As always, as grace builds upon nature, answering the crucial Christian call to holiness may entail acquired natural virtues and always entails natural receptive virtue and supernatural infused virtues. Most essentially, the courage to embrace the Cross comes from the love of God. And yes, to embrace the cross is a volitional act, but it ultimately requires a receptivity to crucifixion, a choice not to exert the will against God's reality, purgation, and grace.

CONTROVERSY ON EFFICACIOUS GRACE

The dynamics of the virtue of receptivity addresses, may even reconcile, the long-standing controversy between the Jesuits and Dominicans as per the interplay between divine efficacious grace and human free will. This controversy entails the dynamics between an empowering grace that facilitates the assent to the truth and choosing of the good and the part free will plays in this. Catholic theology advances that once efficacious grace is present man must consent to it and act accordingly. But if this is true, how does man act freely?

The Dominicans promoted the theories of physical promotion and predetermination, where efficacious grace not only provides the necessary impetus for an action, but even the necessary physical impulsion to a person's faculties in determination of their meritorious actions. The Jesuits promoted the concept of *scientia media* (middle knowledge) whereby God, knowing outside of time what a person will do on his own free will in any given circumstance, providentially allows such circumstances to occur.

But while the loggerheads logic of both the Dominicans and the Jesuits is impeccable, the inevitable fruit— or theological ethos—of either position can be seen to be somewhat poisonous. As usual, the Dominicans tend toward an optimistic Aristotelian eudaemonism and the paradoxical corollary of a grim Calvinistic predestination. In this Dominican position, though virtue is optimistically held to be easy for the elect, vice is pessimistically held to be inevitable for the less favored. On the other hand, the Jesuits tend towards an optimistic Pelagianism and the paradoxical corollary of a grim authoritarianism. In this Jesuit position, though free will is at face value promoted, in the end freewill is only to be denounced.[144]

Receptive virtue appears to resolve this age long quarrel and the inherent contradictions of both sides. For with receptive virtue what a person does is not exert his will to achieve an end, but rather chooses not to exert his will against reality, the will of God, purgation, and grace. Here a person accepts God's end as his own will's end. But note well this is not abandoning nor even diminishing one's own will, for it is an act of love for God, which is also the highest act of the will. Paradoxically, this loving docility of a receptive will has less to do with one's own efforts than does the resistance of a rebellious will.

As per the dynamics of receptive grace, man acts freely but is essentially acted upon. This dynamics of receptive grace is present in the Holy Angels and the Blessed Mother as they cooperated with grace by being receptive to their own inadequacy that was made necessarily manifest by the very presence of this grace. Again receptive grace is simply a choice not to resist God's Allness and the corollary of one's nothingness.

THE MAGNIFICATION OF GOD

The Christian vocation immeasurably transcends the human vocation to be in the image of God, for it is to become a soul that magnifies the Lord, nothing more and nothing less; and there can be nothing more than the Lord God, and all is infinitely less. Still, for Technarcistic Man, this final end may seem rather anticlimactic, and he may ask, "But what about me?" The answer is that "me"—that is, the part of a person that even asks that question—is destined either for annihilation in fulfillment of that vocation or damnation in the rejection of that vocation.

All of God's creation exists for his manifest greater glory.[145] Thus, all creation in its analogous being to God, from inanimate objects to living beings, gives glory to God. Man may best appreciate the starkness of this truth of existence by looking at dumb animals (maybe a beloved pet) and knowing that these creatures live, suffer, and die, ending in utter annihilation for God's greater manifest glory. The human person, and still more the Christian, also exists for the greater manifest glory of God. But man, unlike animals and inanimate objects, cannot go out of existence due to his *imago Dei* immortal soul. In addition to, and because of, his immortal soul, man also differs from the rest of material creation in that he has pride and self-love. It is this human pride and self-love that is meant to go out of existence, that is to be annihilated for love of God and his greater glory.[146]

Created beings are then necessarily sacrificial.[147] Created beings *qua* creatures are also necessarily deficient, which is especially true for those in *imago Dei*. By their nature, beings in God's immortal image, angels and man, have an infinite capacity to be divinized. However an infinite capacity is also an infinite *emptiness*. This emptiness or nothingness is intrinsic to beings created in *imago Dei* and are prerequisite to eith[H6]er divinization or any fall/advent of pride and self-love. For purely spiritual angelic beings outside of physicality, this recognition of an infinite deficiency occurs in the aeviternal moment of their creation. In this moment when the receptive intellect of angelic beings, in the pristine *imago Dei* state, is impacted by Supreme Being, by Supreme Reality, by *I AM*, their cognitive realization is necessarily that *I am not*. This angelic realization that in relation to God, whose essence is existence and hence essentially and totally Other, he is but a contingent being brings into play the volitional choice to love; that is, to either love God or himself. Thus, the angelic existential moment of sanctification or damnation is the psychomoral act to receive-the-real, assent-to-truth, and choose-the-good.

For St. Michael and the Holy Angels in their pristine *imago Dei* state, the response to the recognition and realization that *God is God* and *I am not* is: "*Praise God!*" Theirs is a rejoicing in God's divinity and an acceptance of their contingency. For the Holy Angels there is no turning away from God, but rather a volitional loving and worshipful gazing upon him, through which they achieve the divinizing indwelling. Conversely, for Satan and the Fallen Angels, the response to the recognition and realization that *God is God* and *I am not* is: "No, I want to be God!" Theirs is a hatred of God's divinity and a rebellion against their contingency. For the Fallen Angels there is a turning away from God, a prideful apostasy to a volitional loving and worship of self, upon which they distort the *imago Dei*. The Holy Angels are humility personified, and the Prince of the Heavenly Hosts' own battle cry and thus his name, "Who is like God?,"[148] questions the absurdity of it all. Conversely, the Fallen Angels, the demons, are pride personified, fixated on their own excellence and refusing to accept that even their very existence is a gift of God.

And so too with man. Though the preternatural state of

man (and the created state of the angels) was pristinely *imago Dei*, it still had the deficiency[149] of not being yet divinized. This divinization of God's indwelling could take place only by the person's use of his *imago Dei* faculties to lovingly choose to worship God and only then be able to wax in the indwelled manifestation of God's glory. But conversely, the person could also choose to rebel against and turn away from God, creating in his apostasy an *imago Dei* distorting pride ordered to self-love. So the pride-personified Satan would goad Eve, and Adam, with their deficiency, mortality, contingency, and lack of omniscience,

> For God doth know that in what day soever you shall eat thereof, your eyes shall be opened: and you shall be as Gods, knowing good and evil. GN 3:5

Conversely to Adam and Eve, and in accord with the angelic beings, the unfallen human person of the Blessed Virgin Mary issued a *yes* to her given creaturely emptiness, "the Lord has regarded the lowliness of his handmaid." (LK 1:48) It is this *yes* that would manifest the Divine indwelling of Mary that had already taken place during her life, for she was declared by the Angel of God to be "full of grace." The Blessed Virgin Mary's self-perceived and accepted lowliness, her emptiness, is already the end of immolation; it is already the culmination of fallen man's sacrificial existence that allows sanctification to occur. So all persons in God's image, even the Blessed Virgin Mary and the Holy Angels, indeed even Christ himself (see below) are sacrificial; even if not subject to purgation because not possessive of pride.

Beings created in *imago Dei* (the angels and Man) can choose to say *yes* to their emptiness or rebel against it, and as per the presence of a fallen nature the human person can choose to say *yes* to the annihilation of pride and self-love or rebel against that annihilation. St. Thomas Aquinas affirms that the fires of hell and the fires of purgatory are the same.[150] Thus, the fires meant for the purgative burnt offering of the pride and self-love, for the annihilation of viciousness, imperfections, and defenses that mar the image of God, are inescapable. But the salubrious effects of these fires can be fought, and that is the dynamics of damnation.

A person's ultimate choice is simple and the dynamic of the Christian vocation is simple. Either a person chooses to love God more than he loves himself, and thus decreases so as to allow God to increase, or a person chooses to love himself more than he loves God, and thus fights his decreasing to maintain himself. This choice becomes absolute when a person at death encounters God face-to-face in his particular judgment. Here a person, for love of God, either enters into the fires of purgation, where his pride and self-love are completely annihilated unto his salvation and ultimate fulfillment to be a soul that ever more magnifies the Lord unto all eternity, or a person, for love of self, enters into the fires of hell, where his pride and self-love hatefully fight these fires unto everlasting damnation.[151]

OUR LORD JESUS CHRIST

And what of the virtues of the Son of God Incarnate, Our Lord Jesus Christ Himself, who the Christian is called to emulate? Christ did not have acquired virtue. But still he did struggle mightily with accepting the Father's will when his hour had come, and in his ultimate act of love receptively said *yes* to the Father's will. The Agony in the Garden witnesses to this most amazing fact. One could assert that during Christ's entire life in essence all his prayers and mortifications were ordered toward this *agonia*, this wrestling unto death.[152] No, Christ in his perfection did not need to die to his human self, but nonetheless had to submit his human nature to the experiencing of the spiritual death that is separation from God.

Even before his going to Jerusalem for the final time, Christ would dramatically manifest his life's essential conflict, and God the Father would even more dramatically reveal himself in confirmation,

> Now My soul is troubled, and what shall I say? 'Father, save Me from this hour'? No, it is for this purpose that I have come to this hour. Father, glorify Your name! Then a voice came from heaven: 'I have glorified it, and I will glorify it again.' The crowd standing there heard it and said that it had thundered. JN 12:27-29

It is indeed one single hour that Our Lord referred to as "my hour" in his ministry. No, not the three hours on the Holy Cross, but this single hour when he choose to drink of the chalice in the Garden of Gethsemane,

> ...he began to fear and to be heavy. And he saith to them: My soul is sorrowful even unto death; stay you here, and watch. And when he was gone forward a little, he fell flat on the ground; and he prayed, that if it

might be, *the hour* might pass from him. MK 14:33-35 (*Emphasis* added).

Jesus Christ in his human nature did not much fear physical torture or death, for this was a man who had fasted for forty days. It was not that Christ suffered more than any other man in his physical passion, as some in misguided piety seek to claim and depict, but rather that he suffered more than any other man in his spiritual anguish; for no other man comes close to the perfect intimacy and love he had for the Father. Christ feared and sorrowed unto death experiencing the loss of God the Father.

> And he saith: Abba, Father, all things are possible to thee: remove this chalice from me; but not what I will, but what thou wilt. MK 14:36

Christ was so fearful and sorrowful unto to death because drinking of the chalice would cause him in his human nature to experience separation from the Father. It was Christ's utterly holy dread of this being made "to be sin,"[153] that caused him to verily sweat blood[154] in the Garden of Gethsemane. This fear and sorrow was so immense that Christ needed the succor of an angel,

> Saying: Father, if thou wilt, remove this chalice from me: but yet not my will,[155] but thine be done. And there appeared to him an angel from heaven, strengthening him. And being in an agony, he prayed the longer. And his sweat became as drops of blood, trickling down upon the ground. LK 22:42-44

Note well, it was never ever a question of Christ not doing the will of the Father, but only of his not wanting the consequences of that will. Jesus Christ, who even in his human nature was nothing less than one with the Father, was to experience the supreme devastation of being separated in his human nature from the Father. This separation was *experienced* as a very tearing apart of the Hypostatic Union and thus infinitely deeper than any mere separation of body and blood. This experienced separation, this drinking a chalice of all the sins of the world and thus experiencing of damnation, repulsed Christ to the greatest degree possible by the thought of it;

> God made him who had no sin to be sin for us, so that in him we might become the righteousness of God. 2COR 5:21

While the angel from heaven came to Christ to give him physical strength so as to not faint in his agony, after he drank of the cup there was no such succor. After the drinking of the cup, Christ experienced the most violent and horrendous separation from God in his human nature, and thus mysteriously, because not ontologically, experiencing a separation from his own hypostatic nature as true God and true man. This separation brought the passion of the Incarnation, where Christ first mysteriously "emptied himself," to its fulfillment:

> Who being in the form of God, thought it not robbery to be equal with God: But emptied himself, taking the form of a servant, being made in the likeness of men, and in habit found as a man. He humbled himself, becoming obedient unto death, even to the death of the cross. . PP 2:6-8

Christ said *yes* to experiencing separation from the Father only for love of the Father. His greatest act of the will was to lovingly accept the will of the Father that he not experience the Father's love, the love of God. But though Christ experienced "damnation," experienced being forsaken by the Father, he was not damned. Being damned is a choice a person makes once and for all not to love God, but Christ chose to experience this "damnation," to endure this forsakenness, as an act of love for God. Though Christ experienced the absolute darkness of being forsaken upon the Holy Cross, he would utter in his own most sacred liturgical language the deepest, most loving and intimate prayer of his life:

> And at the ninth hour, Jesus cried out with a loud voice, saying: *Eloi, Eloi, lamma sabacthani?* Which is, being interpreted, My God, my God, why hast thou

forsaken me? MT 27:46

This prayer *"Eloi, Eloi, lamma sabacthani?"* is construed by exegetes to be a unique admixture of Aramaic and Hebrew, and are here surmised to be the only record of the liturgical language Our Lord Jesus Christ used in his most intimate prayer to the Father.[156] Not only in the complete darkness of his crucifixion, but even after his death as he would descend into the very depths of hell, Jesus Christ loved the Father with the same love that was present his whole life, with the same love that would be present in the glory of all eternity.

It is this very perfect receptive and infused virtue so modeled in Christ himself that is the perfection of the Christian. Hence, it is only the purely innocent or the humbled penitent that are found in the most intimate inner sanctum of Christ Crucified. And, as Christ did in regards first to the Blessed Virgin Mary and then to Mary Magdalene, it is to those in this inner sanctum that preeminently experience the glories of his Resurrection.

CRUCIAL CHARITY

The first millennium of Christianity was the age of exuberant faith. Christians of this early Church had an urgent expectation that the Kingdom of God was imminently upon them, and that this kingdom would dramatically spread like an irrepressible conflagration.

The second millennium of Christianity was the age of unbridled hope. Christians of this middle-age Church saw all here below in the context of gaining heaven and the avoiding of hell, while at the same time exerting heroic efforts to transform all here below into an earthly kingdom of God.

But this third millennium of Christianity is neither an age of faith nor hope. Christians of this stark age must rely on the crucial virtue of charity, i.e. love of God, to bring about the Kingdom in a virulently anti-Christic culture and amidst the very ruins of an obliterated Christendom.

In this rebellious third millennium the peoples of an erstwhile Christendom have apostatized from the Holy Faith. In this cynical third millennium it no longer suffices to depend primarily on faith, for faith is at every turn denied. In this delusional third millennium it no longer suffices to delay sinful gratification in the dread of hell, for the existence of hell, indeed the very reality of the here and now, is itself obscured. In this escapist third millennium hopeful anticipation of heavenly bliss is not motivation enough, for there are too many readily available ways to, for the time being, anesthetize oneself. In this enslaving third millennium hope in the earthly triumph of the Church Militant is wanting, for the only tangible ascending kingdom is that of the techno-bureaucratic totalitarian State.

But charity remains when faith and hope wanes. Yes,

charity will suffice in these dark days of salvation history, as well as in the dark days of a Christian's personal spiritual journey. Just as charity is all that will remain in heaven, so too, charity is all that remains, or at least suffices, here below in the deepest fires of purgation.

When faith grows dim in an impenetrable darkness of senses and spirit, when hope gives out in a seemingly hellish damnation, charity can not only endure but wax and conquer. The Christian can in fact allow this darkness and hellishness to turn to the good, for he can say *yes* to that very darkness and hellishness for love of Christ Crucified and thus turn it to a purgation that actually, even superlatively, brings about God's Kingdom.

As the days darken in the third millennium—as faith and hope grow frigid in this ice-age of catastrophic cultural climate change—it is only charity that will keep the hearts and hearths of the faithful aglow. And it is only charity that gives a person the undaunted courage to advance God's Kingdom against all odds. For Christian charity is a pure and unquenchable love that is without self-regard or self-interest and thus, it is not disheartened by humiliation and failure. Indeed, the culmination of charity entails the annihilation of self for God's sake.

It is the charitable, cross-conformed annihilation of the egoistic self that allows God to victoriously wax within the soul and thus the world. So this third millennium of Christianity, in all its annihilating anti-Christic dynamics, must needs be the age of a crucial charity; for only charity suffices for the vitally important conformity of the Christian to the Cross of Christ.

IMMEDIACY OF LOVE

Christianity in the third millennium must be driven by charity. But isn't all Christian activity driven by charity? No, and no in varying degrees; that is, Christianity can be practiced and motivated in varying degrees by self-love and pride. Simply put, Christianity can be practiced imperfectly. Whereas this imperfect practice of Christianity can be expected, it cannot be accepted, as it has come to be, as the standard as well.

Faith—belief in Jesus Christ and a doctrinal assent to the teachings of the Church—requires an assent of the intellect to truth and an exertion of the will against doubt and error. In other words, faith requires a positive thinking that is especially in need of exercise in the throes of vicissitudes. In these throes one exerts faith against the darkness, against the doubt, against the fears.

Hope—a focused intent on the goods of the Faith—flows from faith. Hope is a faith in Divine Providence that segues into a hope in Godly things and in heaven itself. Hope, like the faith from which its flows, requires a positive thinking and exertive willing that needs to be exercised most vigorously in the throes of vicissitudes.

Unlike charity, both faith and hope *may* admit of self-love and pride. A Christian has faith and thus may conform himself to God's truth to gain heaven and avoid hell. A Christian has hope and thus may be motivated and succored by the thought of heaven and heavenly aid. Though the self-love and pride that may be involved in acts of faith and hope do not ordinarily make those Christian acts wrong, they do make those acts imperfect, and thus at times—yes, especially in these faithless and hopeless times —make those acts insufficient.

Imperfect Christian motivation is found in delayed gratification and its appeal to self-interest. The essence of this imperfect egoistic spiritual motivation is the dread of hell and desire for heaven coupled with the fear of a cursed earthly existence and desire for earthly prosperity. But to effectively convert or motivate people to the Gospel in the third millennium will not entail terrifying fire and brimstone oratories on the afterlife, but rather sobering explications of the fire and brimstone realities of this life. It requires the preaching of severe earthly realities undiluted by promises of prosperity. In the third millennium, the acquired discipline of delayed gratification, of forgoing earthly pleasures so as to gain heavenly bliss or avoid hellish torment tomorrow, will not suffice for the conversion of the masses, nor maybe even for the perseverance of Catholics in the Faith.

Neither the fear of hell nor the desire for heaven will keep the third millennium's Technarcistic Man on the straight and narrow, for he has too many ways to distract himself from this world's reality, much less the next's. Yes, the hope of heaven and the dread of hell surely kept many on a straight path when that path made its way through an unanesthetized valley of tears. But not so today, when a superficial but nonetheless deadening bliss can be accessed with the mere turn of a control nob, bottle top, or medicine cap.

Charity admits of an immediacy that faith and hope do not. Both faith and hope when implemented against vicissitudes (and vicissitudes are always present in this vale of tears) are a reaction and thus admit of a two-stage dynamic. But charity even in the throes of vicissitudes is not in itself a reaction to these vicissitudes. Though the fruit of charity may well entail a militant response to evils, charity itself is a courageous receptivity to these vicissitudes for love of God.

Charity involves the simplest binary process.[157] Here

a person says a simple receptive and loving *yes* to the real, true, and good (including the reality of vicissitudes), and to its author, the person of God. Charity is not a reactive exertion of the will but rather a willful non-exertion: a choice not to resist God and his reality. It is a choice that is a perfect act of charity in so far as it excludes the motivation of pride and self-love, for it is a choice that will always admit of the realities of a fallen existence and the painfully purgative decreasing of self.

Charity finds its locus in the Cross. But it is always the Cross that is the stumbling block in doing the will of God. It is always the Cross that is the excuse for rebellion against God. For it is always the Cross that is the essence of both reality and Faith. In the third millennium, man is tech-enabled and hell-bent on escaping not only the Cross of Christ but the cross of reality as well.

At the center of earthly existence is found the Cross, and at this center's unfathomable heart is found Christ Crucified. Thus, the Gospel is not a mere theoretical enunciation, but an exhortative prescription to lovingly embrace reality in all its infinite plenitude. A Christian's existential journey to embrace the plenitude of reality entails living out the vitally important truths of the Faith. In the unrealistic and anti-Christic third millennium this embrace must be done with a most vigorous charity motivated intentionality.

CRUCIAL PRAYER

Just as the theological virtues of faith and hope give way by necessity to charity in this faithless and despairing third millennium, so too the prayers of petition and thanksgiving give way to the prayers of atonement and adoration in this age of egocentricity. For of the four ends of Christian prayer, the first two of petition and thanksgiving may be egoistically oriented. Even the pagans petition the gods for favors, and even a child knows enough to effusively thank a gift-giver so as to incite further gift-giving. But in the third millennium, where God is greatly seen to exist for man, emphasis on petition and thanksgiving can readily obscure true religion where man exists for God.

But not so with the other two ends of prayer, atonement and adoration which are, respectively, ordered away from man and towards God. It is true that there exists a lesser form of atonement prayer that is still egoistic and may seek to atone, propitiate, or appease God in the self-interest of avoiding his withdrawal of favor or punishment. But such reactive atonement, or purgative, prayer is a Christian's imperfect contrition of being sorry for sin because he "dreads the loss of heaven and fears the fires of hell." True atonement or purgative prayer is a higher and qualitative sort of prayer that consists of a receptive *yes* to the decreasing of the pseudo self. It is this purgative prayer that necessarily excludes egoistic motivation because it is intrinsically ego-abnegating.

Ego-abnegating atonement or purgative prayer is motivated by the love/adoring of God, which is the final and highest form of prayer. A person chooses to decrease so Christ may increase; so that he may no longer exist but rather Christ may exist within him; so that he may become a soul that magnifies the Lord. Atonement or purgative prayer is then necessarily accompanied and motivated by adoring prayer. Indeed, the more a person loves God the more he recognizes (even, or especially, if that person is a saint) that he does not love God enough.

Saying *yes* to one's wretchedness, to the humiliation of one's sinfulness and existence, to one's own sorrows and to the world's sorrows, is the essence of purgative prayer and atonement. Inseparably linked to this purgative receptivity, because it is the very motivation for it, is the love of God. It is the receptive prayer of purgation for love of Christ that can be set in motion with every heartbeat, truly allowing one to pray always and then most intensely in the most difficult moments. This is the crucial prayer, where even petition is but a request for graceful abnegation, and where even thanksgiving is but an act of grateful receptivity to this abnegation. Yes, it is this integrated receptive prayer of purgation for love of Christ that fulfills the essential vocation to decrease the self unto becoming a soul that magnifies the Lord. And it is in this purgative act's loving receptivity, its ceasing and desisting fighting against impacting reality and God's will, that one, by definition, is at peace. And it is in the purgative act for love of Christ that the fruit of that love is surprisingly given: the fruit of joy.

X. EXISTENTIAL REALITIES

"Where have you laid him?"
They said to him: "Lord, come and see."
And Jesus wept. JN 11:34—35

What **does man fear**? What is the fly in the ointment of life? What ominously hangs over the head of each and every human person? It is death. And it is suffering, which is but the experiencing of death incrementally.

> Therefore the death of man, and of beasts is one, and the condition of them both is equal: as man dieth, so they also die: all things breathe alike, and man hath nothing more than beast: all things are subject to vanity. And all things go to one place: of earth they were made, and into earth they return together. Who knoweth if the spirit of the children of Adam ascend upward, and if the spirit of the beasts descend downward? EC 3:19—22

"I am not afraid to die," Technarcistic Man often boasts. But his saying, "I am not afraid to die," is proof that he knows not death. Rather he is blind to the realities of his mortality. "We espouse dying with dignity," says the mental health and medical professions. But by saying this, these technarcistic professionals show they understand neither dignity nor death. For these professionals, dignity is but appearances of comportment, even if this comportment is a coma state induced by drugs.

Dying is not about dignity at all, for in dying a person

is stripped of all and undergoes the greatest of humiliations. Rather, dying is about suffering-well the final culminating drama of mortal existence. The ultimate denial of existence is to be unaware of this final, and yes, fearful, drama of life and death, and it is a blasphemous contempt for the dying, and their loved ones, to obfuscate this drama under a narcotic stupor.[158]

In the third millennium mortal fears have been, if not allayed, buried down under material abundance and technological desensitization. An unbridled technarcism has turned the contemporary person away from not only from his mortality but from other basic realities of his physical existence and limitations. Technarcistic Man's denial of realities and limitations range from the ultimate earthly reality of death, to the myriad of vicissitudes of suffering, to even the basic demarcation of the flesh as male and female. But it is these most urgent physical realities in their limitations, and thus humiliations, that are most maturing when accepted. Because third millennium Technarcistic Man depreciates, rejects, or is even unable to recognize these ultimate and most fundamental mortal physical realities, he is also unable to live a mature and fully human life.

MORTALITY & CONTINGENCY

Man is weighed down by the flesh which is a constant visceral reminder of his mortality and acutely non-divine status. The blessed angels have not the rotting flesh, and the brute animals have not the aspirations or capacity, to know the humiliation of the flesh. Indeed, the human being is truly the most pathetic of creatures; for he is made for eternal beatitude but he is not even able to keep himself in mortal existence. Yet God takes on the nature of the most pathetic of creatures and appropriates the rotting flesh in the Incarnation, making the most pathetic of creatures also the most blessed of creatures, for man is the only creature that shares a common nature with God. In his very weakness, then, man finds his greatest blessing.

While mortality, the brutalizing reality of suffering and death, is the most urgent principle of human physical existence, it triggers an even more piercing spiritual concern. This is the concern of human contingency, that is, of not having control over one's spiritual existence one way or the other. Though human contingency is properly a spiritual concern of the Psychomoral Vocation, it is here spoken of in conjunction with mortality and the Incarnational Vocation since it is physical mortality that not only makes man rightly aware of his spiritual contingency but as well may lead him to wrongly surmise that because he will someday cease to exist physically he will cease to exist completely. (So too, this interplay of the Psychomoral and Incarnational Vocation is demonstrative of the interplay of all the Seven Crucial Vocations.)

Unlike the human person's physical existence where he has some influence, he can neither keep himself in spiritual existence nor escape it. Since existence is contingent upon

God loving the being, and since God loves the human person as an analogous *imago Dei* in his immortal rational-volitional image,[159] man can neither exist on his own accord nor not exist. It is this spiritual contingency that is the underlying and ultimate source of all existential fear.

This *imago Dei* contingency, where man is immortal yet existentially helpless, pierces all the more deeply due to *imago Dei* infinite capacity for the divine. The person's infinite capacity for the divine is the source of his deepest existential pain because an infinite capacity is also an infinite emptiness. The human, as a creature created in God's image, is made for immortality as well as divine life, yet is unable to secure it on his own accord. Even if man destroys his physical life he can neither fill nor escape this inherent, infinite emptiness, this infinite capacity for the infinitely divine. As is evidenced in the creation account, adhering to and not rebelling against creaturely contingency, the essential reality that *God is God and the creature is not,* is the very premise of natural law.[160] For the rational creature's (*i.e.*, angels and men) essential proper act and end is to give glory to God, and this must begin by saying *yes* to God being God and the creature not being God.

When a person recognizes his mortality and thus contingency, he knows reality is not tailored to his desires; he knows that the world does not center around him; he knows that God's ways are not his ways; he knows that God is God and he is not. The reality of one's mortality and contingency is the source of all fear and hence all egoistic defenses; indeed, all sin. To seek to escape or rebel against the fearful truths of one's mortality and contingency entails rejecting other existential realities as well (including even the most fundamental demarcator of human enfleshment as male and female). It also entails, to some degree, an apostasy (turning-way) from God.

EMBRACING THE CROSS
OF EXISTENCE

Holy Church has always encouraged the faithful to contemplate the Four Last Things: death, judgment, heaven or hell. It is the Cross itself, the focal point of the pain, that makes the contemplation of these four last things profitable, even joyful. For it is the Cross, if only a person embraces it, that defeats death, expiates judgment, bars hell, and opens heaven. The existential mortal and contingent threat to the human person poses the primary choice to embrace the painful cross of existence or to run from it. This primary existential choice demands a moral response from a person that necessarily entails either vice or virtue. It is at this point that existential anxiety is first encountered. As a person is brought to this chasm of choice he can either accept reality, that is, turn toward God in humble worship, or he can fight reality, that is, turn away from God in prideful rebellion.

In so far as a person is mature he will have a natural courage that allows him to gaze upon reality and thus further facilitate the maturation of ego-abnegation and *imago Dei* dominance. And in so far as a person is psychomorally debilitated and fearful he will either succumb to a blinding despair or seek distractions and anesthetizations that temporarily assuage that despair. The world, the flesh, the devil, and the technarcistic third millennium offer a myriad of distractions and numbing agents that can be partaken of to facilitate a turning away from reality. And in truth it is only the Holy Christian Faith that gives a person the requisite supernatural courage to not only gaze unblinkingly upon reality but to then leap head and heart long (read *reasonably and volitionally*) into the chasm of existence.

An eyes-wide-open look upon reality, and much more so a leap of faith, entails leaving behind lesser goods: that is, the very distractions and anesthetizations prescribed by the myriad of technarcistic escape artists. Indeed, it is when these lesser goods and distractions are consciously chosen to the detriment of higher goods, including and most essentially the good of man's existential reality as a mere creature utterly dependent on God, that a person impedes maturation, is vicious, and sins.

Looking into the chasm of reality can be done with unaided reason, for it is a fulfilling of the natural Psychomoral Vocation. This encountering of reality, mots especially the mortal and contingent existential reality, can either be the catalyst for assenting to the truth and embrace of the good of reality and the subsequent abnegation of the ego and restoration of the *imago Dei*, or it can lead to denying the truth and the good and the further besmirchment of the *imago Dei* with a reality denying defense of a person's egoistic self.

Merely looking into the chasm of reality is not to be confused with religious faith but with the acceptance of a Being that, though beyond comprehension, is nonetheless known to be All-Powerful and responsible for existence. Leaping fully into that chasm of reality is an act of faith, for it is a fulfilling of the crucial Christian vocation. But while looking into the chasm of reality is not yet an act of religious faith, it nonetheless poises one for the leap of faith. A man's acceptance of his own existence's radical contingency and complete dependence on a Being that is totally Other is the realization that he is suspended in, or even free-falling through, midair, with no personal control over his footing in existence.

Once the elementary truth of one's createdness is assented to, it is imperative that a person continue to be open to and seek reality. A person cannot remain in the air, as it were, without having a sense of urgency about the nature of God. On the other hand, complacency is a sign that one has scampered back to illusionary distractions. A complacent attitude about existence and the nature of God is itself vicious, for it means a person has chosen the contentment of lower goods, of distractions, over the highest good, which is truth.

The man who does not seek ultimate truth with his whole heart denies his human nature, which at its essence compels him to be a desperate seeker of truth and of God. As such, the refusal to embrace the existential threat by courageously transcending the intrinsic anxiety of existence leads to vice and subsequently further anxiety. Vicious anxiety plagues the man who has chosen lesser goods to the destruction of higher ones. It requires that a man attempt to deny these higher goods by closing himself off from the fullness of reality. This turning from reality, from God, is at the same time a turning to self. It is thus an act that increases self-love and pride. Reality then becomes not only a threat to one's existence but to one's self-love and pride. Though this self-love and pride is not of the essence of man, as is his existential emptiness and contingency, it can become so extensive and habituated that one can easily mistake it for who he is. To various extents then, vicious anxiety impels the psychomorally debilitated person to deny and escape from reality. For such a psychomorally debilitated person the fullness of reality, light, and truth becomes a source of anxiety, for it threatens his egoistic pseudo-self: both his self-love and pride and the secondary vicious defenses that seek to serve and protect that self-love and pride. God himself, who is ultimate reality, must be denied and escaped. But it is God's light and truth, which is manifested on both the natural and supernatural levels, that is indeed the antidote to existential anxiety, for it is he who gives a man the courage to overcome his fear and face the pain of his existence. Benedict XVI said:

Those who "fear" God "are not afraid". Fear of God,[161]

which the Scriptures define as "the beginning of knowledge" coincides with faith in him, with sacred respect for his authority over life and the world. To be without "fear of God" is equivalent to putting ourselves in his place, to feeling we ourselves are lords of good and evil, of life and death. . . . Instead, those who fear God feel within them the safety that an infant in his mother's arms feels (cf. Ps 130: 2). Those who fear God are tranquil even in the midst of storms for, as Jesus revealed to us, God is a Father full of mercy and goodness. Those who love him are not afraid.[162]

A person can say *yes to that which causes his existential fears*, to his very deficiency, inadequacy, mortality, and spiritual contingency as part and parcel of choosing the good; for it is good in that the person's deficiency, inadequacy, mortality, and spiritual contingency is true, even though it means accepting the ego-abnegation and humiliation of this creaturely wretchedness. This ability to so choose reality, truth, and good—inclusive of one's mortal and contingent inadequacies—while still fully desiring the absolute Supreme Good, is the essential drama of human existence. It is also the intensified, condensed drama of the psychomoralitic and/or conversional process, the heart of which is the moment in which undiluted being, truth, and good are brought to the threshold of a person's innermost awareness.

GOD-GIVEN GENDER

The living, vibrant, and militant Christian ethos requisite for a new Christendom will be made manifest in the resurgence of the Christian family. But the resurgence of the Christian family itself requires nothing less than a new manifestation, indeed a courageous celebration, of the family's essential components: the God-given gender incarnational demarcation as male and female.

Gender here is to be understood as the totality of maleness or femaleness, of masculinity and femininity, of manhood and womanhood. Gender entails not only the biological designation as male or female, as xy or xx,[163] but a person's psychomoral[164] and familial/ social accordance with that designation as well. Gender is determined and normed not to subjective beliefs or feelings or self-identifications, nor to social or political constructs, but rather to immutable and objective biological facts; in other words, *to reality*. Thus, as per reality there is no "theory" of gender; either a person's gender awareness and identification are realistically in accord with his biological sex or unrealistically in discord with it. Likewise, either both society and culture facilitate the uniqueness of the male and female genders or they do violence to them.

In many ways it can be said that between the genders there is not that big of a difference, and yet the difference is crucial. Yes, men and women are both essentially incarnate beings in the image of God, and for the most part they share the same physiology, and of course the same rational-volitional nature. As such, it can be said that male and female are more the same than different, for they are both of the same species, they are both human. In accord with philosophical logic, the difference among individuals of the same species is termed an "accidental."[165] Thus, gender can be considered an accidental, but if so considered, it also must be considered the most important of accidentals; or, if you will, the *most essential of accidentals.*

So while there is *"neither male nor female"* (GA 3:28) in heaven (that is, participating in the beatific vision is not limited by gender, though gender is still present in the glorified body), gender is nonetheless the essential demarcation of the human person here below. Biblically, the first distinction is *"male and female he created them"* (GN 1:27) and the first distinction made universally of a newborn is "It's a girl!" or "It's a boy!"

Gender is defining (and thus limiting) because it is inextricably linked to the biological demarcations of being either male or female. But gender is more than just overt biology. Gender also is a charism that permeates into the very character of men and women as they mature into the unique persons God has destined them to be. Gender charism also exudes from a person into all relationships, all families, and all communities and societies. To facilitate and live in accord with biological gender and the ensuing charisms is *gender propriety.*

While there may be minor cultural and personal differences in facilitating, conforming to, and conveying the true essence of masculinity and femininity, these differences can only go so far if they are to be gender proper. Thus, gender propriety not only actualizes and manifests a person's true nature as male or female, but also limits a person in its call for conformity to that nature. But any recognition in the post-Christian, and now anti-Christic, West of definitive limitations on a person are considered vicious, and in regards to gender, sexist. But if "sexism"—a term coined in the mid-twentieth century—means limiting a person on account of gender then the Church is clearly "sexist." But if the Church is so-called "sexist" it is only because nature itself is. Finally, if nature is so-called "sexist" it is only because its author, God

Almighty, is—and so be it.

HUMILIATION OF THE FLESH

Technarcistic third millennium society and culture does violence to gender because gender is limiting; that is, like it or not, one is either male or female. Limitations on the psychomoral level entail humiliation; hence, from a narcissistic view, gender in its limitations and humiliations is undesirable; and hence, from a technological view, gender becomes an area calling for manipulation or neutralization. But to properly understand and live in harmonious accord with the nature and reality of gender it is necessary to accept its specifying and therefore limiting aspects. Because both the physiology and charisms of gender entail not only aptitudes and gifts but limitations and deficiencies as well, gender is part and parcel of the limited nature and humiliating[166] reality of the human person as a created incarnate being.

A *person* is a rational being; that is, a being that has reason and free will. There are three types of persons. The first type of persons are the uncreated Divine Persons of the Holy Trinity. The second type of persons is the created angelic person of pure intelligence and non-corporeality. The third type of persons is the created human person who is both rational and incarnate. Of course, the latter two types of persons derive from the former Prototype and are persons by the very fact that they, as rational-volitional beings, are *imago Dei*, in the very analogous image of that Divine Prototype.

The aeviternal angelic persons are superior to human persons because they, like God, are purely intellectual/spiritual beings and can reason and will (know and love) without the need or encumbrance of the flesh and senses. That is why the human person is *"less than the angels."* (PS 8:6) The human person is *less* because of his incarnate nature.

Thus, even the most brilliant human, because he must exercise his intelligence through his corporal organicity, is of less intelligence than the lowest angel who exercises his intelligence in a purely spiritual manner.[167] Having a body, or corporeality, then, is in itself a limitation.

Because corporeality is a limitation, it is a humiliation. This limitation/humiliation of corporeality must be the foundational principle of any authentic "theology of the body." This limitation[168] was present even in the preternatural state of paradise. In fact, from the very beginning (before the Fall), because of his enfleshment, Adam experienced an aloneness; a deficiency that was "not good." This deficiency of the flesh would find its remedy in the flesh, for from the flesh was brought forth a companion:

> And the Lord God said: It is not good for man to be alone: let us make him a help like unto himself. GN 2:16-18

After the fall, this limitation of the flesh became a humiliation in all its aspects. As such, in both their spiritual sinfulness and bodily nakedness,

> Adam and his wife hid themselves from the face of the Lord God. GN 3:8

As a result of Adam's apostasy his descendants would suffer a life that was laborious, and subject to sickness, hunger, and death: sufferings and humiliations that are dependent upon physicality. But this Divine punishment, which gave full reign to the fundamental humiliation of corporeality, became as well the antidote to the fundamental sin of spiritual pride.[169]

The fundamental humiliation of corporeality became the very means through which man would be redeemed when the Son of God took upon Himself corporal human nature. In the Incarnation, Christ experiences a sort of "divine humiliation." More accurately, Our Lord experiences *kenosis*, or "an emptying" of what is rightly his:

> [Christ] who being in the form of God, did not consider

equality with God something to be grasped: But rather emptied Himself, taking the form of a slave, being made in the likeness of men, and in habit found as a man. PP 2:6—7

This kenosis differs diametrically from the account of the Fall where man, radically unequal though he was, nonetheless *grasped* to be equal with God, as can be seen in the temptation of the serpent:

...what day soever you shall eat thereof, your eyes shall be opened: you shall be as Gods, knowing good and evil. GN 3:5

So having a material body is a God-given limitation that entails humiliation, and must be either humbly accepted or pridefully and rebelliously rejected. Corporeality's limitation and humiliation is inseparable from gender distinctions, thus the rejection of the essential corporal limitations of gender distinctions is a vicious rejection of God the Creator. The urgent call, especially in the gender-bending third millennium, is for Christian men and women to humbly, piously, and strikingly embrace distinct manifestations of their masculinity and femininity.

THE FEMININE CHARISM

The proper understanding and crucial ethos of God-given gender is intrinsically tied to the appreciation by both men and women of the *feminine distillation*.[170] Aristotle's speculation that woman is an incomplete or under-formed male was incorrect but not without some basis. At face value this point does not appear to have the potential for a positive view of woman, yet it does! Aristotle did not have the advantage of revealed truth, but Holy Scripture states that woman was *taken* from man. Woman, then, is not an incomplete man, but rather a *derivation* of man. "And the Lord God built the rib which he took from Adam into a woman." (GN 2:22.) In an affirmation of the Genesis account, the x can indeed be taken from the xy, but not vice versa.

Woman, if she is to be at all construed as "incomplete" or "half" of man, can also be deemed, if not unqualifiably, *the better half*, at leastwise the purer, sweeter and more integral half. The feminine, as a derivation, can even more aptly be understood as a purified *distillation* of the masculine. As will be seen below, the essential masculine call to fatherhood entails elements not integral to the human person as a creature *qua* creature made in God's image.

Woman in her simple and pure receptivity has an integrity that man has not. Woman is less than a man, but less as in more pure, and therefore to be considered the sweeter, distilled essence of the human person's creaturehood, of humanity itself. A distillation is purer because it is less than the coarser matrix it is derived from. In her pure refinement then, woman is the very nectar of the human race. The feminine distillation, most exquisitely so with divine grace added, is the most life-imbuing of liqueurs, the most soothing of balms. Feminine receptivity and sweetness allows the specific vocation of womanhood, which is nurturing maternity. The receptive capacity allows the maternity, while the sweetness provides the sustenance of that maternity. Whether a woman is a biological mother or not, she is still called to nurture. As St. John Paul II and others have said, "Motherhood is woman's vocation. It is her eternal vocation...."[171]

Yes, it is a man's very husbandly duty to facilitate his wife's being set apart so as to facilitate her holiness. But, of course, a husband cannot do so if she herself does not desire this setting apart. Nonetheless, a woman, especially a wife and mother, ought to be home-loving. A wife and mother finds her place, the place of her vocation, her peace and sanctification, in the home. Note well, *a woman's place is in the home not because she is not good enough for the world but because she is too good for it.* A woman's precious gifts are squandered when she gives herself to the making of a dollar rather than to the making of a home. The world, its corporations, bureaucracies, and agencies are profane entities that are unworthy of a woman's devotion and are unable to avail or value the feminine charism. These profane entities coarsen, poison, and suck dry the maternal heart.

Finally, it must be stated emphatically that today very few, whether inside the Church or out, understand the true value of femininity. In the world today, the feminine is valued in two perversely wrong ways. The first is in a superficial, and most often sinful, erotic valuation. The second is in the defemininizing valuation of a woman in how well she can do a man's job. But, as previously stated, the true feminine charism is receptivity and sweetness. This is the feminine value that mustn't be squandered for anything, much less haphazardly tossed away for naught as is done today. It is this true femininity, along with the childhood innocence that domestically surrounds it, that is to be cherished above all things here below.

THE MASCULINE CHARISM

As counter-cultural as Christian patriarchy is in the third millennium, it nonetheless provides the essential pillars of the Catholic family; and, as per its very counterculturality, the remedy for the third millennium's socio-political ills. Christian patriarchy is also an unchangeable teaching of the Church, being affirmed and expounded upon by the Magisterium for 2,000 years.[172] Truly, no other position of leadership is more absolute than that of the patriarchal headship of the family. The office of familial patriarchy calls for the highest degree of homage, surpassed only by that due to Almighty God; and it is a man's wife who is properly his first, even if only, and most loyal subject. As per the Catechism of Trent,

> "Again, and in this the conjugal union chiefly consists, let wives never forget that next to God they are to love their husbands, to esteem them above all others, yielding to them in all things not inconsistent with Christian piety, a willing and ready obedience."[173]

Suffice it to say here (for it is expounded upon below) that a husband's reciprocal duty is to *love his wife like Christ loved the Church* and there is no greater sacrificial love than this. Indeed, for her and in Christ, a husband is called to respond to his wife's obedient submission by nothing less than he himself "becoming obedient unto death, even to the death of the cross." (PP 2:8) For both a wife's submission unto her husband and a husband's complete immolation for love of his wife derive from Holy Matrimony being the prime typification[174] of the relationship between Christ and the Church.

The hierarchical order requires a woman, for love of God and her husband, to be submissive unto God in the person of that husband. The hierarchical order requires a man, for love of God and his wife, to forsake all other women, and more so to forsake his very self,[175] for that wife. These two dynamics of wifely submission and husbandly forsaking-of-self are essential to the marital relationship and as a Christological typology; they are that from which marriage derives its very Christian sacramental nature.

> Being subject one to another, in the fear of Christ. Let women be subject to their husbands, as to the Lord: Because the husband is the head of the wife, as Christ is the head of the church. He *is* the savior of his body. Therefore as the *church is subject to Christ*,[176] so also let the wives be to their husbands in all things. Husbands, love your wives, as Christ also loved the church, and delivered himself up for it: That he might sanctify it, cleansing it by the laver of water in the word of life: That he might present it to himself a glorious church, not having spot or wrinkle, or any such thing; but that it should be holy, and without blemish. So also ought men to love their wives as their own bodies. He that loveth his wife, loveth himself. For no man ever hated his own flesh; but nourisheth and cherisheth it, as also Christ doth the church: because we are members of his body, of his flesh, and of his bones. *For this cause shall a man leave his father and mother, and shall cleave to his wife, and they shall be two in one flesh.* This is a great sacrament; but I speak in Christ and in the church. Nevertheless let every one of you in particular love his wife as himself: and let the wife fear her husband. EPH 5:21-33 (*Emphasis* added.)

Be aware that this last statement—*for a husband to love his wife as himself and for a wife to fear her husband*—is but the *very minimum requirement* not to sin. It is the minimal natural law requirement of the husband to protect and provide for his wife and for a woman to be submissive to her husband. But in this passage St. Paul says nothing of the specific Christian call for heroic sacrificial marital love (though he does profusely elsewhere), the truly Christ-like love, that entails a husband loving his wife more than himself, more than his very life, and for a wife to be submissive not out of a fearful self-interest but out of a loving self-abnegation. This degree of marital love is one of charity: the loving of one's spouse for love of God. This marital love is the Christian ideal, and certainly in the anti-Christic, anti-familial, and anti-God-given-gender third millennium it is only a wholehearted commitment to this ideal that will suffice.

THE ORIGINAL THEOLOGY
OF THE BODY

Theology of the Body is a popularization of St. John Paul II's writings on the *Original Unity of Man and Woman*.[177] At times this popularization tends to glorify the body and may take the sexual mating aspects of these writings out of context and focus on them almost exclusively and thus disproportionately. But the ancient Catholic "theology of the body" entails chastity, which entails mortification, asceticism, custody of the eyes, ordering of the marital act toward procreation, and the recognition of the superiority of ascetical celibacy for the sake of the Kingdom.

The traditional theology of the body is the theology of asceticism. This original theology of the body is seen in Christ's own taking of a body, who in doing so,

> . . . emptied himself, taking the form of a servant, being made in the likeness of men . . . . PP 2:7

Our Lord did not acquire a further perfection when he took flesh, but quite the opposite. The body is not a perfection to be gloried in, but rather a limitation, and thus an imperfection, that is to be joyfully accepted because it is humbling. More so, man can rejoice in the humiliation of the flesh because it is the means by which Christ shared in the nature of his creatures by "humbling himself, becoming obedient unto death, even to the death of the cross." (PP 2:8) More so, it is man's own ordering of the flesh to the spirit, his own suffering and death united to Christ Crucified, that allows him to share in Christ's Divine Life.

Ultimately all corporal mortification, just as the body itself, is rightly ordered toward the spiritual and psychomoral realm. Hence, physical mortification finds its end in spiritual mortification. *Spiritual mortification is the acceptance of humiliation.*[178] Etiologically, purity or chastity stems from the spirit of poverty; the spirit of poverty stems from humility; and humility stems from reverence for God. Conversely, impurity or lust stems from covetousness (the opposite of poverty of spirit); and covetousness stems from pride (the opposite of humility); and pride stems from a love of self as opposed to reverence for God.

The human person is called to embrace the truth of his existence, to embrace the humiliation both of his vulnerable corporeality and helpless contingency, rather than anxiously fighting or running away from such humiliation. To be receptive to reality in its harshest and most absolute aspects is to be in touch with the most fundamental premise of natural law: again one's mortality and utter spiritual contingency. Though third millennium's Technarcistic Man is not in touch with the brutal impact of mortality, and hence is even less in touch with his utter spiritual contingency, his technarcism can be effectively combated with the spirit of poverty and humility.

The culture of technological materialism and subjective narcissism—*i.e.,* technarcism—is certainly a culture of death (to reference St. John Paul again). This is because, in so far as its technarcistic population is not sorrowfully aware of the curse of death, it is likewise not joyfully aware of the blessings of life. The pervasive power-hungry anti-God ideologies and ethoses of the third millennium have a hatred that knows no bounds in regards to the contingencies of reality, of truth, and of the natural order. Indeed, the very same[179] anti-God ideologues who now deny the absolute definitive proclamation of the newborn as "it's a girl!" or "it's a boy!" preceded this by murderously denying even that "it's a baby!"

XI. The Church

*...and the gates of hell
shall not prevail against it. MT 16:18*

In God's providential unfolding of salvation history, specifically with dogma defined and readily accessible, these latter times have made the living members of the Magisterium less important than ever and the explicated teachings of the Church paramount. But so too, the contemporary era's mass-media technology has made the pope and sundry prelates and priests more accessible than ever, and this presents the very real danger of cults of personality and celebrity. Hence, the dichotomy of permanent, immovable, objective, and definitive—indeed, dogmatic—doctrine versus the volatile, fleeting, subjective, and sensational—indeed opinionated—soundbite or tweet.

In the past, a pope's private life or personality had nothing to do with his papacy (or prelacy or pastorate), in fact, a pope would even dine in solitude so as not to manifest even his culinary needs, wants, and desires. Neither would a pope entertain guests nor be entertained. However, post-Vatican II popes have become quite lackadaisical about separating their personal life from their papal office, and have gone so far as to publish personal writings after their ascendancy to the Chair of Peter; thus blurring the line of what is a formal papal writing. Popes have become even more lackadaisical about personal versus papal utterances.

This ill-defined demarcation between the man who is pope and the office of the papacy began in earnest with John Paul II's reading of his pre-pontificate, that is, private, theological works (*viz. Original Unity of Man and Woman*) at his "Wednesday Catechesis." It was continued by Pope Benedict's writing and publishing of a private theological work (i.e., *Jesus of Nazareth*) while pope. And it has reached its crescendo with the myriad of informal quips and press interviews issued by Pope Francis. To be sure, popes have not only become personalities but celebrities; however, as personalities and celebrities their publications and pronouncements are not necessarily pontifications.

As the lines between the man and the papal office are evermore blurred in popular culture and practice, these lines must needs become evermore clear to the individual informed Catholic conscience of the faithful. This is in God's divine providence; divesting even the papacy itself of that which is extraneous to it, limiting its competency, limiting its power, indeed dethroning the man who happens to be pope. This need for demarcating paradoxically purifies the papacy of the human and extraneous and requires a clear understanding that not only is the man who is pope but the papacy itself is subordinate to the Church.

Because of the fact that dogma has been defined, and in spite of previous condemnations,[180] both Vatican II and most of the post-Vatican II pontifications have been but vacuous attempts to change, embellish, or at least mitigate the sense of Church teachings. Most modern day pronouncements—be they from the Vatican, National Conferences of Bishops, or a local ordinary—are susceptible to this vacuity. For though this is the age of instant and gregarious communication, providentially the Magisterium has very little new to say. As such, there is primarily the need to focus on living out the readily accessible teachings of Holy Mother Church, teachings infallibly secured by that very Magisterium which is now to recede in favor of that Church.

DECONSTRUCTION & PURGATION OF THE PAPACY

Due to the erroneous ideology and culture that equated the Church with the Magisterium, the institutions they ran, the ordained ministry, and those devoted exclusively to the institutional church, historically that very Magisterium was concerned first and foremost with the preservation of its power and prestige when confronted with evil within its own ranks. Most infamously, ecclesial powers buried clericalistic sins so as to avoid scandal to themselves and their institutions, but finally succeeded only in burying the faith of those who were the victims of those sins.

It was these sacerdotal scandals that put the final nail in the coffin of an overriding triumphalism. It was these scandals that finally accomplished what schisms, imprisonment of popes, usurpation of kings, ecclesial rebellion, Kulturkampf, or social revolutions could not. The influence of the Catholic Church's living Magisterium —that is the prestige, power, and authority of the *persons* who are the holders of the offices of the papacy, curia, and episcopacy—was completely vanquished from the public square with the sordid sacerdotal scandals of the latter 20th Century. In the third millennium the monarchical political power of the papacy, its prelates and princes, is no more. And may God be praised as his salvation history (the coming of his kingdom) unwaveringly unfolds; for by the grace of God the ideology of clericalism in its ensuing sinful abuses and cover-ups only crushed itself.

Paralleling the brutal chastisement of the sacerdotal scandals, has been the self-imposed deconstruction of the papacy by the series of *circa* third millennium popes.

This deconstruction of the papacy began in earnest with the charismatic John Paul II. With John Paul II's celebrity status and worldwide and mass-media fueled popularity came certain commonality as well. Truly, it was John Paul II's very spontaneity, his very rich and vibrant humanity, that (undeniably infused with grace) was the source of his charismatic appeal. Then came the favorite of the traditionalists, Benedict XVI, who because of his reputation as a conservative/traditionalist, would further and quite substantially deconstruct the mystique of the papacy with his shocking, but totally valid, abdication. In the wake of Benedict's abdication came Francis, with his social liberalism and theological progressivism, jettisoning of many monarchical trappings, unprecedented accessibility to the press, and unbridled expression of his personal opinions. Even more so than his formal issuances, it is Francis' opinions that are seemingly less than orthodox, but have at the same time shown the limitations of the papacy; *viz.*, the pope is not always right nor the embodiment of Catholicity much less holiness. Francis has quite rapidly, and, *please God,* finally succeeded in reducing the papacy to its relatively perfunctory role in the third millennium of Christianity.

The lesson to be learned, or rather relearned, is that Peter is not the Church, but exists as the foundational slab for the doctrinal building up of the Church, which Peter himself infallible directs. As per God's providential salvation history, as Peter accomplishes his mission, he, that is the man who is pope, correspondingly becomes relatively obscure and less prominent as the foundational slab underneath the dogmatic edifice he has constructed.

> Jesus replied, "Blessed are you, Simon son of Jonah! For this was not revealed to you by flesh and blood, but by My Father in heaven. And I tell you that you are Peter, and on this rock I will build My church, and the gates of Hades will not prevail against it. I will give you the keys of the kingdom of heaven. Whatever you bind on earth will be bound in heaven, and whatever you loose

on earth will be loosed in heaven. MT 16:17—19

It is Peter that is used to infallibly unpack the dogmatic truths from the Deposit of Faith, truths that will constitute the Church's essential nature regardless of who the man is that occupies the Holy See. Most essentially, the Church's members, her faithful from peon to pope, are ranked not in accord with office but in accord to the degree they assent to and live out these truths. Yes, with the Magisterial task complete and all essential dogmatic truths defined, that Magisterium has worked itself out of its most vital job, and hence must become less as the Church becomes more, indeed all.

Note well again, that in God's providence after Our Lord designates Simon as the Rock, he immediately rebukes him, and all future popes, prelates, and priests, for meddling in the "things of men," in the things of the world, in the things of power and politics, in things not within their competency:

> But Jesus turned and said to Peter, "Get behind Me, Satan! You are a stumbling block to Me. For you do not have in mind the things of God, but the things of men." MT 16:23

Thus the Church is not to be equated with the persons who are her popes (or prelates and priests), for if she is she surely could not claim to be the Spotless Bride of Christ. If the Church is seen as essentially the office of the Magisterium, then she could not be indefectible save in the most rare of occasions, and she certainly would be capricious. If the Church is seen as but her political and worldly power, then she certainly would be seen in decline. But the Church miraculously transcends her human elements, administrative structures, and worldly positioning. This transcendence is the very *proof* that the Church is unlike any other historical institution, all others of which have risen then, in a matter of time, have fallen; it is the tangible proof that she is truly the indefectible Spotless Bride of Christ.

Those in this third millennium that seek the remedy

for the severe, but still accidental, crisis in the magisterial bureaucracies of the Church by the coming of a savior pope, much less a bishop or pastor, are not abiding by Divine Providence nor attuned with salvation history, but rather are exacerbating and prolonging any crisis. Salvation history insistently teaches the faithful that their following of Christ and his Church, that their very salvation, is not in the hands of a pope or a priest. Rather, it teaches that their faithfulness is in their own hands; that their faith is their individual responsibility and the responsibility of those in closest authority over the individual, which is the family.

The faithful laity's vision must not depend on the standards of whoever might be pope, or bishop, or pastor, but be fixed only on the standard of the Cross. Indeed, popes, prelates and priests exist solely to facilitate the faithful's vision and holiness. Here, in this God-ordained time, the common maxim often heard in conservative circles, "Don't be more Catholic than the Pope," is seen to be nothing less than heretical. Here, the true and orthodox position is known to be, *"You can never be too Catholic."* Here, it is understood that the Pope himself is subject to the Church. And here it is clear that each Catholic's conscience informed by the Holy Church is the ultimate Vicar of Christ.[181]

RE-LOCUS OF ECCLESIAL AUTHORITY

There is likewise an inexorable shift in, and thus need for, a clearer recognition of the locus of ecclesial authority[182] in this third millennium. In light of the dangers of personality cults made possible by technology, the man who is pope (or prelate or priest) is providentially less important than ever due to the virtually complete defining of doctrine and its full and ready accessibility. The same technology that has facilitated personality cults has also allowed the great majority of the faithful to have direct access to the teachings of the Church, with many among them engaged in the deepest theological scholarship outside of mainstream institutions and/or the privileged academic and/or clerical ranks.

There is, then, a synergistic impetus for the locus of authority, of theological knowledge, and of moral judgment to take place on the grassroots—that is, familial and individual—level. Churchmen must heed the impetus of salvation history and not seek to go back to an unseemly authoritarianism, but rather to empty themselves of all conceits and desires for domination, and to even empty themselves of just prerogatives, so that the faithful may flourish in a full maturity. For popes, prelates, and priests exist for the faithful, not vice versa.[183]

This relocation of authority and apostolic impetus is all in keeping with the Catholic principle of *subsidiarity*. Subsidiarity demands that authority and governance be implemented at the most fundamental level possible. In the third millennium, for the first time in salvation history, this subsidiarity is possible at its most fundamental level of the faithful themselves, of the family and the individual informed Catholic conscience. This is truly providential and timely, for only such a locus of authority, governance, and personal initiative will suffice for the third millennium of the Church. The unfolding of salvation history in the third millennium calls for the Christian *qua* Christian to no longer blindingly acquiesce as inferiors to the ecclesial "experts," but rather for the informed Catholic conscious of the Christian to be rightly considered as superior. As such, the third millennium is the time for the Christian family to be rightly recognized as the essential ecclesial unit (*ecclesia domestica*) to which all ecclesial structures—be they chanceries, universities, or the Roman Curia itself—are ordered and not, as in the past, vice-versa. It is then as well the time for the small faith community, which is in essence the particular and endlessly varied union of families, to be recognized as the dynamo of Christian ecclesial and cultural growth, and for the parish to properly be seen as a sacramental center ordered towards the facilitation of these varied small faith communities.

So too, it is providential in this age of technological totalitarianism, bureaucratic brutality, and celebrity cultism, that a Christian be free from their enslaving influences. This freedom is found in adhering to the truth, both natural and revealed, and to its ever deepening and pervasive spirit. To combat totalitarianism, servile obedience must be imbued with the spirit of the law and thus transformed into courageous love. Such a love of truth, the good, and Christ is freeing, and more so freed of all that is tainted by worldly dominance, of all coercion based in egoistic servile fears, and of all provocations based on respect for persons.

THE ESSENCE OF THE CHURCH

To flourish in the Christian life an ecclesial existence is required, for in some manner or another there is no salvation outside the Church. The Church is Holy Mother Church, and she nourishes her children from her founts of grace.[184] Some condemn the Church as being too harsh. But she is never harsh. It is nature that is harsh. In other words, it is the good God who is harsh. But Holy Mother Church, like her personification in the Blessed Virgin Mary, is always maternal and only seeks, if anything, to palliate the harshness of reality and the cross. Though she has the power to bind and loose, the Church in her maternal clemency only binds the faithful to the minimum under the pain of sin and avoids placing stumbling blocks upon the Way of the Cross. Yet the Way of the Cross is nonetheless the only way the Church espouses, and as a good mother, she encourages in her children the very ultimate in Christian heroics and holiness.

In fact, it is the cross, both the crossed "t" of truth and the grace that flows from the cross, that is the essence of Catholicism. No, it is not even the unique and superlative gifts of the sacraments that is Catholicism's specific difference, but rather her truth and grace, of which the sacraments are special portals thereof. This means, contrary to common opinion, Catholicism differs from Protestant sects not merely by her sacraments, nor from Eastern sects by her papacy, but by the *fullness of the Gospel* which she possesses in her deposit of faith, which is simultaneously the fullness of truth and of grace.

In this third millennium, and in God's divine providence, for all intents and purposes, the definition of all dogma has been fulfilled, rendering the Church herself, rather than the Magisterium that infallibly explicated that dogma, as clearly paramount. But then what is the Church? To begin with existentially, the Church will tangibly exist as long as there is but one sole baptized believer on earth. That is, not one sole pope, prelate, or priest; not one sole curial bureaucrat; but one sole baptized believer.

The Church has been in the past too conceptualized, and even more so manifested, as per worldly terms. Namely, it has been conceived as a perfect society according to the Greek sociopolitical model of the *polis*. In this conceptualization, the Church is seen as a complete and perfect society, akin to the complete and perfect secular state,[185] but with a superior perfection. But the Church is not a society[186] at all, much less akin to a secular one. Concisely put, Our Lord declares, *"My kingdom is not of this world."* (JN 18:36) So the Church (much less the State) is not the perfect worldly society, neither in nature nor organization.

This means the Church on earth, as the Spotless Bride of Christ, does not derive its essence from its corporate structure. The Church's perfection consists in her fullness as the Church on earth, in purgatory, and in heaven. This perfect Church is not a society but a body: the Mystical Body of Christ. The Church is called a body because it is a living entity; it is called the body of Christ, because Christ is its Head and Founder; it is called the mystical body, because it is neither purely physical and earthly nor purely spiritual and heavenly, but a singular supernatural entity.[187]

To have a salvific ecclesial existence is to be part of the Church via nature and grace. This means on the natural level, and as *imago Dei*, assenting to the Church's truth and volitionally living out these truths, and then having this nature infused with faith, hope, charity, and grace on the supernatural level.

Though there is a fundamental credal demarcation that makes one a member of the Church, assenting to the basic truths of the Faith is not by itself sanctifying or salvific. In fact, it is only in knowingly dissenting on Church teachings that deal with sanctification and salvation or the converse of sin and damnation—which are the subjects of the Church's infallibility on faith and morals—that cause a *de facto* separation from the Church.

THE ONE TRUE CHURCH
OF CHRIST

From Holy Mother Church is derived the fullness of truth, and it is this truth that mandates her authority. From her infallible deposit is derived the tenets of the faith that are the *sine qua non* of Christian existence and best guarantor of a truly human existence. The Holy Catholic Church, unlike any other institution or corpus of knowledge, claims with a divine boldness that her teachings are absolutely infallible. Furthermore, the Church enunciates and catalogs these teachings in the most definitive way so as to subject them to the searing scrutiny of reason. These concise and unambiguous philosophical and theological formulations, meticulously detailed in logical expostulation and recorded in her own dogmatic archives, would leave the Church in a precarious position indeed if not for the divine guarantee that is uniquely hers.

Her absolute claim to be the one true Church of Christ, infallible in matters of faith and morals and authoritative in their teaching, means that what the Church proclaims definitively is without exception the truth. If but one instance can be found where she is or was wrong, if even one of her formally taught truths can be shown to be false, if but one truth she holds can be shown as contradictory to the other myriad of truths she holds, then the whole ecclesial edifice crumbles. It is the bold assurance that the edifice stands against not only all philosophical scrutiny but against the very Gates of Hell that is the tenor of the Catholic mindset. When a believer gains this Catholic mindset through faith and reason it procures for him the superior vantage point of the Holy Faith. This superior vantage point of the Faith provides a perspective that allows for a critical and insightful discernment that is not possible without grace. While false faith can blind one to the truth, the Catholic Faith as completely rational empowers reason to go beyond its own ability to see the truth.

If there is one term, other than those proper names of God Himself, that is central to Catholicism, it is truth. It is in truth that eternal life is found. It is man's ability to know the truth that makes possible his ability to love the good. It is a Christian's very ability to know the truth and love the good that makes possible his partaking in salvation, and it is the act of knowing and loving that is his eternal destiny in the beatific vision. Christ states,

> And this is eternal life: to know Thee, the one true God, and Jesus Christ whom Thou hast sent. JN 17:3

All of Christianity hinges on the Church being true. It is the Church that validated the authenticity of Holy Scripture; it was the Church that validated the orthodoxy of Christology; it was the Church that defined and dogmatized the Christian faith. But the boldest truth of all proclaimed by the Church is her claim to be absolutely true throughout.

SPECTRUM OF ORTHODOXY

On the spectrum of orthodoxy truths play out between the right pole of traditionalism and the left pole of progressivism.[188] The only valid traditionalism is that which hearkens back to the touchstone of the Cross of Christ and the only valid progressivism is that which moves toward that same Cross of Christ. Traditionalism exceeds the boundaries of orthodoxy when it becomes hidebound. Progressivism exceeds the boundaries of orthodoxy when it becomes modernist. Traditionalists tend to compartmentalize the Faith and exclude both the spirit of law and the integral implementation of the Faith. Progressives tend to compromise the Faith and include the spirit of the world and its subsequent dilution of the Faith.

A so qualified "hidebound" traditionalism is stultified and a so qualified "modernist" progressivism is worldly, and they are so designated specifically because they exclude one another. A hidebound traditionalism exceeds the spectrum of orthodoxy on the right by compartmentalization and an *exclusive* emphasis on the letter of the law that stultifies the spirit of the law. Whereas, a modernist progressivism exceeds the spectrum of orthodoxy on the left by nondiscrimination and an *inclusive* openness to worldly values that contradict or supplant orthodox truths.

It is in professing the Holy Faith with rational certitude and living it with loving conviction that both the hidebound traditionalist and the modernist progressive are deficient in. The hidebound traditionalist, for all his fierce dogmatism, lacks the rational certitude that his faith can withstand the onslaughts of the world's contradictions. Thus, the hidebound traditionalist also fails in loving conviction to engage that world, nay even to engage members of the *status quo* church itself, as he seeks in self-love to protect himself. Contrary to their posturing as zealously adhering to the letter of the Faith, the hidebound traditionalist's lack of deep and certain faith leads to a defensive and fearful closed-off position. Their faith is tenuous and rigid, it cannot withstand the storms of the modern world, much less the gales of regularization; nor, for that matter, the doldrums of mainstream commonality.

The modernist progressive, for all his socialistic rhetoric, lacks the loving conviction to confront the world with the fullness of the Faith. Thus, the modernist progressive also fails in rational certitude to espouse the prophetic truth and so compromises with that world, even unto the betrayal of Christ and his Church. For the modernist progressive, contrary to their confrontational claims to the spirit of the Faith, it is a lack of courageous love that leads to a compromised and cowardly position. Their love is superficial and socially specific, it cannot endure the deep and universal onslaught of the world, the flesh, and the devil, much less the curative purgation of the Holy Cross.

Hidebound traditionalists are those who are traditional but not adequately progressive. This is part and parcel of the traditionalist not delving deeper into the spirit of the law for fear of losing the letter of the law; though a letter of the law can be an accidental (such as rubrics) that obscures the essential. Whereas the modernist progressives are those who are progressive but not adequately traditional. This is part and parcel of the progressive not being convicted of the truth for fear of losing the spirit, but a spirit that is not purely of the Gospel. The hidebound traditionalist is apt to fall into material heresy when the letter of the law and material practices begin to impede a deeper understanding and practice of the faith. Whereas the modernist progressive is apt to fall into formal heresy where the spirit and values of the world's positions become ensconced as heretical formal ideals.

PROGRESSIVE TRADITIONALISM

The vitally important truths, that is, the *sine qua non* dogmatic truths, of the Holy Faith are the same yesterday, today, and forever; and this is the essence of traditionalism. But so too, these truths that can never be denied can always be lived out with greater integrity in a person's or a community's life, they can be implemented more saliently in one's current milieu, according to their deeper spirit, and this is the essence of progressivism. Both the progressive pollution of the world that blurs and the traditionalist compartmentalization that disintegrates are prohibitive of orthodoxy and orthopraxy and specifically exclude an authentic Christian ethos from being lived out.

As such, the pristine orthodox Catholic position is neither an unbalanced traditionalism nor an unbalanced progressivism to the exclusion of one or the other. Rather the orthodoxy position amalgamates traditionalism and progressivism in a synergistic harmony. Such a balanced synergy does not make the orthodox position less radical and salient but rather more so, for the truth is more pointed because more crucial[189] and the good is more militantly promoted because more apropos to the very errors of the times.

With his steadfast faith, the progressive traditionalist with courage and zeal engages the world, or even the *status quo* church, and is likewise courageously and totally open to the deepening call of the Spirit. With his steadfast love, the progressive traditionalist with courage and zeal preaches the Gospel to the world, even in expectation of the world's persecution,

> If the world hate you, know ye that it hath hated me before you....Remember my word that I said to you:

> The servant is not greater than his master. If they
> have persecuted me, they will also persecute you. JN
> 15:18,20

As per the dynamics of the virtuous mean and the either excessive or deficient vicious extreme where one vice can be seen as more in keeping with the virtue,[190] it can be said that the excessive or hidebound traditionalist position is apt to be more in keeping with orthodox Catholicity because it assents to all dogmatic and moral truths of the Faith, and the worldly or modernist progressive position is apt to lack orthodox Catholicity because of the supplanting of certain dogmatic, but usually moral, truths of the Faith with those of the world.

Hidebound traditionalists fall into the trap of the letter of the law and compartmentalization, whereas progressives allow their faith to be diluted and polluted by the world. Aboard the Barque of Peter, hidebound traditionalists stowaway in cramped lifeboats of superficial certainty, fearful and distrusting of the captain and crew, but also acting as if the ship's sea-worthiness itself is in question. Modernist progressives abandon the ship altogether as they foolishly leap into the secular sea in the hopes of reaching mirages of worldly shores.

For the hidebound traditionalists, be their lifeboat still aboard ship (that is, be they in the spirit of schism) or be their lifeboat cast-off (that is, be they in formal schism), their cramped, lifeboat existence is due to their attributing too much to the letter of the law and to the man and office. Hidebound traditionalists equate not only the man with the office, but the office with the Church herself. Thus if there is a personal crisis of pope or prelates the hidebound traditionalist sees the Church as in crisis and sinking. For modernist progressives, their drifting farther and farther from the Church and drowning in a worldly sea is due to their attributing too little to the Church. For modernist progressives equate not only the office with the man but the Church herself with sinful and fallible men, and thus construe the Church as sinful, fallible, and not seaworthy. But it is the progressive traditionalist that, by both gazing upon the world's stormy seas and by studying the Church's certain charts, can ably man the Barque of Peter on the true course of salvation history.

SPECTRUM OF ORTHOPRAXY

As can be noted in the discussion of the spectrum of orthodoxy, there is a concurrent spectrum of orthopraxy. The spectrum of orthodoxy is found along the horizontal line of reason and truth and the spectrum of orthopraxy is the vertical line of volition and love; neither are possible without the other. Truth and love are inseparable, for truth both precedes and succeeds love, and love is truth's essential dynamic. When a person loves the truth, he fully embraces the truth as the good. Love, then, is the embracing of the truth, the culmination of knowing the truth. The quality and ardor of a person's love depends on the validity and depth of his knowledge. A person must first know something before he can love it, though love can impel him to want to know more about it and thus be enabled to love it even more. Once the truth is known, love goes out toward that truth in a certain ecstasy, which in turn allows further knowledge of the truth, which in turn draws reality further into the knower/lover.

While the horizontal spectrum of orthodoxy and its plurality of truth is kept within orthodox bounds by the mandate of crucially defined truths that are of vital importance to the Holy Faith, the vertical spectrum of orthopraxy and its spirit of charity takes place through the mandate to love God and to love man in a simultaneous, and thus valid, manner.

> If any man say, I love God, and hateth his brother; he is a liar. For he that loveth not his brother, whom he seeth, how can he love God, whom he seeth not? 1JN 4:20

The inseparable spectrums of orthodoxy and orthopraxy entail the assent to vital truths and their implementation as the good. All the vital truths of nature and grace that fall within the horizontal spectrum of orthodoxy are pulled together, integrated, and become one as per the intensity of charity in the vertical spectrum of orthopraxy. Together, the horizontal spectrum of truth and orthodoxy and the vertical spectrum of charity and orthopraxy intersect to form the Cross' full spectrum of the Faith.

AN ECCLESIAL EXISTENCE
CASE STUDY

As per the spectrums of orthodoxy and orthopraxy, a case study of Karol Wojtyła, the consummate man of Vatican II, may be helpful. Wojtyła was, like the other Rhineland fathers, a product of the traumatic epicenter of a war-torn Europe. And he, like the other Rhineland fathers, was undoubtedly a progressive. But Wojtyła, unlike some of the progressives, was and remained firmly Catholic. He assented to the truths of the Faith and hence could only be so progressive as to keep within the left bounds of the spectrum of orthodoxy.

Wojtyła abided by the strictures of orthodoxy whether he liked them or not. Thus, he reiterated that women could not be admitted to the ordained ministry because "the Church has no authority whatsoever to confer priestly ordination on women."[191] However, he then went on in the document (and subsequent policies) to promote the empowering of women as much as possible in the non-ordained ministries, and hence the phenomenon of women chancellors.

Although a progressive, Wojtyła was seen largely as a conservative. This is because, albeit often near to the left-limits of the spectrum of orthodoxy, he was indeed within those limits. However, those who viewed him, those both of the world and many so-called Catholics, were outside those left limits of orthodoxy, and thus Wojtyła was to the right of them and thus seen from their liberal perspective as conservative.

Because Wojtyła was very progressive in many ways, traditionalists balked at his canonization. But it is not positioning along the horizontal axis of orthodoxy that determines if a person is a saint or not. It is not being correct on all the issues that indicates sanctity. So long as a person is within the bounds of traditionalism and progressivism, it is the vertical axis of love of God and man that determines heroic sanctity. Wojtyła demonstrated on a world-stage a remarkable love of God and man, suffering the lasting wounds from an assassin's bullets but still vigorous in his preaching and traveling. Finally, suffering unto death the disease of Parkinson but never once uttering a word about retirement, Pope John Paul gave himself to man, the Church, and God until the end. Thus, though not right on all the issues, there is absolutely no justification for balking at Saint (even if not necessarily "Great") John Paul II.

ECCLESIAL TAPESTRY

The corpus of Catholic truth and love is like a magnificent tapestry that has been woven over the ages. Indeed, this tapestry entails all truths, natural and supernatural, and all that is true and good, both of man and creation, and of Divine Revelation. The existence of such an unmatched monumental tapestry testifies to the divine nature of its Weaver and the indefectible nature of his ecclesial loom, the Church.

A weave of tapestry is made up of threads that are horizontal warp and vertical weft. In the ecclesial tapestry of truth and love it is the threads of truth along an axis of orthodoxy that make up its horizontal warp and give it its form and design. It is the threads of charity along an axis of orthopraxy that make up this tapestry's vertical weft and give it its color and vibrancy. This weave of truth and charity integrates the ecclesial tapestry and holds it together.

The truths of the Faith that make up the horizontal spectrum of orthodoxy are all pulled together by the vertical spectrum of charity. As this spectrum of charity's vertex symbolizes, it soars up to the love of God and then necessarily reaches down to his creation and humanity.

It is indeed love that covers a multitude of sins, including, as such, material heresies. Again, it is advanced that the third millennium is the age of charity and that means the emphasis is not on dogmatic truth that, in any case, is now a given since now definitively enunciated. It is not assenting to the truth that is the hard part, but living it out. The horizontal warp of truth without the vertical weft of charity become dead letters of the law and soon unravel. The vertical weft of charity without the horizontal warp of truth become vaporous sentiments and soon lose their vibrancy. The proper weave of horizontal truth and vertical charity form the crucial intersect of ecclesial existence—the vitally important center pattern of the Cross—which repeatedly and always marks the sweet spot of Catholicism.

XII. Integrity of the Holy Faith

The sabbath was made for man,
not man for the sabbath. MK 2:27

There is no celebration of Holy Mass on the most sacred day of the year, the day of our redemption, Good Friday. For the Holy Sacrifice of the Cross is absolutely sufficient unto itself,

> Jesus knowing that all things were now accomplished, that the scripture might be fulfilled, said: I thirst. Now there was a vessel set there full of vinegar. And they, putting a sponge full of vinegar and hyssop, put it to his mouth. Jesus therefore, when he had taken the vinegar, said: It is consummated. And bowing his head, he gave up the ghost. JN 19:28-30

Every other day of the year, indeed all the Masses offered thereon, make present this Good Friday; all these days, and all devotions and prayers, are ordered toward this crucial and singularly essential day. For it is Christ Crucified that is the ultimate reality at the very heart of human and Christian existence.

What is amazing about Christianity is the Crucifixion not the Resurrection, even though resurrection is the Christian's certain hope. Again, Easter Sunday seen in retrospect of Christ's divinity is incomparably glorious but not amazing. It is to be reasonably expected that God would raise his hypostatically united human nature from the dead. But it is the retrospect that Easter Sunday provides and its proof of Christ's divinity that makes Good Friday amazing. It is astoundingly amazing that the tortured and crucified Jesus was indeed God Almighty!

Yes, it is Good Friday, not even the greatest feast day of Easter Sunday, that is the central, most astounding, and holiest day of the liturgical year. Yet Good Friday, the holiest day of the liturgical year, has no liturgy intrinsically attached to it.[192] There is no liturgical fanfare or spectacle proper to Good Friday, for in its intimacy it is as sublime as a Christian's own daily death and as subdued as his own final breath. Good Friday, like the altar itself, is stripped of all non-essentials. At the Crucifixion there were no sacraments or ceremonies, but only Christ *Crucified*, the source of all sacraments and the object of all ceremonies. At the Crucifixion there was only the essential intimate weeping and ministration of the faithful[193] that so disposed their hearts to allow Christ's sacrificial redemption to be accomplished. On Good Friday, even if there is an accompanying liturgy, a priest is not required.[194] At the Crucifixion there is only the suffering Christ, both High Priest and Spotless Victim, and the weeping faithful at the foot of his cross.

Good Friday, like the final moments of every person's earthy existence, is a gathering gloom that ends in profound darkness. Man does not rise from the dead in this earthly vale of tears. But still, as a Christian enters into the depths of darkness and sorrow on Good Friday and issues an intimate *yes* to the annihilation of existence in union with Christ Crucified he too is then able to enter into the glories and joys of Easter Sunday. In fact, the sorrows only heighten the joys and the joys only deepen the sorrows. Good Friday, then, is the touchstone for all piety, the source of all grace, and even, rather most especially, the Holy Sacrifice of the Mass is simply a direct and immediate portal to it.

INTEGRITY VS COMPARTMENTALIZATION

In the intrinsic integrity of the Holy Faith, the Mass and all other liturgies and devotions derive from, are to be seen in the light of, and come together in the Holy Sacrifice of the Cross. Reciprocally, the Mass and other liturgies and devotions are ordered to facilitate the integral living out of the Holy Faith. In sum, the Holy Mass and other liturgies and devotions are neither sources nor ends in themselves but means to Christ Crucified and the faithful's union with him.

However, the integrity of the Holy Faith in practice, that is in its liturgies, devotions, and spiritualities, began to slowly compartmentalize in the High Middle-Ages and then became predominantly compartmentalized in the latter quarter of the Church's second millennium.

In the early Church the Holy Mass and Eucharist were hidden mysteries that were revealed only *after* a person became a Christian. A person in the early Church did not convert so as to receive the Eucharist, but rather to receive Baptism. It was not the Mass but rather the truth of the Gospel and its proffered salvation that drew a person to this initial conversion.

Indicative of these dynamics of conversion, in the Profession of Faith that is recited upon becoming a Christian there is nothing about the Mass or Eucharist. Indeed, in the early Church the Holy Mass was a clandestine affair, a mystery that was not even witnessed, much less entered into, before Baptism and the Profession of Faith. Back then the Holy Mass was surely a mystery, for though the early Christians entered most deeply into the mystery of the Eucharistic Sacrifice, as only those who are on the cusp of martyrdom can, the early

Church still had but a vague understanding of its ontological nature.

The First Mass was a hidden affair in an upper room; where the beginning Masses of the early Church were offered deeply cloistered from the world in the depths of the catacombs; and where even Masses in the Romanesque period were offered in the shadows of womb-like chapels with rounded domes, thick walls, and cavernous arches. But with the advent of the high Middle-Ages came liturgies offered under the sun-bright lights of precariously towering stained glass houses propped up by contrived flying buttresses and topped with endless Gothic ceilings and towering spires that sought to pierce the very heavens.

In conjunction with the Middle-Age's architectural advancements came scholasticism and the philosophical definition of Christ's Eucharistic physical presence. Unprecedentedly, Pope Urban IV's bull *Transiturus* (August 11, 1264) established the first new universal feast of *Corpus Christi*. Urban IV commissioned St. Thomas Aquinas, who ontologically defined the Mass and Eucharist, to write the hymns for this feast. Thus, the philosophical definition of Christ's Eucharistic physical presence was accompanied by an ideological and devotional component. However, the establishment of *Corpus Christi* was considered a very progressive act, and even an invalid one, since it was the first ever papally decreed feast for the Church Universal, and it fell quickly into obsolescence as the thirteen subsequent popes disallowed its continued implementation.

It was Pope John XXII (1244-1334), who was an advocate of the *Pope as Supreme Ruler of the World*,[195] that would revive the defunct bull *Feast of Corpus Christi*. John XXII, who chose to live opulently as a supreme ruler in the papal courts of Avignon, could justify royally extravagant papal processions by including the carrying of the Eucharist in them. John XXII's apparently fervent devotion to the Blessed Sacrament may as well have been due to his viewing it as a magical amulet against the sorcery he feared was being waged against him.[196] In any case, it was from John XXII's lackluster and somewhat scandalous pontificate forward that a certain strain of devotionalism that used lavish spectacle in conjunction with the Holy Sacrifice of the Mass and the Eucharist began to take firm hold. As this form of devotion to the Holy Mass and Eucharist grew so too did the compartmentalization of the Mass and Eucharist, resulting in the lessening of the faithful's intimate encounter with the Lord in them, as witnessed by the ever decreasing reception of Holy Communion.

COUNTER-REFORMATIONAL COMPARTMENTALIZATION

The compartmentalization that was advanced by a devotional emphasis on Eucharistic spectacle versus intimate communion would become full-blown in the Counter-Reformational reaction to the damnable Protestant denial of the Holy Mass and Christ's Eucharistic physical presence. Though the Council of Trent had just dogmatically reiterated a fully integral Faith, it was during the Counter-Reformational period that the practical integrity of the Holy Faith began in earnest to fragment due to the Catholic reaction to the Protestant heresy.

The understandable and well-intended Catholic Counter-Reformational reaction was to overemphasize all that Protestantism heretically denied: most especially the Holy Mass, Eucharist, and priesthood. This reactionary emphasis led to the compartmentalization of the Mass and Eucharist from their transcendental reality, be that reality the Holy Sacrifice of Christ on the Cross or the purgative sacrifice of the Christian in daily life. As such, this overemphasis on the Mass and Eucharist actually reduced their efficacy or leavening within the faithful. Catholics thus began to overemphasize and myopically define themselves by their participation in the Holy Mass and show of devotional zeal toward the physical presence of the Eucharist.

In fact the widely used term "Real Presence," has both an orthodox and a heterodox understanding. It was the heretical priest, and precursor of Protestantism, John Wycliffe (c. 1320's—31 December 1384) that first used the term "Real Presence" as an alternative to transubstantiation. Wycliffe used "Real Presence" as a compromise term to suggest a high view of the sacrament while in fact denying the Catholic doctrine of transubstantiation. As per the definition of transubstantiation at the Fourth Lateran Council in 1215, the exact orthodox terminology is "real body and real blood of Christ." The term "Real Presence" doesn't occur. The orthodox understanding connoted by this terminology is that Christ's "real presence" is not limited to the Eucharist, but that the Eucharist entails, in addition to his real spiritual presence, that Christ is also actually physically present. However, the addition of Christ's real physical presence is no more real than his spiritual presence, otherwise there is a heretical materialism. In fact, even Christ's physical presence is not limited to his Eucharistic presence, *viz.*, in apparitions.

So Christ is not *most* or, more heretical still, *only* really present in the Blessed Sacrament. Rather, Christ is uniquely tangible and accessible, *indeed edible*, in his Eucharistic Presence. This is why there is an insurmountable contradiction between the misleading pious assertion that the Blessed Sacrament is the most important entity in a Christian's life and the fact that a Christian, even those known for high sanctity, are not fixated on the Blessed Sacrament 24/7. Indeed, a Christian can become discouraged if he aims at such a fixation, rather than appreciating the subtleness and familiarity of the Eucharist and its influence on him. Thus, it is not Christ's physical presence in the Holy Mass or the Blessed Sacrament that makes these gift so amazing and precious, but rather the fact that the Holy Mass is a portal that allows a person to be at the moment of Christ Crucified.

Nonetheless, in an overreaction to the Protestant heresy and an ensuing compartmentalization, the liturgy of the Mass would continue to become more and more lavish and would be seen as the very *raison d'etre* of the Church, resulting in the integral ethos of Catholicism becoming disjointedly compartmentalized. This Counter-Reformational compartmentalization and centralization of the Holy Mass and its corollary fixation on the Holy Eucharist, which culminated in the advent and promotion of perpetual adoration, has no historical or doctrinal basis in The Council of Trent or elsewhere.

> No trace of the existence of any such extra-liturgical cultus of the Blessed Sacrament can be found in the records of the early Church. As has already been pointed out in this latter article, the attempts formerly made to demonstrate the existence of a custom in the early Church of showing special and external veneration to the Sacred Species when reserved for the sick break down upon closer investigation.[197]

> To this day in the Greek Church no practice of genuflecting to the Blessed Sacrament is known and in fact it may be said that, though it is treated respectfully, as the Book of the Gospels or the sacred vessels would be treated respectfully, still no cultus is shown it outside of the Liturgy. During the first ten or twelve centuries after Christ the attitude of the Western Church seems to have been very similar. We may conjecture that the faithful concentrated their attention upon the two main purposes for which the Blessed Eucharist was instituted, viz. to be offered in sacrifice and to become the food of the soul in Holy Communion.[198]

This fixation of the Holy Eucharist is seemingly reasonable due to an erroneous syllogistic logic: *God is ultimately all that matters; the Eucharistic is God; therefore, the Eucharist is ultimately all that matters.* The faulty reasoning here does not take into account that, though the Eucharist *is* God, this does not mean that God *is* the Eucharist; that is, God is not limited by the Eucharist. This means that the Faith as well is not limited by the Eucharist.[199]

Again, this reasoning and subsequent compartmentalization of the Holy Mass and Eucharist has no doctrinal basis. The Council of Trent always painstakingly describes the Mass and Eucharist as transcendent, which is the very opposite of compartmentalized. The Council of Trent is the paramount council on the Eucharist, for Trent needed to staunchly and definitively express the orthodox understanding of Christ's Eucharistic physical presence that the Protestants were denying. However, in all of Trent's pious and scholarly elaboration on the Holy Eucharist there is not even an allusion to it being an end in itself. Rather, Trent always denotes the Eucharist's transcendent nature.

> For the victim is one and the same, the same now offering by the ministry of priests, who then offered Himself on the cross, the manner alone of offering being different.[200]

The Eucharist is manifestly not about itself as a sacrament but about Christ Crucified and those he seeks to feed,

> Then Jesus said to them: Amen, amen I say unto you: Except you eat the flesh of the Son of man, and drink his blood, you shall not have life in you. JN 6:54

In understanding the above passage the *de fide* understanding that a person is saved if he dies with the remission of original and mortal sin, which can occur without ever having received the Blessed Sacrament, must be reckoned with. Therefore, this eating of Christ's flesh and drinking of his blood *must necessarily* refer to salvific union with Christ Crucified and must then transcend reception of the Eucharist, which nonetheless remains the direct sacramental manifestation of salvific union with Christ Crucified.

FURTHER VATICAN II
COMPARTMENTALIZATION

Vatican II, which as per the liturgicalism of the 400 years that preceded it, was first and foremost all about the Mass and only exacerbated the compartmentalization of the Holy Faith. In fact, the Catechism of Vatican II formalizes this compartmentalization. As per the *New Catechism of the Catholic Church*,

> The Eucharist is "the source and summit of the Christian life." "The other sacraments, and indeed all ecclesiastical ministries and works of the apostolate, are bound up with the Eucharist and are oriented toward it. For in the blessed Eucharist is contained the whole spiritual good of the Church, namely Christ himself, our Pasch." (CCC 1324)

The phrase "source and summit of the Christian life" is the cornerstone for the rest of the above paragraph and all the ensuing pieties and practices that compartmentalize that Eucharist. However, the phrase "source and summit of the Christian life" is not an ancient maxim of the Church but was taken from a mere parenthetical aside of a Council notorious for its ambiguity and lack of rigorous terminology.

> 11. It is through the sacraments and the exercise of the virtues that the sacred nature and organic structure of the priestly community is brought into operation. Incorporated in the Church through baptism, the faithful are destined by the baptismal character for the worship of the Christian religion; reborn as sons of God they must confess before men the faith which they have received from God through the Church. They are more perfectly bound to the Church by the sacrament of Confirmation, and the Holy Spirit endows them with special strength so that they are

more strictly obliged to spread and defend the faith, both by word and by deed, as true witnesses of Christ. Taking part in the Eucharistic sacrifice, *which is the [source and summit] of the whole Christian life*, they offer the Divine Victim to God, and offer themselves along with It.[201] (*Emphasis* added).

It is this parenthetical aside that has become in practice a dogmatic statement, and it is cited as such in a vast amount of post-conciliar statements, including numerous times in the *New Catechism of the Catholic Church*.

The post-Vatican II Church carried, and even accentuated, elements of the Counter-Reformational compartmentalization of liturgicalism, clericalism, and parishism. Make no mistake, the prelates and priests of post-Vatican II, be they progressives or conservatives, were, and are no less, clericalistic than their pre-Vatican II predecessors.[202] Vatican II only increased and formalized the liturgicalism, clericalism, and parishism of the 400 years previous to it. The spirit of Vatican II went so far as to equate the quality of Christian life with involvement in liturgical ministry, which harmed both the charisms of the laity and the priesthood. Consequently, in regards to liturgicalism, clericalism, parishism, and compartmentalization Vatican Council II ended up being less a reformation than a continued deformation.

To construe *Lumen Gentium's* parenthetical comment that the Eucharistic Sacrifice "is the source and summit of the Christian life" in an orthodox manner, the use of the term "Eucharist" must be understood not as *Eucharist qua Eucharist* but as *Eucharist qua Jesus Christ Crucified*. Indeed, the *New Catechism* does this in explanation of that statement, *"For in the blessed Eucharist...namely Christ himself; our Pasch."* The strict characterization of the Eucharist as the source and summit, or end all, of the Faith compartmentalizes the Faith, the Christian Life, and even Christ himself. The erroneous implication being that Christian life is all about the Mass and the Eucharist, rather than the Mass and the Eucharist being all about Christ and him crucified and the faithful's embrace of him. The whole of Christian existence is not all about going to Mass, but is about living each day and moment in union with Christ *Crucified*, which is also to be in union with the Holy Mass.

The compartmentalizing and focused isolation of the Eucharist that occurred from the Counter-Reformation to the post-Vatican II era does violence to this sacrament's transcendent *mysterium fidei*, which is of the very charism of the Holy Eucharist. Again, in striking contradistinction, the *Dogmatic Council of Trent* describes of the Eucharist as transcendent, the very opposite of compartmentalized.

> "These three things, then, which are clearly distinguished by their reference to past, present and future times . . . ."[203]

Interestingly enough, it was Paul VI who not only took *mysterium fidei* out of the words of institution[204] but out of context as well. In his encyclical *Mysterium Fidei*, Paul VI strongly reaffirms Christ's Eucharistic physical presence and the true nature of the Mass as a sacrifice. However, his very labeling of his encyclical "Mystery of Faith" denotes falsely equating the supreme mystery of the Holy Faith as transubstantiation; a wrong equation, again, that grew with the counter-reformational compartmentalization of the Mass.

As the very words of consecration denote, the supreme Mystery of the sacrament of the Holy Faith is not the Eucharist but the Redemption of Christ on the Cross,

> *Hic est enim Calix Sanguinis Mei, novi et aeterni Testamenti: Mysterium fidei: qui pro vobis et pro multis effundetur in remissionen peccatorum.*

> "For this is the Chalice of My Blood of the new and eternal Testament, the Mystery of Faith; which shall be shed for you and for many unto the remission of sins."

The Holy Eucharist (and all other sacraments as such) is

not *the* Mystery of Faith, but "*of* the Mystery of Faith." The Holy Eucharist and the seven sacraments emanate from the Mystery of Faith and have as their very reason for being the facilitation of the believer's entering into and becoming one with the supreme "new and eternal Testament, the Mystery of Faith," that is Christ Crucified.

DEVOTIONALISM

In facilitating conjunction with this compartmentalization of the Mass and Eucharist from the Holy Faith came the spiritual movement known as the "French School of Spirituality." The French School of Spirituality, herein more specifically termed "devotionalism," was, like liturgicalism and the newly emphasized devotional cultus of the Blessed Sacrament, the Catholic answer to both the heresies and the spiritual energy unleashed by the Protestant Reformation. This devotionalism was the dominant spirituality in the period between the Counter-Reformation and Vatican II. Devotionalism remained the spirituality of choice of conservatives and traditionalists in counteraction to the post-Vatican II errors that were so akin to the Protestant Reformation's heresies.

In reaction to the heretical rejection of the Holy Mass and the Blessed Sacrament, devotionalism advanced a singular focus on the Holy Mass and the Blessed Sacrament, which then for the first time in nearly two millennia of Christianity became the central and nearly exclusive feature of the Holy Faith. But this singular focus on and intense devotion to the Eucharist would only end up isolating the Eucharist from the lived out Holy Faith and thus reduce its efficacy and its very reason for being.[205]

As part and parcel of this new centrality of the Eucharist came newfangled duties that entailed making reparation for the "neglect, indifference, and ingratitude" of the faithful for the Blessed Sacrament. That is, quite absurdly, the faithful were to make reparation for Jesus' reparational sufferings. In devotionalism, a devotee is to be outraged that Jesus Christ was being neglected, left alone, abandoned, and forgotten on the altar, and therefore Jesus must be consoled. But God has given his Divine Presence in the Blessed Sacrament as a lavish gift for the succor and strengthening of Christians, not so he can be consoled, much less succored and strengthened. In devotionalism there is a subtle but grave error that sees man as existing for the Blessed Sacrament rather than the Blessed Sacrament existing for man, so that man could exist for Christ.

Devotionalism, as admirable as some of its sentiments and intentions may be, would synergistically combine with the other deficient and even erroneous elements of the Counter-Reformation. Devotionalism's emphasis on appeasing and pleasing God would be combined with notions of blind obedience and infantilism that stemmed from nominalistic tendencies that sought to appease a God of arbitrary law and order. So too, devotionalism's emphasis on external displays of piety, holiness, and mysticism would combine with both a waxing clericalism and an elitism among those in evangelical vows.

The result of devotionalism, in synergistic combination with these other erroneous trends of the Counter-Reformation, was the overall compartmentalization of the Faith, including the eventual compartmentalization found in Catholic Action and parishism previously discussed[206] and the liturgicalism discussed below.

In counter-response[207] to the Protestant emphasis on a "personal relationship with Jesus," devotionalism emphasized setting aside blocks of time for prayers and devotions, personal perfection, and the external manifestation of both. In sum, to exhibit the external practices and posturings of devotionalism was the Catholic equivalent to the Protestant's "being saved." In both cases a "pious persona," appearing either holy or saved, was paramount.

Devotionalism was synergistically combined as well with the rise of a new Spanish mysticism that emphasized the interior life and achieving personal holiness. For as external as this French devotionalism was and as interior as Spanish mysticism was, both devotionalism and mysticism shared a disconnect with the lived out Holy Faith. French Devotionalism was disconnected and compartmentalized in the chapel from the lived out Holy Faith. Spanish mysticism was apt to be disconnected and compartmentalized in the cloister and more so in the interior castle of the imagination (mistakenly called contemplation) from the lived out Holy Faith. In French Devotionalism a Christian's piety culminated in his time spent in the chapel, whereas any time spent in the chapel should properly culminate in a Christian's pious embrace of Christ Crucified in the home and community. In Spanish Mysticism a Christian's holiness culminated in his supposed ascent of his personal ladder of perfection within his own private interior castle, where Christian holiness is properly ordered toward the advancement of God's Kingdom in the home, community, and Church rather than a Christian's own personal advancement, spiritual or otherwise.

DYNAMICS OF DEVOTIONALISM

The dynamics of the French School of Devotionalism is similar to that of all primitive religions, it reduces religion down to the pleasing and/or appeasing of God by external signs of worship. But because French Devotionalism was Catholic these external signs of worship, at least ideally, also require a congruent inner disposition.

In devotionalism, the devotee seeks to not only make up for his own offenses but, even more so, the offenses of others. Here, the devotee wrongly interprets "making up for what is lacking in the sufferings of Christ" as the need to add his own redemptive efforts to Christ's so as to somehow enhancing the infinite sufficiency of Christ's sacrifice.[208] But again, it is not the sufficiency but the efficacy of Christ's sacrifice that is lacking due to the indisposition of a person.

In devotionalism, the devotee identifies as another Christ and by his own positive acts of penance, adoration, and devotion "saves souls." In devotionalism, it is the quality and quantity of the devotee's acts of reparation, appeasement, adoration, and worship that makes the impactive— indeed, pleasing, appeasing, and salvific—difference. In devotionalism, becoming perfect was to be a "prayer warrior," and more so a heroic mystic, rather than a *humble penitent*. In devotionalism, the Christian life is about exerting oneself in vigorous spiritual exercises and worship so as to excel at appeasing and pleasing God.

In devotionalism, a Christian's time and effort spent in prayers, devotions, and liturgies designates him as being holy, rather than these activities rightly being seen not as ends in themselves but as aides to becoming holy. But devotions are a means to facilitate the ultimate Christian end of holiness, *viz.*, the decreasing of self for love of God and

Christ's subsequent increase.

In devotionalism, the devotee was motivated to save souls as if man's part in saving souls was something other than embracing his own cross and ego self-abnegation for love of Christ. "Offer it up for the poor souls" was the maxim, but this was actually a coping mechanism that deflected the humiliation and sorrow, the *purgative piercing*, of a person's own heart. Such a spirituality is contrary to being receptive to one's wretchedness and subsequent self-abnegation for love of God. In devotionalism, a devotee is ego-gratified by the idea that he can in some way replicate, and even augment, Christ's sacrifice on the cross, which deflects from the devotee's own immediate purgation.

In keeping with the dynamics of acquired virtue, it is the exertion of the will, rather than the specific Christian virtue of receptive acquiescence of the will, that is the hallmark of devotionalism. Devotionalism calls upon the devotee to exert his will in the worship and adoration of Christ so as to exalt Christ. This same exertion of the will is further implemented to even make a devotee Christ's "humble" servant, which is made manifest by acquired virtues. But again,[209] acquired virtues are not specifically Christian and may well find their locus in the pride. In devotionalism, worship and adoration are done through scripted exertions, or "spiritual exercises." Repetition of words, be they endless novenas or other formulas of devotion, and the dedicated use of mentation and the imagination through habitual daily meditation is also seen as essential. But again, these spiritual exercises depend primarily on the exertion of the will.

In devotionalism, devotees are exhorted to exert his will in rote devotional practices so as to become other Christs but at the same time are contradictorily expected to give up their volitional autonomy. Jean-Jacques Olier was a primary leader of French Devotionalism and founded the Sulpician Order that took over much of the seminary training in the counter-reformational Church. He wrote,

> It is necessary for the soul to be in fear and distrust of self . . . . It should make its pleasure and joy depend on sacrificing to Jesus all joy and pleasure which it may have apart from himself. And when taking part in those things in which by Providence it is obliged to be occupied, such as eating, drinking, and conversation with creatures, it must be sparing in all, must discard what is superfluous, and must renounce, in the use of them, the joy and pleasure to be found therein, uniting and giving itself to Jesus as often as it feels itself tempted to enjoy something apart from him and not himself.[210]

In devotionalism, the call to holiness is indeed promoted, but this holiness was seen as a mystical infusion from above made manifest by an external devotional rapture. Indeed, here a person was deemed "holy" because of their ardent and prolonged participation in prayer, devotions, and worship. Thus, a person's holiness could be judged by their frequency of Mass attendance, their time in Eucharistic adoration, and the quantity and quality of their other prayers, meditations, and devotions. To be considered a *bona fide* leader[211] in the French school of spirituality, a person necessarily had to be considered a mystic.

In devotionalism, a hallmark of holiness is a religious stoicism[212] where no authentic passions were to be shown in interpersonal relationships. This stoicism, as part and parcel of devotionalism, is to be expected. Since in devotionalism one does not distinguish between, and thus has little awareness of, the ego and psyche passions, the ego passions, that is pride and self-love, are apt to make a mess of interpersonal relationships, especially in the cloister. As such, in devotionalism, the passions are strictly relegated to the devotional realm. During spiritual and mental exercises the devotee is encouraged to evoke sorrow and outrage at the sufferings of Jesus and to provide compassion, comfort, and relief for him, not only for his earthly life but also for his sacramental existence as well. Thus, it is paramount in devotionalism to be fixedly devoted to the Sacred Heart of Jesus; that is, his human, emotional nature. The Blessed Sacrament is paramount to evoke such sentiments.

But sorrow and outrage are strange bedfellows, especially when the passions have not been properly demarcated as egoistic and psychic. Nor is reparation the same as contrition. Contrition is primary to becoming one with Christ Crucified, not trying to balance the books. Neither is contrition the imagined blotting out of all of one's need for purgation (which is manifested in a mania for indulgences), nor is it the imagined "comforting" of Jesus.

A CONTRITE SPIRIT AND BROKEN HEART

Christ *Crucified* is the atonement, and it is the Christian's receptivity to the contrition of humility and sorrow, evoked by God who is all-good and deserving of all love, that allows Christ's propitiatory act to be redemptive. Our Lord Jesus Christ does not in fact need the faithful to exalt him, or to take away his pain, or to defend him, much less help him redeem others.

Jesus only "needs" the faithful to avail themselves of his salvation by being receptive to their own purgation for love of him, and in this way to also impact the members of his Mystical Body. To be united to Christ Crucified is not about the faithful alleviating his sorrow and pain but about saying *yes* to their own.

This decreasing of self for love of Christ so he may increase is what the Holy Christian Faith is all about. All aspects of the Holy Faith—be they offices, ministries, devotions, liturgies, or the Holy Mass itself, exist solely to facilitate this purgation and sanctification which comprises the essence of bringing about the Kingdom of God.

XIII. Liturgy

And when ye pray,
you shall not be as the hypocrites,
that love to stand and pray in the synagogues
and corners of the streets,
that they may be seen by men...
MT 6:5

VATICAN COUNCIL II was all about the liturgy of the Mass. Indeed, Vatican II's first and flagship constitution, *Sacrosanctum Concilium*, was on the Eucharistic liturgy. Indubitably, Vatican II will be forever and singularly associated with the reform of the Mass. But while Vatican II was all about the Holy Mass, most tellingly, it wasn't at all about the Holy Cross!

Being all about the Mass, and not at all about the Cross, shows where Vatican II went wrong,[213] for it wasn't the Mass that urgently needed reform but the living out of the Faith, which again is all about the Cross, about carrying it and being conformed to it. While the popes, prelates, and *periti* of Vatican II rightly perceived there was at leastwise a malaise in the Church, their own deficient theology and elitist compartmentalization, which was a major factor in that malaise, caused them to seek the remedy primarily in reforming the liturgy of the Mass, and secondarily in the restructuring of their own magisterial bureaucracy. Thus, in seeking a solution to the malaise of the Church, Vatican II only succeeded in promulgating the very compartmentalization, liturgicalism, and clericalism that was a major cause of that malaise

Vatican II sought to address, as did the decades long and already pervasive liturgical movement, what was widely perceived as a disconnect between the 20th Century's faithful and their attendance at Mass and other formal sacramental, liturgical, and parish functions. But though there was certainly a disconnect, it wasn't a disconnect between the faithful and the Mass (and other sacraments, liturgies, and parish functions) but between the faithful and their integral living of their Christian faith outside of Mass (*etc.*). Even after the breakup of Christendom and the death throes of the World Wars, the faithful (be they lay, consecrated, or ordained) for the most part, maintained their duties as per the Mass and much of their other external disciplines, devotions, and associations. But Mass attendance, *etc.* notwithstanding, the faithful were still becoming more and more secularized in a post-Christian and increasingly anti-Christian, mass-media propelled, popular culture.

LITURGICAL VS PERSONAL REFORM

Immediately before Vatican II there were more (traditional Latin) Masses being said and attended than ever before; there were more vocations to the consecrated and priestly life than ever before; there were more new churches, evangelical houses, and schools being built than ever before. Indeed, the Church was flush with money, especially in the emerging superpower of America, which spread the wealth of the American Church throughout the Universal Church. But though at an apex of Catholic indicators, the faithful on the grassroots level, on the familial level, continued to slide down the slippery slope of secularism.

The reason for the pre-Vatican II disparity between the faithful's formal religious practices and concurrent increased secularization was compartmentalization, which, as previously noted, found a catalyst in devotionalism and came to fruition in the Catholic Action movement[214] and its inherent parishism. In a counterproductive effort to remedy this disparity, Vatican II spent the bulk of its energy on promulgating liturgical reform.

Whereas the principles of personal reform would have entailed remedying the disconnected compartmentalization of the faithful by exhorting them to be less secular and more conformed (*enculturate*) to Christ Crucified, and thus to the Mass, the principles of the Vatican II liturgical reform instead made the Mass more secular (*inculturate*). But it wasn't the sacredness of the Holy Mass that was the problem, but the secularization of the faithful. The need to locate the Mass as a wellspring within the greater context of Christian life went astray by locating the Mass within the greater context of secularity, social justice, politics, and political correctness.

Instead of facilitating the faithful's entering into the Holy Sacrifice of the Mass so as to be fortified to sacrificially carry their cross in daily life, the reforms of Vatican II only muted the nature of the Mass—*viz.,* the renewal of the Holy Sacrifice of the Cross—and thus also muted the essential Christian call to carry the cross in daily life. Rather than exhorting the faithful to pick up their cross and follow Christ in a militant and evermore countercultural manner, to intentionally conform their increasingly secularized hearts to the Holy Cross of Christ, Vatican II conversely ended up muting the Holy Cross.

Without the faithful's assent to their primary vocation to embrace the Cross of Christ in their daily lives the Holy Sacrifice of the Mass and other external practices of piety lost their urgency and their meaning. Thus, the spirit of Vatican II only ended up obfuscating the objective sacrificial nature of the Mass, and its very *raison d'etre* that was the subjective intimate vulnerability of the faithful in their abnegating embrace of the Cross. The Spirit of Vatican II, and its subsequent reforms, conformed to and compromised with the increasing interior secularity of the faithful who themselves where conforming to and compromising with an increasingly anti-Christic culture.

LITURGICALISM

Liturgicalism wrongly holds the liturgy, most especially the Mass, to be the definitive Christian act.[215] But liturgy is rather a means to the definitive Christian act and end; that is, the liturgy is a source of grace and compendium of practices that facilitates the definitive Christian act, which is self-abnegation for love of Christ that is derived from union with him crucified. A Christian does not go straight to heaven if he dies while attending Mass or while chanting in the monastic choir, but rather when he dies for Christ, be that death a white or red martyrdom. It is the liturgy's *raison d'etre* to facilitate that dying for and with Christ.

Liturgicalism also entails the erroneous belief that the Mass is more pleasing to God the more perfect the externals of it are. But the Mass is objectively and infinitely pleasing to God because Christ's sacrifice was infinitely pleasing to God. It is prideful arrogance to think man can add to the perfect sacrifice of Christ on the Cross. All that man can do is order his heart properly so as to avail himself of that perfect sacrifice, and thus make his subjective sacrifice acceptable and the objective sacrifice efficacious. Truly, the externals of the Mass are ordered toward facilitating the rightful disposition within man and not the disposition of God; as if God can be manipulated through man's efforts!

> And whereas such is the nature of man, that, without external helps, he cannot easily be raised to the meditation of divine things; therefore has holy Mother Church instituted certain rites, to wit that certain things be pronounced in the mass in a low, and others in a louder, tone. She has likewise employed ceremonies, such as mystic benedictions, lights, incense, vestments, and many other things of this kind, derived from an apostolical discipline and

tradition, whereby both the majesty of so great a sacrifice might be recommended, and the minds of the faithful be excited....[216]

The proper disposition to be excited is a broken spirit and contrite heart,

A sacrifice to God is an afflicted spirit: a contrite and humbled heart, O God, thou wilt not despise. PS 51:17

However, liturgicalism entails a Pelagianistic and egoistic perfectionism, that absurdly aims at enhancing the Mass through man's efforts to make it more pleasing to God, and thereby somehow increasing its already infinite sufficiency. Liturgicalism's aim to enhance the Mass is not only contrary to its objective infinite sufficiency but antithetical to the very subjective disposition that is required of the faithful to efficaciously avail himself of that sufficiency. For liturgicalism and Pelagianistic perfectionism facilitates a prideful and haughty heart, whereas what is requisite for an acceptable sacrifice is a heart of abject humility, one that fully assents to the Gospel truth of,

So you also, when you shall have done all these things that are commanded you, say: We are unprofitable servants; we have done that which we ought to do. LK 17:10

To offer the Holy Sacrifice of the Mass is to but do what was commanded by Our Lord and its sufficiency has nothing to do with man's unprofitable efforts but only with Christ's perfect Sacrifice on the Cross. Indeed, this infinitely sufficient Sacrifice's subjective efficacy requires the worshiper's personal recognition of unprofitability.

Stemming both from liturgicalism's erroneous locating of the offering of the Mass as the definitive Christian act and the Pelagianistic belief that its objective sufficiency can be enhancement by man's efforts, is the concurrent error that overemphasizes the cultural and artistic accidentals of the liturgy. Liturgicalistic overemphasis on cultural and artistic accidentals distracts from and/or obfuscates the nature of the worship, prayer, and sacrament. Liturgicalism entails spectacle or activity that is inordinately pleasing to man, be it pleasing to his egoistic sense of accomplishment or his physical senses in general. In its overweening appeal to man, liturgicalism countermands the sacrificial abnegation and humble adoration that is of the essence of acceptable worship.

The Vatican II liturgical reform was infected by the error of liturgicalism. Again, the fathers of Vatican II, clerics all, wrongly, but not surprisingly, presupposed that reforming the Mass was the key to reforming and re-invigorating the faithful. Vatican II thus sought in liturgical reform the cure-all for the ills that plagued the Church. This means that the *Novus Ordo* Mass was not spawned, as traditionalists claim, from a Protestant mentality but rather from a Counter-Reformation mentality; a mentality that in its myopic focusing on the Mass was indeed an overreaction to the heretical Protestant rejection of the Mass.[217]

Liturgicalism can be present both in a traditional solemn high Mass with priest, deacon, sub-deacon, a bevy of altar boys, and a cluster of candle bearers, as well as in a *Novus Ordo* Mass with two drum sets, everybody and his sister in the sanctuary, and liturgical dancers. While the former example of a traditional Mass has propriety that the latter example of the new Mass lacks, this does not necessarily mean that the former traditional Mass example is the height of liturgical propriety. While the latter *Novus Ordo* example may be inordinately pleasing to man due to its entertainment value and stimulation of ego-emotion and sentimentality, the former traditional Mass example may be, and even more insidiously, inordinately pleasing to man due to its imbuing the celebrant and congregation with a Peleganistic sense of self-satisfaction. So too, the traditional Mass in its most elaborate forms is overlaid with beautiful, but auditorially incomprehensible (especially if not in the vernacular) polyphony; or even located within extravagant, even if elevated, entertainments, such as symphony Masses. Though such grandiose traditional Masses certainly have merit as artistic productions, the very distraction of the artistry will render such productions to some degree improper.

Even those who, in reaction to the secularized liturgicalism of Vatican II, promote a "high" or traditional liturgy are apt to claim that the faithful give greater glory to God by their "active participation" in the Mass; be it by serving the Mass or singing in the *schola*. However, it is not vocal participation, much less pomp and circumstance, that makes the Holy Sacrifice of the Mass acceptable, but, again, a broken spirit and a contrite heart. Our Lord reiterates that it is such a spirit and heart that is the acceptable spirit of prayer in the very temple itself,

> Two men went up into the temple to pray: the one a Pharisee and the other a publican. The Pharisee standing, prayed thus with himself: O God, I give thee thanks that I am not as the rest of men, extortioners, unjust, adulterers, as also is this publican. I fast twice in a week: I give tithes of all that I possess. And the publican, standing afar off, would not so much as lift up his eyes towards heaven; but struck his breast, saying: O God, be merciful to me a sinner. I say to you, this man went down into his house justified rather than the other: because every one that exalteth himself shall be humbled: and he that humbleth himself shall be exalted. LK 18:10-14

It is this contrite and humble sort of heart that in its proper disposition allows the faithful to enter most deeply into the Holy Sacrifice of the Mass.

LITURGICAL PROPRIETY

Though traditionalists oft times like to play the part of omniscient theologians—either assuming to know the intent of the ministers (as with the confecting of the Eucharist) or pretending to understand the mysteries of sacramental conferral (as with ordination)—questions of the validity of the Holy Mass are unwarranted save in the most extreme, and in the most obvious, cases. And though progressives often like to play the part of liturgy police—as is the case with their reading out of the Church those who would participate in a traditional Mass unsanctioned by the diocese—illicitity is often but a superficial legalistic characterization that is easily overridden by the license of informed Christian conscience.

While the issue of either validity or licity is often tangential, unwarranted, or inapplicable, the liturgy can still be evaluated as per propriety. The concept of propriety allows the evaluation of the liturgy without either pontificating on validity or bloviating on licity. Again,[218] propriety is a most unique word, contradictorily meaning either "that which conveys true essence" or "that which conforms to current societal norms." In that Christian liturgy is intrinsically tied to the Divine, which is outside of time, and specifically to the Crucifixion, which transcends time, it especially is proper in accord with the first definition.

Liturgy, then, is proper when it conveys the true essence of worship, prayer, and sacraments. Liturgy is improper to the degree it entails incongruous and/or overemphasized accidental aspects that obscure the true essence of worship, prayer, and the sacraments. The true essence of the Mass in particular—but the source of all worship, prayer, and sacraments in general—is the sacrificial oblation unto Almighty God, which in its infinite sufficiency is the Sacrifice of the Cross. Once again, for the worshiper to efficaciously enter into this true essence of the Mass requires his own proper disposition of vulnerable intimacy, so as to "make up for what is lacking in the sufferings of Christ." (CO 1:24).

To evoke the true essence of worship, prayer, and the sacraments, the liturgy properly excites in the faithful two key elements: that of its nature as a sacrificial oblation unto Almighty God and the vulnerable intimacy of the participant. These two seemingly contradictory elements— sacrificial oblation in light of God's awesome omnipotent grandeur versus vulnerable intimacy with God as Father— makes perfect sense and are perfectly one when the Christian lovingly kneels at the foot of the Holy Cross. For it is at the foot of Christ the King Crucified that the Christian in vulnerable intimacy, and in his abjectness both as a mere creature and as a sinner, lovingly relinquishes himself unto God's mercy.

The liturgical accidentals of the Mass, then, are primarily cultural and artistic and are ordered to resonate with the worshiper so as to effect the objective reality of sacrificial oblation and the subjective disposition of vulnerable intimacy. Such accidentals can derive from ancient culture or contemporary secular culture, from fine art or popular art. Liturgical propriety as anchored to exciting within the faithful a proper disposition is then tied to some extent to cultural vagaries. Technarcistic Man has different tendencies than man of the Middle-Ages. What might have inspired pious fear in the faithful of the Middle-Ages, today may only feed the ego and inure it from the reality of the Cross. What may have evoked sacrificial oblation unto Almighty God in the past may only diminish vulnerable intimacy in the present. But regardless, liturgical reform is proper in so far as it further manifests Christ Crucified and facilitates a broken spirit and contrite heart.

LITURGICAL INCULTURATION
& ENCULTURATION

Liturgical reform entails both inculturation (*i.e.*, conforming a liturgy to man and informed by a current culture) and enculturation (*i.e.*, conforming man to a liturgy informed by Christ Crucified). The conundrum for liturgical inculturation in the third millennium is that the culture has its inception in the very rejection of Christ, is essentially anti-Christic, and thus cannot be much utilized.[219] This fact will lead to a liturgy that while tied to the ancient world will eliminate some ancient accidentals that in their obsolescence impede the true essence of the Mass and the worshiper's proper disposition, but will not necessarily replace these with accidentals from the current anti-Christic culture. A proper third millennium liturgy, then, will be simplified and characterized by a certain monastic minimalism.

As per liturgical enculturation, or conforming man to Christ Crucified, the conundrum is that third millennium Technarcistic Man is on the natural level already inured from the cross of reality and thus not at all disposed to be a sacrificial oblation intimately vulnerable at the foot of Christ Crucified. This fact will again recommend a certain monastic austerity, indeed a contemplative quiet, in the liturgy so as to facilitate the union with Christ Crucified.

In the Third Millennium especially, but even in every day and age, liturgical propriety is most assuredly conveyed by a sacred simplicity. Even in overt signs of worship. Less is sometimes more. Traditional rubrics rarely prescribe a prostration, but quite often a genuflection. This is because liturgical propriety also requires the balancing of the sacred and the simple with the appreciation of diminishing returns.

Whereas the sacred puts the worshiper in the proper relationship to Almighty God, the simple prevents that worship from becoming self-absorbed, which would mitigate against the proper relationship to God and the requisite self-abnegation of the worshiper. God Almighty is not akin to some pagan god that desires extravagant displays of piety, much less productions, but rather, again, only a broken spirit and contrite heart.

In that inculturation is rightly ordered to enculturation, it is best to bar third millennium popular culture from the formal liturgy so as not to taint that liturgy with unchristian values or connotations. So too, barring popular culture from the liturgy presents to the faithful as an edifying example of counterculturality purified of secularity; a counterculturality which can be implemented in their own lives. However, the barring of the current profane anti-Christic culture does not automatically mean that anything "classical" is necessarily proper, for even the learned sophistication associated with classical education—be this education in the liberal, fine, performance, or liturgical arts[220]—itself can militate against the intimate vulnerability required for the sacrificial oblation.

LITURGICAL CRUCIALISM

Whereas a traditional Mass that evokes a high-brow prideful attitude, a dilettante interest, or an elitist connoisseurship of the classical is improper because it does not dispose one to the requisite vulnerable intimacy, a *novus ordo* Mass that evokes undue self-centered emotions via music and interaction between the worshipers is improper because it does not adequately manifest the essence of sacrificial oblation.

Though the dialogue *novus ordo* Mass is supposed to make participation more active, this activity is not necessarily conducive to the requisite intimacy. This is because a person, in his intimacy, is subjective and spontaneous of heart, but this subjectivity and spontaneity can be impeded by the participation in the objective office of the Mass, a participation that is only required of the priestly celebrant. Indeed, the depth of the Mass, the treasury of all its readings and prayers, can be said to be beyond the ken of any person to fully enter into in the course of a single life, much less the course of a single liturgy.

So too, though the high traditional Mass is supposed to make the sacrifice grandeur, its musical production is not necessarily conducive to the requisite sacrificial oblation. This is because a person, in his sacrificial oblation, is necessarily ego dystonic and self-abnegating; in other words, ordered away from self and towards God. But this ordering can be impeded by the spectacle, artistry, and ego-gratification of the liturgical performance. Liturgical intricacies and complexities, even rubrics, can be impedingly distractive and/or ego-gratifying. Thus, for instance, plain chant may be deemed to be more proper than polyphony, for though polyphony is beautiful in its melodious intricacies, this very beauty and intricacy can become an end in itself and at the same time obscure the prayer (especially if not in the vernacular) and thus obscure the actual meaning and sentiments of the sacred texts being sung.

In general, the liturgicalism that may occur in the traditional Mass emphasizes the sacrificial nature of the Mass to the detriment of its intimate personal nature, and the liturgicalism that may occur in the *Novus Ordo* Mass emphasizes the intimate personal, and even more problematic social, nature of the Mass to the detriment of its sacrificial nature. However, both the elements of sacrificial oblation and intimate vulnerability that are properly present in the Mass work in complete synergistic integrity and require each other for their own perfection.

Liturgical propriety, then, not only entails the objective elements of the sacrificial and sacramental, as per the nature of God and man, but rightly affects man's subjective dispositional propriety. What makes the Holy Mass objectively sufficient is the renewal of the unbloodied sacrifice of the Cross, and what makes it subjectively efficacious is for the worshiper, in intimate vulnerability, to have a broken spirit and contrite heart, the requisite disposition for deep receptivity. As such, may it be surmised that a Mass most proper was likely offered in the dim and grim recesses of a concentration camp or at the painful and poignant bedside of a dying loved one? For in such scenarios man adds nothing to the sacrifice but the most paltry requisite elements of matter and form and is most well-disposed in his wretchedness and broken vulnerability.

The very reverence proper to the Holy Sacrifice of the Mass, then, is not one that stems from the spirit of awe, nor should the liturgy seek to evoke such a spirit. Indeed, God is intentionally hidden in his awesomeness and the mental effort and exertion of the will required to evoke the sentiment of awe is unconducive to the requisite sentiment of a receptive, broken, and contrite heart for love of Christ

Crucified.

Note well, the Mass, aside from all the liturgical circumstances that surround it, is essentially but the one moment of confection. At this moment, the most ancient liturgical custom prescribes for the priest to hunch over the bread and utter the words of consecration inaudibly, without even an elevation of the Sacred Species. Such a muted and intimate confection of the Holy Eucharist disallowed the accidentals of that Eucharist, its appearance as bread, to distract from the Crucified Christ, to whom they are a portal. Again, the most ancient liturgical custom prescribes in the confecting of the Precious Blood that the priest's words of consecration reverberate only within the chalice. These words of consecration are muffled so as to silently echo in the abyss of timelessness, so as not to be bound to the here and now.

That is the Holy Mass: consecration, crucifixion, compunction. The Mass is so simple in essence. Liturgically it calls for but a piercing of the faithful's hearts, hearts withdrawn and undistracted from all save the Crucified Christ. The proper liturgy of Holy Mass essentially[221] evokes in the faithful a response that is but the groaning of a pierced heart. In its essence then, the liturgy of the Holy Mass is properly a relatively silent and austere affair, where neither verbosity nor spectacle should distract from the immediacy of the act of atonement.

XIV. Holy Mass &
The Blessed Sacrament

" . . . do this in remembrance of me."
LK 22.19

In that the **Holy Sacrifi**ce of the Mass derives completely from, and is a manifestation of, the Holy Sacrifice of the Cross it adds nothing to the sufficiency or appeasing properties of that Sacrifice of the Cross. For the Sacrifice of the Cross is in itself *infinitely* sufficient and appeasing. This then necessarily means that the Mass does not exist for God, who is infinitely appeased by Christ's Sacrifice on the Cross, but rather the Mass exists for man so that man may more efficaciously avail himself of the Sacrifice of the Cross.

By allowing man to worship God by entering into the very moment of the Sacrifice of the Cross the Holy Sacrifice of the Mass facilitates the efficacy of the Sacrifice of the Cross. Specifically, the Holy Mass, and the fruit of Holy Communion, were instituted to facilitate a contrite and humble heart, thus remedying "what is lacking in regards to Christ's sufferings" (COL 1:24). This attitude is encouraged by the Catechism of Trent:

If, therefore, with a pure heart, a lively faith, and affected with an inward sorrow for our transgressions, we immolate and offer this most holy victim, we shall, without doubt, obtain mercy from the Lord, and grace in time of need.[222]

It is not the Holy Sacrifice of the Cross that must be made acceptable—for already the slain Lamb of God is infinitely acceptable, worthy, and sufficient—but rather man that must be made acceptable. Thus the Holy Mass was not instituted to enhance in any way that Sacrifice of the Cross, but it was instituted to remedy the indisposed hearts of the faithful, which are the only "lackings" in the Sacrifice of the Cross.

Thus efficacious participation in the Mass entails a properly disposed heart that is placed at the foot of Christ Crucified. In an uncompartmentalized way, a properly disposed heart is brought to the Mass, further disposed by the Mass, and then lived-out from the Mass in further disposition. The liturgical unbloody Sacrifice of the Mass calls for the faithful to *add the blood* in the lived-out sacrifice of daily Christian life. Indeed, it is the very participation in the Cross of Christ in daily life that causes a Christian to verily pine away for the Holy Mass and to hunger and thirst mightily for the Most Blessed Sacrament of the Altar.

EUCHARISTIC PARTICIPATION

To enter deeply into the mystery of the Holy Sacrifice of the Mass is not an issue of liturgical activity but of personal intimacy. The depth of participation in the Holy Mass, be it of the laity or the celebrating priest in his own person, depends on one's subjective disposition. The requisite intimate and deep subjective disposition of the heart is best evoked not merely by participation in the formal externals of the liturgy, but rather by the interior cultivation of the person in everyday, vale-of-tears, life.

In distinction to the Christian's participation in the Mass, the priest in *persona Christi* (as opposed to in his own concurrent person) does not depend at all on his subjective disposition but rather on a mere modicum of objective intent; that is, an intent to do what the Church intends, with the addition of the requisite form and matter. The fact that the confecting of the Eucharist is accomplished objectively means it necessarily entails the very subordination of the subjective person of the man who is the priest.

The Holy Mass then, in its objective and infinite sufficiency, is not made more meritorious by the actions of the priest, much less by the quality of the liturgy or the participation of the laity. To hold otherwise, which was a prevalent Counter-Reformation error and is an enduring and prevalent traditionalist error, is to fall into a heretical Gnosticism. So too, to hold otherwise is quite conducive to a prideful clericalism, which is exactly the opposite disposition for an acceptable sacrifice on the subjective level.

An orthodox understanding of the Mass' sufficiency and efficacy recognizes the infinite and unquantifiable sufficiency of even one single Mass. But without such an orthodox valuation of the Mass, a person may somehow wish to increase the Mass' sufficiency by either an anxious desire to embellish and enhance the Mass or by an anxious desire to multiply the sheer number of Masses. Again, such a deficient realization, if not theoretical understanding, of the sufficiency of the Holy Mass, was a prevalent Counter-Reformational reaction to the Protestant denial of the Mass.

The Holy Mass and all the sacraments have their *sine qua non* in the Holy Sacrifice of the Cross. In a most direct manner, the Mass and the Eucharist are manifestations of that very sacrifice. Therefore, the more a soul becomes one with Christ Crucified the more that soul becomes one with him in the Mass, and the more a soul exalts the Holy Cross the more that soul adores the Holy Eucharist. For it is Christ Crucified and the Holy Cross that are the essence of the Mass and the Eucharist.

THE MOST BLESSED SACRAMENT

The fact that the Holy Sacrifice of Christ on the Cross, in and of itself, has infinite sufficiency means that the provision of the Mass by the Lord Jesus Christ was not necessary but purely gratuitous. Such a gift of Christ's very self under the mode of the most mundane of foods—thus rendering this priceless gift of himself so readily, plentifully, and easily obtainable—is truly a squandering of himself for his faithful's sake. Indeed, the very name *Eucharist* means "thanksgiving" for this most blessed of spendthrift gifts.

The Holy Mass and Holy Eucharist are gifts that, though they exist for salvation, are above and beyond what is required for salvation, which finds its absolute sufficiency in the death of Christ on the Cross. This means that the Christian does not exist for the Mass and Eucharist, but rather that the Mass and Eucharist exist for the Christian so that the Christian may exist for Christ. A subtle distinction to be sure, but nonetheless *a crucial one*. Christ instituted the Eucharistic Sacrifice so,

> He might leave, to His own beloved Spouse the Church, a visible sacrifice, such as the nature of man requires....[223]

So again, God does not require the Mass, for the Son of God's sacrifice on the Cross was infinitely sufficient. Rather, it is for the needs of man that the Mass was instituted. Not only does the offering of the Holy Sacrifice of the Mass allow man to formally engage in a ceremonial sacrifice as per the requirements of his human and religious nature, but more importantly it provides the superlative medicinal boost of grace to become holy; a growth in holiness that primarily takes place outside of Mass in the daily sacrifice of dying to self in union with Christ Crucified. The Mass, while at the same time a mystical portal to the past death of Christ on the Cross and to future eschatological glory, is in the present given to nurture and preserve the soul.

> It must, therefore, be diligently explained what the Sacrament of the Eucharist signifies, that the faithful, beholding the sacred mysteries with their eyes, may also at the same time feed their souls with the contemplation of divine things. Three things, then, are signified by this Sacrament. The first is the Passion of Christ our Lord, a thing past; for He Himself said: *Do this for a commemoration of me*, and the Apostle says: *As often as you shall eat this bread, and drink the chalice, you shall show the death of the Lord, until he come.* It is also significant of divine and heavenly grace, which is imparted at the present time by this Sacrament to nurture and preserve the soul. Just as in Baptism we are begotten unto newness of life and by Confirmation are strengthened to resist Satan and openly to profess the name of Christ, so by the Sacrament of the Eucharist are we nurtured and supported. It is, thirdly, a foreshadowing of future eternal joy and glory, which, according to God's promises, we shall receive in our heavenly country. These three things, then, which are clearly distinguished by their reference to past, present and future times, are so well represented by the Eucharistic mysteries that the whole Sacrament, though consisting of different species, signifies the three as if it referred to one thing only.[224]

Christ certainly did not institute the Eucharist so that man has something more to adore, something additional to do, so as to placate and appease God. Rather, Christ instituted the Eucharist to make his salvific act of sacrifice on the Cross immediately present, and to nourish and comfort man in his becoming one with Christ Crucified. When one appreciates, is receptive and responsive to, this charism ("gift" indeed!) of the Eucharist, he will then necessarily adore and worship the Eucharist. But it is not that God needs or thirsts for man's adoration, but rather that he desires man to recognizes his own absolute neediness, his own soul-deep thirst, and so come to Christ in an intimate, self-abnegating love.

The definitive essence of the Holy Mass is not in the fact that it is unbloodied, for a lack is not a specific difference. Rather, the definitive essence of the Holy Mass is its allowance of man to participate *in vivo* and outside of time in the redemptive Holy Sacrifice of the Cross, and to be subsequently nurtured by the Eucharistic fruit of that Cross. Nor is the Eucharist's specific difference that it is God but that it is God as edible fruit of the Holy Cross. Thus, the Eucharist is not given specifically to man so that he can worship God by means of it but it is given to man so that he can be nourished by it. In participating in the Holy Sacrifice of the Mass a person unites himself to Christ Crucified and purgatively decreases himself, and then in the reception of Holy Communion this same Christ increases.

"Do this in remembrance of me," (LK 22:19) points to another time and place; that is, what is to be done in remembrance is a means, a portal, but not an end in itself. In synergy with this transcendence of time, the Eucharist in its very veiling in mundane accidentals demands the transcendence of the actual senses so as to encounter the unveiled Christ. And once seeing beyond in faith, the adorer in love communes most intimately with the Crucified Lord as he brings to his communion an intimate receptivity, which "makes up for what is lacking in the sufferings of Christ." (CO 1:24). Here, the adorer says *yes* to his own crucifixion, his own purgation, his own humiliations and sorrows. In so saying *yes* to his own daily crucifixion, the Christian will thirst deeply and pine ardently for the Holy Eucharist and will be so disposed as to enter fully into the sacrificial act of the Holy Mass. The subjective efficacy of the Mass is rooted in the heart of man conformed to Christ in self-abnegating intimate vulnerability.[225]

It is the very fact that the Holy Mass and the Holy

Eucharist are not necessary for salvation that renders these gifts from the Lord Jesus Christ to his Catholic faithful so uniquely precious, so stupendously gratuitous, and so exceedingly lavish. The Eucharistic celebration is not so much about the faithful's dutiful giving to the Lord, but about Our Lord's spendthrift squandering of himself for the consumption of his beloved faithful.

In the same vein, it is not dutiful participation in the Eucharistic celebration that makes one a good Catholic, but rather a person participates in the Eucharist so that he can be nourished in his striving to *be a good Catholic* in his everyday life. In recognizing that the Mass and Eucharist are not essential to the Faith, a Christian gains a much deeper and fuller appreciation of and thankfulness for these most prodigious of gifts!

THE SUBTLE SACRAMENT

The Holy Eucharist is not the superlative sacrament. The superlative sacrament is Holy Baptism. The Holy Eucharist is not even the penultimate sacrament, for that would be sacramental confession. This is because both baptism and confession can remit soul damning sin, original/mortal and mortal respectively, and thus procure salvation; whereas the Holy Eucharist can only remit venial sin, and it is the remission of mortal sin that is necessary for salvation. But the Holy Eucharist is certainly the *Most Blessed Sacrament*: the totally gratuitous, sweet, incomparable food that strengthens a Christian to carry his cross, to nourish a Christian in the throes of his own life and passion, to accompany a Christian in the trauma of passing from this mortal coil to life-everlasting.

The first Mass itself was offered by Our Lord in preparation for the Passion. Note well, that though the apostles had all just received the Eucharist, one still betrayed Christ unto death, another betrayed him at his death, and all but one fled. Thus, a Christian is not saved at the Holy Mass, nor by the reception of the Eucharist, but is afforded a boon of strength and grace so as to help him embrace the Holy Cross and thus be saved. Again, it is not the communicant but the martyr that goes straight to heaven.

An overemphasis on the Blessed Sacrament that dislocates it from the overall Gospel message and overall Christian life actually diminishes appreciation for the Eucharist's true charism. This charism is symbolized by the propriety of unleavened bread being used for transubstantiation, for the Blessed Sacrament is itself a leaven of the Christian life. Understood as a leaven, the proportionalizing and locating of the Blessed Sacrament within the overall Gospel message and the overall Christian life only increases a true devotion to it. The Gospel message is about Jesus Christ and it is about man, and the Christian life is about embracing the Cross for love of God, and thus the Holy Eucharist must be seen as per its relation to Jesus Christ, to man, and to the embracing of the Cross.

Our Lord promised the Holy Spirit, rather than the Holy Eucharist, and this is what he specifically emphasized when he said he would be with us "for all time," (JN 14:16). Nor is the Eucharist mentioned in any of the creeds. Much like the lack of praise Christ could have lavished on the Blessed Virgin Mary, his surprising lack of praise of the Blessed Sacrament would be readily understandable if he were seeking to avoid a devotion that would become compartmentalized from the larger corpus of the Faith, and indeed to avoid a devotion to the Eucharist that would in its compartmentalization do violence to the Eucharist's very own charism. For when the Eucharist or the Mass is so compartmentalized and overemphasized their efficacy is only impeded.

Like devotion to the Blessed Virgin Mary always being about Jesus,[226] the Blessed Sacrament is always about Christ Crucified. So too, like the charism of the Blessed Virgin Mary, the charism of the Blessed Sacrament is about nourishment. Thus, both the Blessed Virgin Mary and the Blessed Sacrament are to be loved and availed of in an intimate manner. The Blessed Virgin Mary, then, is most properly seen not so much as a queen but as a mother; more aptly seen in her perfect femininity and maternity rather than in her authority and superiority.[227] In the case of the Blessed Sacrament, Christ is most properly seen not so much as Christ the King but as the Lamb of God, more in his sacrificial nourishment of the Christian than in his Omnipotent Otherness. The Blessed Mother intercedes for us, wraps her children in her clement maternal mantle, so that they are not overly fearful of Christ the King and Pantocrator, and this same Almighty Christ wraps himself in the Eucharist so that his faithful are not overly fearful to intimately commune with him.

Just as Christ walked the earth in a familiar manner, just as he came to man as a commoner, just as he began calling his disciples friends at the Last Supper, so too does he come to us in the Eucharist. Yes, we revere and love him, but we are not overwhelmed or fearfully awed by him, save theoretically. Christ chose to appear only once transfigured, and this was on Mount Tabor not at the Last Supper. Thus, there is no need, nor even is there an exhortation, for the faithful to evoke imagination and emotion unto a fearful awe of the Eucharist as the Omnipotent God. In fact, to do so is beyond human ability, for the Omnipotent God is beyond human comprehension.

> Thou canst not see my face: for man shall not see me and live. EX 33:20

Rather, Jesus Christ comes to his faithful in the Eucharist as the Lamb of God; in his incarnational kenosis state that is emptied of his equality with God.

The Holy Eucharist is not so much to be looked at but looked through. The Lord Jesus Christ did not give himself to the faithful in the Blessed Sacrament so as to tax them with a mental and emotional exercise where they exert themselves to see the mundane accidental species as God Almighty. Rather, the Lord gives himself to the faithful in the Blessed Sacrament so that they, in loving remembrance, may gain a transcendental portal beyond accidentals, time, and place unto his act of eternal propitiation and redemption on the Holy Cross. There is no need, as some devotional works encourage, for the adorer to work himself into a frenzy of awe over being in God's presence, rather the adorer need only have a modicum of simple faith, and more so the love, to see Christ Crucified beyond appearances, time, and place. Truly, it is only love that can gain access to this mysterious portal, and thus reason, though not suspended, must finally give way to and depend on that love.

Rather than trying to muster fervor via volition and positive thinking, if the Christian accepts that there is an intended veil entailing a certain indirectness, that allows a certain familiarity, then one is able to enter into the Holy Mass in the depths of his authentic, yes wretched, self and thus is able as well to intimately receive and lovingly adore the Blessed Sacrament. The ideal disposition at Holy Mass, at Holy Communion, and even at Adoration, can be seen in the disposition of St. John the Beloved, the Apostle of the Eucharist, at the Last Supper and first Mass:

> Now there was resting on Jesus' bosom one of his disciples, whom Jesus loved. JN 13:23.

It is the reciprocal love between Christ and St. John that epitomizes the essence of devotion to the Holy Eucharist, and this love, knowing no bounds, can always increase. But only a basic faith is needed in this devotion to the Blessed Sacrament. It is indeed the same basic faith that holds Jesus Christ to be the Son of God; that holds his Church and Scripture as under his assured auspices; that holds Christ's words as authoritative and actualizing. Just as God said "Let there be light," and it became light, so too, as Christ said "This is my body," it became so and becomes so at every Mass. From there on in the Mass, a Christian need not focus on the accidentals of bread and wine but on Christ Crucified that transcends those accidentals and place and time.

The basic act of Christian faith believes a son of a carpenter, a Nazarene, a Jew crucified to death, is himself the Son of God. It is the very same sort of Faith that believes that a piece of bread and a cup of wine becomes the Body, Blood, Soul, and Divinity of Jesus Christ. In this the Eucharist gives all men the opportunity to believe just as the contemporaries of Jesus did: from Mary, to Joseph, to the shepherds and the magi, to the apostles and disciples, to St. Dismas and the Centurion. Or conversely in this the Eucharist is given the potential not to believe, just as some of the contemporaries of Jesus did not: from Herod and his henchmen, to the Pharisees and the high priests, to Pontius Pilate and the Jewish mobs.

To become a Catholic, that is, to have access to redemption, requires only that a person believes; *viz.*, professes the Faith as per the Apostle's Creed, and is baptized. A Catholic may be a saint and never have attended a Mass (such as a baptized infant or the martyrs of certain Catholic populations that were generations without priests). Indeed, attending Mass is not even an intrinsic requirement of the Christian life, but rather an obligatory discipline imposed by the Church. For it is not attending, no matter how often,[228] the Holy Mass, or the other sacramental and devotional activities, that makes a Christian holy, but rather attending Mass facilitates a Christian being holy in his daily Way of the Cross.

The Mass and Eucharist do not save in and of themselves, but manifest in a superlative sacramental way Christ Crucified who does save. Again, one can be saved without attending Mass, but not without dying unto himself in union with Christ Crucified. As most blessed as it is, it is not the reception of Holy Communion[229] that assures salvation but martyrdom in this world and the fires of purgatory in the next.

LIVING THE MASS

The Holy Eucharist is Jesus but Jesus is not the Eucharist; for Jesus Christ transcends and is not limited by the sacramental species of the Eucharist. While the Holy Eucharist is the most exquisite means of unification with Jesus Christ and the very summit of the liturgy, it is still not essential for incorporation into the body of Christ, nor even to holiness. For the Eucharist itself derives from the singular salvific act of Christ Crucified, who transcends and is not limited by that Eucharist. Again, the highest and only essential Christian act is that of self-abnegation for love of Christ, be it a life-long purgative white martyrdom, a life ending with salvific red martyrdom, or a receptivity to the fires of purgation at one's particular judgment. Nonetheless, the Holy Eucharist superlatively fortifies a Christian to so die to himself.

The minimalistic standard of lay spirituality that characterized the interim between the Counter-Reformation and Vatican II necessarily entailed a compartmentalization of Christian life. This minimalistic standard of lay spirituality and compartmentalization of Christian life discounted and de-emphasized the dramatic vicissitudes and heroic love entailed in familial life, which is fundamental to, and makes up the bulk of, human and Christian life. But in the Counter-Reformational compartmentalization of Christian life, the family, as the center of Christian life, was supplanted by the parish. Here, Church attendance became the hallmark of a person's Catholic faith rather than the daily carrying of the cross. Here, the unbloodied Holy Sacrifice of the Mass became an end in itself rather than a superlative grace to facilitate union with Christ Crucified in the everyday bloody sacrifice of existence.

It does not take courage to attend Mass, but attending Mass facilitates the deepest courage required for the intimate and daily embrace of the Holy Cross. It is in the home —be it a sorrowful mother steeped in the life and death drama of bearing and raising children or be it a sacrificial father striving to feed and fight for his family—that the Holy Cross is most intimately and prevalently embraced. It is primarily within the confines of intimate family life that blood is added to the absolutely sufficient Unbloodied Holy Sacrifice of the Mass, thus rendering that Mass sanctifyingly efficacious for the faithful in their purgative union with Christ Crucified.

XV. Specific Christian States

Not every one that saith to me, Lord, Lord
shall enter into the kingdom of heaven
but he that doth the will of my Father
who is in heaven.
MT 7:21

T**he deeper a person goes** in Christian spirit- uality, the simpler it becomes. Indeed, it comes down to the simplest binary process of love. It is a question of either *0* or *1*, *yes* or *no*. It is the choice to undergo utter self-abnegation for love of Christ Crucified or to reject such abnegation and Christ for love of self. This is the crucial Christian vocation to which all the more specific Christian states are ordered.[230]

To the degree a Christian embraces the Holy Cross he adheres to his vocation. In the Christian familial state the Holy Cross is encountered in the bombardment of the myriad of purgative vicissitudes: be they of marital, communal, ecclesial, or sociopolitical existence. In the evangelical state, the Holy Cross is encountered in the intentional, intense, and immediate living out of penitential vows. In the ordained state, the Holy Cross is encountered in the formal victimhood intrinsic to the priesthood. So too, in any special or unique vocation there is always a humiliation and sorrow equivalent to the degree that the vocation is authentically from God and is faithfully adhered to.

The errors caused by the past's de-emphasis on the crucial Christian vocation—that is the baptismal call to holiness—and the corollary over-emphasis on priestly and evangelical (a.k.a., religious) vocations is now exacerbated in the third millennium with confusion about the natural vocations as well, be these natural vocations of *imago Dei* human maturation, familial existence, or even gender. As such, vocational definition and discernment has been gravely muddled and given rise to an unprecedented vocational crisis both on an individual and collective level.

The remedy to the third millennium's vocational indefiniteness, confusion, and crisis is to base the discernment and fulfilling of the electoral vocations (familial, evangelical, ordained, or special) on a prerequisite assent and adherence to the given natural and supernatural vocations (Psychomoral, Incarnational, Familial, Sociopolitical, Baptismal, and Ecclesial). Here, note well, that the prerequisite natural and supernatural vocations are givens that need not be *discerned* but must be *assented* to. Thus, these given vocations properly precede and take precedence over the Electoral Vocations that are variable and discernible.

Though often given a preeminence that puts the cart before the horse, discernment of a person's Electoral Christian Vocation properly comes only after he has begun to embrace his given natural and supernatural ones. A woman really cannot become a good mother in the 3rd Familial Vocation or a good nun in the 6th Electoral Vocation until she has embraced her femininity in the 2nd Incarnational Vocation. A man really cannot become a good father in the 3rd Familial Vocation or a good monk, or a good priest, in the 6th Electoral Vocation until he embraces his masculinity in the 2nd Incarnational Vocation. A person cannot die to himself for love of Christ in the 4th Baptismal Vocation until he dies to himself for love of reality in the 1st Psychomoral Vocation. A person cannot become a good Christian *anything* in their final Electoral Vocation until he begins to truly seek holiness in the crucial Baptismal Vocation. As such, when dealing with either discernment or crisis of a specific Electoral Vocation, it is most advantageous to shore up the prerequisite given vocations, both natural and supernatural. When this prerequisite vocational work is done the clarity for the discernment and/ or remedy of the crisis of the Electoral Vocation is supplied.

VOCATIONAL CATEGORIES

Strictly speaking, that is ontologically[231] speaking, there are only two qualitatively unique Christian vocations, that of the crucial Christian baptismal state and that of the ordained state. For it is only these two states that are conveyed by the reception of indelible marks (ontological changes) upon the soul. The only other indelible sacramental marks upon the soul, confirmation and episcopal consecration, do not involve qualitative changes but quantitative increases. Confirmation quantitatively deepens the mark of baptism and episcopal consecration quantitatively deepens the mark of ordination. As such, and in keeping with the need to avoid vocational compartmentalization, it is most concise to conceptualize the two ontological Christian vocational states as either the *Christian (baptized) state* or the *Christian plus ordained state.* Note well, that just as confirmation is ordered toward facilitating the baptismal vocation, so too is priestly ordination and episcopal consecration completely ordered to facilitating the crucial Christian baptismal vocation.

In addition to strictly classifying vocations ontologically as either the Christian or the Christian plus ordained, there is the common and practical usage that classifies vocations as either lay or evangelical/religious (and more recently, as single or married). In post-Trentian, Counter-Reformation theology there was, and is still, a prevalent tendency to blur the lines between this practical understanding and the strict ontological understanding of vocations. This blurring was due to the devaluation of the crucial Christian vocational call to holiness, and this devaluation's corollary equating of the fullness of Christian life with the evangelical and ordained states. The results were an inconsistent theology and deficient spirituality of vocations.

In the faulty vocational conceptualization prevalent in Counter-Reformational theology and spirituality not only is there a tendency to overlook the crucial Christian vocation but there is a glaring inconsistency in considering the evangelical state as a formal vocation but not so considering the marital state as one. But, of course, a Christian does indeed have a vocation even if he is not in evangelical vows or ordained: it is the crucial Christian vocation that all other vocations are ordered to. In addition, if the evangelical state is to be spoken of as a vocation, then the marital state much more so should be spoken of as a vocation; for the marital state is conveyed sacramentally, whereas the evangelical state is not.

Again, reactionary Counter-Reformation theology played a part in this faulty vocational conceptualization. The Protestant heresy denied the Holy Mass, Eucharist, and sacramental confession, and thus so too it denied the priesthood. But the Protestant heresy also denied the validity of the evangelical life and the sacramental nature of marriage. The Counter-Reformation reaction to these denials was the overemphasis[232] of not only the Mass, but of the priesthood and the vowed evangelical life. And while there was a reassertion of the sacramentality of marriage (made especially urgent with Henry VIII's multiple marriages) there was nonetheless an overemphasis and overvaluation of the ordained and evangelical states that entailed, even if unintentionally, the corollary degradation of the lay faithful. This degradation of the lay faithful itself was fueled by the Counter-Reformational reaction to not only Protestantism's denying of the priesthood and the evangelical counsels, but also due to the full dependence of Protestantism on the ministry of *de facto* laity (regardless of the Protestant supposed ordinations[233]).

In the following explication of a crucial ethos theology of vocations, both the ontological and the practical understanding of vocations are incorporated and integrated. The incorporation and integration of both senses of vocation assures that a vocational theology is kept unambiguous, pastorally useful, and within orthodox bounds. The marital, evangelical, and ordained states will be considered as the three typical practical vocational states, and a fourth as well is admitted for any special vocational state. While taking into considered the different practical vocations, on the strictly ontological level the marital/familial and evangelical states remain the same crucial Baptismal Vocation and the unique Priestly Vocation is fully ordered toward the facilitation of that same crucial Baptismal Vocation.

THE INTEGRITY OF THE SPECIFIC CHRISTIAN STATES

The marital state is both a natural law imperative and a supernatural sacrament. From the marital state emanates the familial state, and all other states are made possible by the marital and familial states. Indeed, the single person[234] is still properly part of a familial social unit, as are vowed evangelical and ordain persons (see below § *Evangelical Chastity* for the error of familial alienation). The marital state and ensuing familial milieu is then the source of the evangelical state, which is properly seen as the flowering of the marital and familial state. Marriage vows are the ordinary and sacramental means of sanctification for the faithful, whereas evangelical vows are the extraordinary and penitential means. In regards to the ordained state, it exists to minister unto the faithful, be they in the familial, evangelical, or the persons who are in the self-same clerical states.

The crucial issues to be discerned in the married/familial state are what it means to be a husband and father, a wife and mother, and a family. The crucial issues to be discerned in the evangelical state are the meanings and proper manifestations of celibacy, poverty, obedience, and cloister. In the ordained state the crucial issues to be discerned are what it means to be ordained, to offer ministerial sacrifice unto God, and to sacrificially minister unto the faithful.

As is elaborated upon in Chapters X and XVI, the renewal of the marital/familial state entails the celebration of God given-gender, the instilling of devotion to the feminine and the family, the enshrinement of the mother as the heart of the home, and the implementation of patriarchal familial authority in both the sociopolitical and ecclesial realm.[235] Such a renewal requires the recognition and advancement of the family's sacrosanct status, and its designation as the primary focus and locus of both the Church and civil society. In practice this means a reordering of both sociopolitical and ecclesial structures to facilitate small faith communities of families. Furthermore, as per ecclesial reform, both the evangelical and priestly life should be ordered toward, and integrated into, the facilitation of the family, which remains the matrix of all the faithful.

(The marital and familial state has been herein addressed elsewhere and thus will not be elaborated upon in the following. The clerical state has been addressed elsewhere as well, and thus will be elaborated upon to a lesser extent than the evangelical state; but some principals of the evangelical state apply to the clerical state, indeed to the familial state, as well.)

VATICAN I REFORM OF EVANGELICAL LIFE

Vatican II infamously called for the reform of evangelical (*a.k.a.*, religious) life. The qualifier "infamously" is indeed warranted due to the near complete collapse[236] of evangelical life in the wake of this call. But why the collapse? As they were in regards to perceiving the general malaise of the faithful, the Council Fathers were right in perceiving a malaise in evangelical life; but, again as with the faithful, they were wrong in their proffered remedies. *Perfectae Caritatis* (Decree on Adaptation and Renewal of Religious Life) was one of the last works of the Council, which was now after three long years entering its final phase. *Perfectae Caritatis* is a rather nebulous document, which may be attributed to other more important documents taking precedence over it, and to the understandable fatigue of the prelates and *periti* who were tasked with tying-up the many remaining loose ends[237] of the Council's work.

While *Perfectae Caritatis* would issue the license "to make allowance for adequate and prudent experimentation"[238] there was, again like in the Council overall, few specifics, and definitely nothing specifically about the essence of true Christian reform being ordered to an interior conform to the Holy Cross of Christ. But when reform is not ordered specifically toward the Holy Cross it will inevitably go astray as per the influence of the world, the flesh, and the devil. Hence, the Vatican II reforms went astray, unto both the great apostasy of the faithful and, to the issue at hand, the destruction of much of evangelical life.

There was a great need for reform of the evangelical state in the pre-Vatican II Church; the infantilism, elitism, and fear-based perfectionism was unchristian to say the least. There is still a need for such reform in the third millennium; but the need is not with those evangelical communities that embraced the "reforms of Vatican II," for these communities have, for all intents and purposes, ceased to exist, destroyed by those very reforms. Rather, the reform needed is with those conservative communities that remained faithful and with new or renewed faithful evangelical communities. Again, the aim of all true Christian *reform* is to *conform* to the Holy Cross.[239]

For faithful evangelical communities of the third millennium it is not good enough to stay stagnant, much less attempt to go back to a pre-Vatican II ethos. Stagnation is not an option, because stagnation is but conservatism and conservatism cannot withstand the onslaught of the anti-Christic culture, nor an inexorable ecclesial metamorphosis providentially mandated by salvation history. A conservatism, or a pre-Vatican II ethos, cannot adequately address the spiritual needs of today's technarcistic population from whom vowed evangelicals are drawn. Indeed, radicality (or an extreme quantitative degree) in following the Gospel is the specific difference of evangelical life. It is only a radical heeding of the spirit of the law and subsequent reform/conform to Christ Crucified that will suffice for the thriving of evangelical life, and hence Christian life itself, in the third millennium.

THE EVANGELICAL STATE

The evangelical lay state is a more perfect state than the non-evangelical lay state in that its additional vowed obligations are more stringent than the obligations of baptismal vows, as well as of marital vows. But though the requirements of the evangelical vows go beyond the vows of baptism, they themselves derive from baptism. For it is from baptism that the call to holiness derives; and though the vows of baptism do not mandate the obligations of the strictest poverty, chastity, and obedience, they do call the Christian unto the ultimate end of Christian discipleship: *absolute self-abnegation for love of Christ*. As such, the evangelical state is to be seen as a more intentional and intense living out of the baptismal vocation and as a harbinger to the absolute self-abnegation that awaits all who will eventually be saved.

The evangelical state can rightfully be seen as the flowering of the family and of the marital vows, which provide the vowed evangelical's incipient physical and spiritual matrix. Again, the difference between the marital/familial state and the evangelical state is not one of ontological quality but actual quantity. In the evangelical state the marital vows of exclusivity, procreation, and indissolubility blossom into the vows of poverty, chastity, and obedience.

The life of those vowed to the evangelical counsels, then, is not only a flowering of the family, but a magnification of the crucial Christian vocation that is the call to sanctity. Thus, in the evangelical life all that which applies to the lay state is intentionally intensified. This integrated locating of the evangelical state within the corpus of the faithful allows it to be fully effective as a prophetic and vivifying presence within the Church. In that the evangelical life is not qualitatively but only quantitatively different from the baptismal state, its specific vows of poverty, chastity, and obedience must be seen as inherent in all Christian life. The evangelical counsels are all about embracing the Holy Cross with intentional and radical intensity. When seen as inherent in the crucial Christian vocation, the evangelical vows are understood in their essential meaning as the Christian ideals of poverty, chastity, and obedience made binding and taken to their overt quantifiable limits.[240]

Evangelical life is to be spent at the foot of the Cross, as undistractedly as possible from the concerns for the flesh. To be so undistracted requires not only a graceful poverty that entails a certain freedom from financial concerns, but as well, being undistracted by fundraising, recruiting, honors, or flatteries. Of course then, pride and self-love have no place at all in the evangelical state. Again, the evangelical counsels of *poverty*, *chastity*, and *obedience* apply in some degree to all Christians for they are of the moral realm where they overlap into each other in their emanation from the virtue of humility.

In the different stages of life, different counsels are the key to growth in humility, virtue, and sanctity. Obedience, or the curbing of a person's will out of pious love (especially love for one's parents) is the key to the virtue and sanctity of the child. Chastity, or the ordering of a person's passions out of love for the highest goods, is the basis of sanctity for the adolescent and young adult. Poverty, or the sacrificing of a person's innate wants and needs for love of God and others, is the basis of sanctity for the adult. So, if a true loving obedience is instilled in a child he will have the basis for purity as an adolescent, and this chastity will then dispose him well for the poverty of giving his life to Christ, family, and Faith as an adult.

The evangelical state, then, like all specific states, is about the Christian life. That is, ultimately, the evangelical state is not about being a monk or nun, much less about being a Benedictine, Carmelite, Franciscan, *etc.*; nor is it about this or that monastery; rather, it is about, and ordered to, the fulfillment of the baptismal promise. When seen in this context, an evangelical is able to keep his focus on Christ, and is best able to avoid succumbing to any group-thinking or in-group power dynamics, which are incongruous occupational hazards of the evangelical state.

The intentional ordering of evangelical life toward its true baptismal end, and its proper locus within general Christian life, is an example of the dynamics of true reform where the essential ideal is intentionally sought and other defects are rectified. In such a reforming of evangelical life elitism most especially must be excised. Elitism is to the evangelical what clericalism is to the priest. In elitism, an evangelical takes on spiritual, and even oft times material, aristocratic airs: *"Thank God I am not like mere laity; yes, even like my family there in the back of the Church."* This elitism results in a compartmentalization, or tearing asunder, of the integral body of Christ where all Christians are equally and essentially called to the ultimate and supreme baptismal vocation of holiness. But this compartmentalizing and vain elitism is avoided when the evangelical state is properly seen as being on the continuum of the baptismal promise.

THE EVANGELICAL COMMITMENT

In essence, the evangelical vows are a voluntary personal choice to radically fulfill one's baptismal promises. As such, a mature and more perfect understanding of, and commitment to, evangelical life fully realizes that the vows are not to be made to a bishop, superior, or community, but to the person of Jesus Christ. As such, these vows are not ultimately incumbent upon ecclesial authority, for they transcend that authority. However, public vows made in the presence of the Church, that is of the faithful, are subject to the scrutiny of the Church (and thus the formal scrutiny of the Magisterium) as to their propriety. Note well, that while ecclesial authorities can never replace or mitigate a person's informed Catholic conscience in regards to their commitment to Christ—that is, one is always free and justified in the following of Christ—it is nearly always correct, and an important safeguard, to seek dispensations from vows when going to an overtly less intense state of Christian existence.

Evangelical vows, like unto the marital vows, are made to one particular person. This means that the various circumstances of Christian vows are ultimately inconsequential. As is enunciated in the marital vows, the commitment to the particular person withstands all circumstances:

> ". . . for better, for worse, for richer, for poorer, in sickness and health, until death do us part."

For the evangelical, this means that even the particular religious community one enters is inconsequential when it comes to one's commitment to Christ.

But, again, evangelical life has been infected with infantilism, vows were often wrongly seen as being made to the bishop, or to the superior, or to the community. Only Christ himself (and quite obviously neither a bishop nor superior) has a spousal relationship with the evangelical. The truly mature evangelical does not depend at all on ecclesial authorities in his commitment to Christ, but on his own informed Catholic conscience and volitional act of love.

In that a person who makes evangelical vows commits himself to Christ first and foremost, the evangelical must faithfully follow Christ, even if, in the extreme, that means leaving his community, indeed even if it means living this commitment out in obscurity or even ignominy. Yes, such a deep purgation can well be involved in leaving a comfortable, respectable, and secure communal existence. All things being equal, it is always acceptable to go to a formally more austere and contemplative state (*e.g.*, going from an active evangelical community into a contemplative community). But in practice going from a formally more austere state to a less formally austere state (*e.g.*, from evangelical life to marital life) can also entail a more intimate union with Christ Crucified. As is always the touchstone for Christians, this means any change in the circumstances of evangelical life or any vocational state should be a further advancement toward or embrace of Christ Crucified. The dynamics of vocational change should then be the proverbial "going from the frying pan into the fire," that is, going into a more intense and loving purgative experience.

EVANGELICAL POVERTY

With evangelical poverty, as always with Christian values, it is the spirit that is of the essence. The spirit of poverty entails both simplicity and penitence. Simplicity entails an intentionality that seeks the Kingdom of Heaven and gives up legitimate worldly goods.[241] This spirit of simplicity is an ascetical prioritization of values. In this intentionality and prioritization, those in evangelical life are not to be distracted by the things of men and of the world.

Penitence entails not just the turning away from evil but the giving up of valid goods for love of God and others. This penitential spirit is not mandatory but voluntary, with its very voluntariness properly an act of sacrificial love that excludes self-love. No, it is not necessary to vow the evangelical counsels to go to heaven. The true spirit of the evangelical counsels is not motivated by a safe, secure path to heaven, but rather by a love of God that has no self-reference, that is, by a love untainted by self-love.

Evangelical poverty entails not needing to be too concerned with material sustenance: a luxury not afforded to the family. This does not mean that physical poverty is not made manifest in evangelical life, but that all is ordered toward an existence that is not distracted by too much material concern. However, this does not justify the opposite phenomenon where those vowed to evangelical poverty live in nothing less than palatial monasteries. Nor is the spirit of evangelical poverty the spirit of fundraising. When a community of evangelicals spend their energy raising funds rather than raising their own simple sustenance, when they seek a great influx of cash rather than seeking to minimize the need for cash flow, they are far from the spirit of poverty, and are only live action role-playing at being a monk or a nun.

EVANGELICAL CHASTITY

In examining the evangelical counsels on a continuum with and flowering of the basic Christian vocation, evangelical chastity must be a more radical deepening of the spirit of marital chastity. Chaste comes from the Latin castigare, which means "to correct; to purify; chastise, punish." Thus, chastise and castigate have a similar meaning and the same etymology. What is important to note in this etymology of chastity is that its inculcation involves a purifying correction and even punishment; that is, it is penitential.

For a married man, on the natural level, chastity entails the giving of his life for the sustenance and protection of his wife and family:

> In the sweat of thy face shalt thou eat bread till thou return to the earth, out of which thou wast taken: for dust thou art, and into dust thou shalt return. GN 3:19

For a married Christian man on the supernatural level, chastity also entails the giving up of polygamous marriage and a deepening of his sacrificial devotion:

> Husbands, love your wives, as Christ also loved the church and delivered himself up for her: That he might sanctify it, cleansing it by the laver of water in the word of life. EPH 5:25—26

For a married woman on the natural level, the acceptance of chastity entails inherent purgations:

> To the woman also he said: I will multiply thy sorrows, and thy conceptions: in sorrow shalt thou bring forth children, and thou shalt be under thy husband's power, and he shall have dominion over thee. GN 3:16

For a married Christian woman on the supernatural level,

chastity entails the spirit of openness to life and its joys and sorrows, and the spirit of Christian submission:

> Let women be subject to their husbands, as to the Lord: Because the husband is the head of the wife, as Christ is the head of the church. He is the savior of his body. EPH 5:22—23

In keeping with locating the evangelical counsels on a continuum with, and flowering of, the basic Christian vocation, for a man who vows the evangelical counsel of chastity the giving of his life for his family becomes the giving "himself up" directly for Christ and his Church. This evangelical chastity for a man must also deepen the mortification of the body and spirit that would be entailed in providing for and protecting the family by the "sweat of his brow" in a lifestyle that is intentionally, and even severely, penitential.

For a woman in the evangelical state, chastity entails her direct submission to Christ himself and her embrace of the universal sorrows of the Church. Her sorrows must be multiplied mightily as she fulfills her vocation to become a woman of sorrows, whose heart is pierced constantly, as was Our Lady's. This evangelical woman, in her very radical chastity, forgoes any respite from sorrow, forgets not the pangs of a pierced maternal heart, but rather "hath sorrow, because her hour" is now and always at the foot of the Holy Cross.

EVANGELICAL OBEDIENCE

In evangelical life, the rule must always take precedence over the desires of a superior, and the spirit of the law must always take precedence over the rule, that is, the letter of the law. Thus, in evangelical life, as in Christian life, obedience to one's informed Catholic conscience is paramount.

Evangelicals in their vow of obedience should be the freest and most spontaneous of God's faithful, for in everything they do they are called to radically heed the spirit of the law and the impetus of love. For evangelical vowed obedience is based on a loving self-abnegation, in which even the most mundane act is one of decreasing the self so as to increase the Lord within the soul. An evangelical obeys his superiors in the mundane (or amoral) order regardless of the superficial rhyme or reason, and in doing so heeds the deepest and ultimate rhyme and reason of his human existence: that of becoming a soul that magnifies the Lord. Evangelical obedience in the mundane order, then, is based not on blind obedience but quite the opposite: it is based on the highest moral obedience. This highest moral obedience is a result of the highest love, it is the giving up of goods that are lesser so as to decrease one's pride for the increase of Christ.

When evangelical obedience is seen essentially as the loving choice to decrease the pride and self-love so that Christ may increase, the atrociousness of an evangelical obedience done so as to gain the approbation of a superior, or even God, is made clear. In its most insidious form, the evangelical obeys so as to be seen as humble which aggrandizes his ego. This is a dynamic of acquired virtue that may facilitate a functional community life but does not facilitate a good Christian, much less evangelical, life.

When an evangelical performs an act of obedience

motivated by a desire to be approved to the extent it stems from and feeds pride it mocks true evangelical obedience. For an evangelical is called beyond the bare minimum, beyond a calculating and stultifying piety based on servile fear. A person's piety is primarily based on fear if it is based on the fear of losing heaven or gaining the fires of hell; that is, on the approval or disapproval of God; or even more servile yet, the approval or disapproval of one's superiors.

True evangelical obedience is an act of love for God that entails the decreasing of the pride and self-love. Indeed, evangelical obedience is traditionally considered not so much as a placing of oneself under the command of others, but as a giving-up of one's privileges, honors, or commands. Significantly enough, when a false or servile obedience is rendered, due to fear of humiliation, it leads to infantilism, a very significant occupational hazard of the evangelical life. As mentioned before,[242] infantilism, the spirit of servile fear, and the standard of blind obedience had even been raised to an ideal of the Christian state and, more so, the evangelical state. But infantilism, the spirit of servile fear, and blind obedience, are in fact antithetical to evangelical obedience, for they violate the human person in his *imago Dei* nature and, much more so, the Christian in his Christic nature.

This means evangelical obedience never entails the abdication of a person's informed conscience with matters concerning faith and morals. Here the evangelical, as one vowed to the highest Christian ideals, must exhibit the *highest freedom* in his assertion of the absolute Christian's right to do his duty to God. This means, far from being an automaton, the evangelical must always be responsive to the dictates of the Holy Spirit, should always be in touch with informed Catholic conscience, and should always go far beyond the letter of the law, and beyond stultifying servile fear.

Herein lies the paradox of evangelical obedience: because of his indifference to mundane matters and his subjugation of egoistic desires, due to his seeking always to act so as to decrease self and increase Christ, the evangelical is both the most regular in the realm of the superficial and mundane, and the most spontaneous in the realm of the spirit. In the evangelical's very docility he accepts mundane regulations and duties without a second thought, for he is focused on loving God by dying to self. But so too in his docility, the evangelical is responsive to the Holy Spirit, whose ways our not men's ways. When the ego is truly decreasing, all will be well, even if prophetically disruptive or even apparently disobedient.

EVANGELICAL AUTHENTICITY

Evangelical life is meant to accelerate psychomoralitic abnegation and Christic sanctification, to minimize distractions and allow the sacrament of the moment, to remove coping mechanisms and facilitate a full openness to reality. When the trappings of evangelical life, even the Rule and cloister themselves, are used to avoid the abnegation and vicissitudes of existence it becomes a mockery. The Rule is apt to become a pure pharisaism, a letter of the law that betrays the spirit. The cloister walls are apt to form an ivory tower of elitism that insidiously feeds pride. Evangelical life can become a perverse parody that defensively inures the Christian against true humiliation and sorrow, against the very vicissitudes of life; that is, against the Cross itself. Not only is *"man not made for the Sabbath but the Sabbath for man"* (MK 2:27), but neither is the monk or nun made for the cloister nor for the Rule but rather the cloister and the Rule are made for the monk or nun.

While the evangelical life is the life of perfection, it is not specifically the life of perfected acquired virtue. This is because acquired virtue is not a specific, or even mostly, Christian virtue. Indeed, when a person is fixated on seeking perfection, spiritual or otherwise, he is necessarily egoistic. The evangelical life (and essentially the Christian life) is not about perfecting oneself, but of decreasing oneself, so that no longer does one live but Christ lives in the soul. This abnegation of self and corollary *imago Dei* manifestation and Christic indwelling is what authentic human and Christian existence entails. Again, since acquired virtue[243] can be congruent with pride it is susceptible to the occupational hazards inherent in the evangelical state. In addition to an egotistic pharisaism, these hazards include authoritarianism, infantilism, and elitism. But most pointedly, in regards to the pursuit of evangelical perfection, there is the hazard of stoicism. For stoicism may have an appearance of perfection but is only superficially "perfect," and is sorely lacking in receptivity and authenticity.[244]

To a large extent, the standard of stoicism was adopted by many monastic communities due to their embrace of the French school of spirituality, or devotionalism. But stoicism is fundamentally just a disciplined coping mechanism. Stoicism defends against those realities a person cannot do anything about, and so appeals to Christians who might seek to enter the cloister to inure themselves from the earthly realities that are so insistent in the world. But the existence of the cloister is only justified and praiseworthy as a means to enter more deeply into the *overwhelming realities of existence.*

These overwhelming realities of existence are the ultimate realities, and openness to them is essential to entering into the full drama of human and Christian existence, and to the flourishing therein. These ultimate realities are the most devastating: the present reality of the irreversible past, its guilt, failure, and all the loss of the good now gone; and the present reality of the irresistible future, its suffering, death and all the loss of the good now had.

Resigning oneself to things one cannot change is rational, but not being bothered by these things, these ultimate realities, is not. To hold, as is the stoical ideal, that *"If I can't do something about it, it doesn't matter,"* is a coping defense of the ego. This defense is the arrogant, prideful refusal to be overwhelmed. That, for the ancient stoics, meant taking one's life once one can no longer keep up the stoical pretense; for the Christian, as a moral equivalent, it sometimes meant entering the cloister. The solution stoicism proffers is to not be bothered by these deepest and most impacting of realities. Stoicism, as a high-functioning ego coping mechanism that protects the ego from ultimate reality, is something only strong, and apparently virtuous, people can implement. Such stoics are focused on what they can do; they are often high achievers; they excel at acquired virtue.

Conversely, authentic Christian asceticism is not about keeping up a pious and placid persona, but about loving God first and foremost, and not being afraid to be overwhelmed or of letting others see that you are overwhelmed. Authentic Christian asceticism does not aim at trying to appear to be perfect or even aim at being perfect, but rather aims at loving God in constant abnegation of the egoistic self.

Such abnegation will necessarily entail and make manifest the stoically forbidden passions, both those of the ego and those of the psyche. Though they are not to be given primacy, nonetheless, when the egoistic passions are confronted with abnegation, they will manifest themselves. Human, and more so Christian, life is messy. A stoic will not allow his egoistic passions to be made manifest because, paradoxically, it would be humiliating for others to see that one does indeed have pride and self-love, and thus it is better to maintain a stoical and all-so-humble front.

While the egoistic passions must not be catered to in the spiritual and Christian communal life, this does not mean that a stoical and superficial pious persona is to be adopted; quite the contrary, it means the deeper psychic passions, which are always in accord with reason, ought to be most dominant. Therefore, as the prime example, a person, as a contemplative, is called to be an authentic man or woman of sorrows, which is of the psychic passions, but not one of sadness/self-pity, which is of the egoistic passions.

Once pride and self-love are demarcated and properly seen as unacceptable elements of the Christian, much less evangelical, life, then a spirituality (replacing the egoistically-influenced devotionalism) and monastic milieu that promotes authenticity can be implemented. This promotion of authenticity entails the maturation and manifestation of the person in his *imago Dei* individuality and the diminishment and subduing of the ego. So too, the brutalizing and inauthentic parody of seeking to prevent all particular friendships (and again, all friendships are necessarily particular) in the name of preventing egoistic friendships is avoided when such a demarcation between the image of God and the ego is clearly made. Such an understanding of *imago Dei* individualism and authenticity also facilitates the flourishing of the soul-deep (and non-egoistic) passions so that human, and indeed Christian, flourishing can occur.[245]

EVANGELICAL PIETY

The holy virtue of piety is a sub-virtue of religion. Obviously then so-called "religious" life would be expected to strive to embody piety. On the natural level piety is specifically the love and honor of God and parents. The natural virtue of piety is built upon by Holy Spirit's supernatural gift of justice which infuses a deeper pious love, honor, and devotion to Christ and to a person's Christian parents and family. Furthermore, as a special gift of the Holy Spirit, it perfects the virtue of religion, which is the practice of justice toward God. Indeed, a piety infused by the Holy Spirit produces an instinctive filial affection and devotion to God and to a person's parents especially. As per the Catechism of the Catholic Church, filial piety entails the following:

> The divine fatherhood is the source of human fatherhood; this is the foundation of the honor owed to parents. The respect of children, whether minors or adults, for their father and mother is nourished by the natural affection born of the bond uniting them. It is required by God's commandment. (CCC 2214)

Thus it is an impious travesty and a lie to proclaim that one loves and honors Christ but fails to love and honor one's parents. Scandalously, self-proclaimed "religious life" has traditionally gone against the virtue of religion and its sub-virtue of piety by not only allowing such impiety to grow within its ranks but to institutionalize it. Under the auspices of detachment, the vice of turning away from one's parents and family-of-origin was, and is, promoted and practiced as a very virtue of evangelical life.

The evangelical counsels are located on a continuum with the basic natural and Christian vocations. Thus those in evangelical vows do not give up family per se, but marriage.

Even in the strictest cloister there is no justification for any diminishment, much less scorning, of familial piety and intimacy. Quite the opposite, for just as in accord with Catholic sensibilities a person grows closer to a departed loved one, so too should a person grow closer to a family member departed to the cloister. However, as a part of the compartmentalization that occurred in Christendom I, the compartmentalization of evangelical life led to the discounting, and even disdaining, of familial piety, and so violated both natural and divine law. No, it is not virtuous to discount parental authority, ties, or influence just because one is entering the evangelical state (or the marital or clerical state). Our Lord showed the way:

> "Why were you looking for Me?" He asked. "Did you not know that I had to be in My Father's house?" But they did not understand the statement he was making to them. Then he went down to Nazareth with them and was subject to them. LK 2:49—51

In fact, Christ not only would delayed his ministry but would later hastened his very "hour" as well as per his Mother's desires at Cana.

Nor did the Lord Jesus Christ isolate himself from his family and closest friends during his "hour" and passion. Those most personally intimate with Christ were with him,

> Now there stood by the cross of Jesus, his mother, and his mother's sister, Mary of Cleophas, and Mary Magdalen. JN 19.25[246]

Likewise, those in the evangelical state are meant to be most intimately united to their families in their own and their family's holy passions. It is truly this intimacy between evangelicals and their families that is the most obvious and direct means to vivify the Church at large.

The vow of chastity is grossly perverted when it is used as a justification for the violation of familial piety and that piety's requisite intimacy. Such a perversion found its way into evangelical rules where a person in the cloister was forbidden to even embrace his parents, grandparents, and siblings. Not only are such strictures inhuman but inconsistent. Whereas at one time it was considered a form of mortification (though extreme and imprudent) to completely forgo the converse and embrace of other people (as was the case with the enclosure of anchorites[247]), it is grossly disingenuous for cloistered sisters or brothers to be allowed to embrace only their fellow evangelicals and not their own parents. There is no justification, scripturally or otherwise for only bishops or priests to be allowed to be in the direct, or non-grated, presence of cloistered evangelicals.

In the very self-same passage that has often been associated with the call to the evangelical state (cf. MK 10), Christ challenges the rich young man to embrace holy poverty, he rebukes his disciples for preventing the little children from coming to him, and he reiterates the necessity of honoring one's parents. The most basic hermeneutical reading of Scripture requires that it be read in contextual integrity and thus this passage as per the Lord Jesus Christ's very words inseparably unites the evangelical counsels with familial intimacy and bonds and the giving of the honor owed to one's parents. But part and parcel of Counter-Reformational compartmentalization, the cloistered life (and those conservative and traditional orders that still seek to implement that life) contrary to Christ's words promoted the severing of familial intimacy and bonds, and the mitigation of the honor due to parents.

Historically, the Middle Ages saw a magisterial usurping of the lay Catholic secular authority, which was an overreaction to the need to mitigate the authority of secular rulers in regards to their dominance of the Magisterial aspects of the Church. With this usurping of lay Catholic secular authority came necessarily the undermining of familial authority as well, for familial authority is the essence of any just and legitimate secular authority. And just as there was an overreaction that not only allowed the Holy

See freedom from secular coercion but actually eviscerated and usurped Catholic secular power, so too if there was a need to mitigate the absolute authority of *pater familias*[248] it resulted in a vicious overreaction that degraded the family and parental authority and transgressed the Fourth Commandment.[249]

The archaic evangelical rules of familial alienation manifests an unseemly mistrust of an evangelical's (or priest's) lay family members. In further confounding of authentic Christian and evangelical values, such familial alienation rules also facilitate the creation of stoical defenses against the pain—indeed the excruciating poverty —of the physical and daily separation from family entailed in the evangelical state.

Instead of a mistrust of parents and family, piety –on the natural, Christian, and most especially evangelical level —demands an intimacy with and honoring of them above all other personages. For the authentic evangelical life entails not a stoical inuring from pain but, quite the contrary, an intentional piercing of the heart that facilitates a closer, most intimate, and synergistic union of the evangelical with his parents and family in Christ Crucified.[250]

ORDAINED MINISTRY

After Holy Baptism,[251] the Church's greatest power is sacramental absolution, and her sweetest gift is the Holy Eucharist. As such, the Church's most specific, and thus quintessential, ministry is that of her priesthood that uniquely imparts that absolution and confects that Eucharist. The priestly ministry exists to offer sacrifice unto God and succor the faithful with the sacraments. In this third millennium's post-Christian days, priests are chaplains whose efforts, and even heroics, are no longer specifically employed on the front-lines of missionary fields but rather in ministrations to the embattled faithful, who themselves are now on the front-lines, and who themselves are now the primary witnesses to the Holy Faith. Like medics on the battlefield who win medals of heroism (indeed Catholic *padres* have always excelled in battlefield heroism[252]) it is not priests that fight the battles but they who before the battle shrive and nourish the faithful and they who after the battle tend to the wounded and anoint the fallen. But even this great gift of the priesthood—this quintessential ministry with its charism of Holy Mass, Eucharist, and Sacramental Absolution—is not to be seen as the essence of the Church but rather as a direct manifestation of the Church's essence, which is Christ Crucified.

The crucial functions of the priesthood entail the confecting of the Eucharist and the administering of the sacrament of confession. Following on this, but still secondary because not unique to the competency of those in Holy Orders, are the spiritual and corporal works of mercy,[253] including the preaching of the Gospel. These works of mercy are especially fitting to the priesthood because of the priestly ideal of universal fatherhood, as facilitated by priestly celibacy and the relative freedom from familial obligations that it entails, that obligates and allows a priest to aid the community of faithful as needed.

Ordination Entails Formal Subordination

The foundational Christian state of baptism entails the ontological remittal of original and actual sin. This ontological decreasing of the pride, and/or its effects, is essential to all Christians in their spiritual transformation. In the evangelical vows of poverty, chastity, and obedience there is intentional, accelerated, and an all-inclusive self-abnegation that is the end of all Christians.

Unique to the ordained state there is the formal ontological subordination of the man unto the office of Christ's priesthood. But unlike the sacramental baptismal state, and more so the intentional evangelical state, due to the fact that priestly ordination is a formal imposition of a power not intrinsic to the man, this does not in itself impose a practical self-abnegation. In fact, priestly ordination can often, if the man is not properly ordered to it, lead to self-aggrandizement.

Because of this formal but not practical subordination that is entailed in priestly ordination, it is of paramount importance that the man intentionally subsume his entire self under the office. Because the priesthood of Christ derives not one *iota* of its efficacy from the man, the intentional subsuming of the man under the office of the priesthood is in keeping with the formally subsuming of a priest's entire being, his personality and talents, under the person of Jesus Christ. This subordination of the man is why celibacy is proper for the priest.[254] Precisely stated, because ordination formally entails an ontological subordination to the priesthood of Jesus Christ it properly calls for the practical subordination of the priest's person.

Thus, the proper elevation of the priesthood, as a unique

presence among men, is simultaneously the proper humbling of the man in his person. Let not the man who is a priest obfuscate Jesus Christ. Rather, let him rest in his nothingness as an instrument through which Christ works; let him not be seen in his person but in his office. Undoubtedly, when the priest exercises his primary charisms, at the confection of the Eucharist and the absolving from sins, he is effectively and operationally not his own person at all but the person of Christ.[255] As a spouse of the Church, who herself is the submissive bride of Christ, the priest must not allow his *self*, even his talents, to obfuscate Christ.

The priest is chosen from among men to give up even that which is rightfully his as both a man and a Christian. As such, the priest is properly called to give up not only a wife and family, but renown as well. Though not vowed to a physical poverty, the priest is called to accept a deeper poverty, the poverty of person. The ordained must in fact give up their identity, for a priest is not his own. His own opinion does not matter, his own person does not matter, his own interests do not matter. He exists simply to offer sacrifice to God and for the faithful. *No one exists for him.* Aptly as another Christ, this is indeed similar to Our Lord's own *kenosis*, or emptying of self, when he became incarnate as both priest and victim.

Ordination to the priesthood, then, entails subordination of the person. The charism of priesthood, its gifts and powers, derives directly from this subordination of the man unto the person of Christ. This is the very purgative crux of the matter in the vocation of priesthood: a subordination of person, of a man's personal gifts and talents, a very sacrificial offering of self, so that the high priest Jesus Christ is made manifest, in persona, unobscured by the person of the man. Clericalism is therefore an insubordination.

This subordination of self unto office is true too, and even more so in the fullness of the priesthood, for bishops or the pope. The bishop's third millennium charism is primarily to work behind the scenes with his priests. Indeed the bishop is not the super-priest of his diocese whose pastoral and oratorical, and ministerial skills are valued as paramount for the thriving of Christian life. Rather, the bishop may even tend to remain rather aloof pastorally from the faithful as he fulfills his duty to be the "servant of the servants of God" who are his priests. But, as such, a bishop in his relatively behind-the-scenes ministry must be careful to eschew any trappings of royal sequestering or privilege. What applies to bishops applies even more so with the Pope, whose third millennium charism is primarily to work quietly with these bishops, and not, as it were, to become an object of sightseeing, or even an object of pilgrimage, and much less an object of a personality cult.

HOLY PRIESTHOOD

Again, the charism of the priesthood is offering the Holy Sacrifice of the Mass and dispensing Sacramental Absolution. Secondarily, it is preaching and teaching. But so too, the charism of the priesthood is the priesthood itself. The mere presence of a priest, even if he is not bringing Christ's Eucharistic physical presence, is in and of itself a blessing, for his[H7] being the presence of the High Priest Jesus Christ. This indeed makes the priest a unique being among men. But at the same time, it makes the man who is a priest, his accomplishments and talents, unimportant. It takes no superlative personal ability to fulfill the most specific duties of priesthood, for confecting the Eucharist and sacramental absolution depends little on the man.

The man who is a priest bears within himself the priesthood of Jesus Christ. His mere presence can suffice to ward off the onslaughts of hell. His mere words can bring Christ down to the altar or bring forgiveness to the sinner. Thus, he must not obscure or impede Christ within him by promoting himself in any way, shape, or form. He must, always and everywhere, not only order his pride and self-love but intentionally subordinate always to the priesthood. Whatever excellence a priest may have in his person must be of no concern to him, much less must he be concerned with its display. Yes, the priest is called to be the most self-abnegated of men. His is not the bodily penance of the penitent, nor the poverty of the evangelical, nor the vicissitudes of the familial, but rather the diminishment of the man, and not just the vicious man, but the virtuous and talented man as well. He, like no other, must heed St. John the Baptist's example and *"decrease so that [Christ] may increase."*

The need to distinguish between the ordained office and

the man is crucial so that the man does not appropriate, misuse, or abuse the office. The man who is a priest can only fully realize this distinction by being inculcated in a deep humility. Again, while chastity, poverty, and obedience as evangelical counsels are appropriate to the ordained, it is humility that is crucial. But since humility cannot be the subject of a vow, it must be enshrined as the ideal.

This is why the ancient rite of the Mass imposes upon the celebrant, especially, a humility from beginning to end. So too, the traditional rubrics that call for a priest to face *ad orientem* is primarily correct in its subsuming of the man unto the office, i.e., its obscuring of the man. Such a subsuming and obscuring is also facilitated in anonymous confession. However, the reforms of Vatican II only tended to highlight the man who was priest, rather than emphasize his subordination.

As per the Lord Jesus Christ's own preference, the best men for the priesthood are the "salt of the earth." Christ even warned his first priests about losing the savor thereof:

> You are the salt of the earth. But if the salt lose its savor, wherewith shall it be salted? It is good for nothing any more but to be cast out, and to be trodden on by men. MT 5:13—16

These first priests were indeed the most down-to-earth of all men: they were taken from the ranks of common fishermen, not from the elite ranks of scribes and Pharisees. A per Christ's vocational direction, the simple and solid, not the flashy and erudite, make the best priests. Indeed, the very patron saint of priests is the most common, and even less than common, Saint John Marie Vianney. All of this goes contrary to the "rock star" image of priests that many, especially conservative, vocational programs seek to promote. But unlike Protestants who idolize the man or the preacher, Catholics are not respecters of men. In Catholic theology a man is called to priesthood not because of his talent but simply *because.*

XVI. New Christendom

*I have come to cast fire upon the earth;
and how I wish it were already ablaze!*
LK 12:49

Utterly **irredeemable** are the apostate Western cultures of an erstwhile Christendom. The World Wars were the convulsing death-throes of Christendom I, and what would result from this drawn-out agony was not a mere post-Christian culture, but an anti-Christic one. This was because no person or society, and especially those whose cultural and familial lineage is Catholic, can ever remain merely indifferent to the Gospel. Hence, the new West is apostate, hatefully rejecting the Gospel, the Church, and even God-given natural law. Indeed, the new West has as its very specific difference, as its very spiritual core, this hateful rejection of Christ.

The new apostate West has built up antibodies against the Gospel, has grown hostile toward the Church, and has rebelled against reality itself. Unlike cultures of ancient paganism that were steeped in familial piety and natural law, and thus well poised to receive the Gospel, the new apostate culture of the West fosters the sacrilege of impiety, and promotes all sundry abominations against both rejected revealed law and natural law. As such, the new Western culture—as well as the vast majority of cultures under its world-wide influence—is a spiritually demolished dystopia, an uninhabitable, toxic moral wasteland, virulently anti-Christic and utterly irredeemable.

Nevertheless, a new grassroots Christendom can sprout

up amidst the ruins of the dystopic macro-culture of the third millennium, but only if Christians fully realize this culture's toxicity and irredeemability. For then Christians—no longer breathing the putrid and mind-fogging airs of immorality, no longer being subsumed into and enslaved by the diseased body politic, no longer engaging in the soul-deadening anti-Christic culture—can begin to effectively cultivate a new Christendom amidst the very reality of the West's ruins. In light of the third millennium macro-culture and ensconced power structure being, unlike the ancient pagan West, utterly irredeemable, the advent of a third millennium Christendom will be much different from that of Christendom I.

In the third millennium, no longer will the strength, indeed indefectibility, of the Holy Faith be made manifest in institutional might and wealth, in papal pomp and circumstance, in the pretenses of prelates, princes, and priests, or even in worldly artistic and scientific accomplishments. At this point in history, the Church has too much institutional baggage, too much scandalous wreckage, to expect to impress, and subsequently convert, the common man with her accidentals of dominance and success. Nor does the Church any longer have the luxury to play the worldly games of the now incorrigibly corrupt powers-that-be. Rather, the Church is to be reduced down, as in distilled and purified, to her crucial essence, and this essence is clearly not of this world.

The advent of a third millennium Christendom is not about raising up big beautiful cathedrals but about raising up big beautiful families. Christendom II will be unlike the now collapsed Christendom I, where Catholic cities and towns were demarcated by their largest and most opulent buildings being ecclesial structures. In Christendom I, a people's piety was measured by the size and wealth of their churches, chancelleries, monasteries, etc. Yes, even nuns and monks who took the vows of poverty contrarily lived in veritable palaces. But far more glorious than the most magnificent

Gothic cathedral is the humblest Catholic family in their faithfulness to one another, to Christ, and to the Holy Church. And in this third millennium these Christian families will sprout up amidst the ruins, flowering amongst the weeds, to eventually create an enduring Christendom; a Christendom that cannot be stomped out or toppled because rooted in each and every family and the hearts therein in which Christ reigns.

SOCIOPOLITICAL LAY COMPETENCY

Neither the rule over the erstwhile Christendom nor the establishment of a new Christendom is the competency of popes, prelates, or priests. In the case of Christendom I, even thought it was established by lay Catholic leaders (the most notable being Pepin the Short and Charlemagne) this lay leadership was eventually usurped by ecclesial authorities which led to the weakening and eventual demise of that Christendom. In the case of a new Christendom, efforts that are conceived, led, or spearheaded by the modern magisterium have only resulted in stillborn failure (*e.g.*, the Catholic Action Movement) and will continue to fail in the future. In fact, due to the authoritarian and usurping nature of magisterial "programs," or even clericalistic parish programs, the Holy Spirit's work with the lay faithful—with Catholic families and mothers and fathers—to bring about the intended grassroots Christendom is actually impeded.

Ever since the Christian conversion of pagan peoples—from the Romans unto the Germans—there has been a need to reign in the excessive personal and sociopolitical power and privilege of patriarchs and princes. This was necessary even after formal conversion, for personal practices such as polygamy (the flagship manifestation of pagan patriarchal power and privilege) could only be slowly curtailed. Popes and prelates were also rightly concerned not only with the abuse of personal power but also about a political power that, if given free-reign, would dominate the Magisterium itself.

So there was a real need in the second millennium to mitigate both a secular patriarchal immorality of brute dominance and a secular Caesaropapism that would dominant the Church. However instead of stopping at a rectification of the excesses the magisterium itself began to employ a brute dominance over, and usurpation of, the lay sociopolitical competency. As the magisterium continued to eviscerate the authority of Catholic princes, and itself usurp lay sociopolitical rule, the Christendom that was extended due to these princes became as a result increasingly weakened. Even more grievously, where pagan patriarchal and familial authority (which was based on natural law even if at times it transgressed that law) should have been truly Christianized (as grace builds upon nature) it was instead eviscerated unto the point where Catholic manhood was emasculated and the family reduced to a subordinate sociopolitical and ecclesial status. This magisterial usurpation—be it by popes, prelates, or priests— of proper lay competency and authority eventually resulted in the complete loss of Christendom and continues unto the third millennium to grievously harm Holy Mother Church, impede her mission, emasculate her militancy, and forestall the advent of a new Christendom.

Christendom is, by definition, a sociopolitical fruition of the Holy Faith, and thus properly a competency of the lay faithful. Popes, prelates, and priests are of a kingdom not of that sociopolitical world. Rather their *raison d'etre* is to minister unto the lay faithful, who themselves have the competency and sacred duty to establish Christendom. The establishment of a sociopolitical Christendom is the lay faithful's sacred vocation and duty because the family is the very cell of any God-ordained, be it natural and/or supernatural, sociopolitical entity. The Church of the third-millennium world will only impact that world through the thriving of her lay faithful, of their families and their endeavors, for it is rightly the lay faithful's charism to be the Christian leaven within the world.

The Church, in her purely priestly and Magisterial state, is called to give up, in an ecclesial kenosis,[256] that which could even be rightfully hers as a sociopolitical or worldly entity. Why is it so hard to understand the Lord Jesus Christ's most clear and emphatic chastisement of a worldly papacy?

> Get behind Me, Satan! You are a stumbling block to Me. For you do not have in mind the things of God, but the things of men. MT 16:23

Why is it so hard to understand that the apostles, and as such all priests, prelates, and popes, are not to be *"like the princes of the Gentiles"* in a lording over exercise of power. Why is it so hard to accept the solemn words of Christ as he faced execution: *"My kingdom is not of this world."* The social reign of Christ the King, when wrongly seen as the reign of ecclesial authorities, has been tried repeatedly and, inevitably, repeatedly failed.

The danger is not in the Church misusing her spiritual power and purpose, but the danger is of men misusing the Church for their own power and purposes. But this does not mean that Catholics are not to be impactive, even militantly so, of the sociopolitical realm, but rather that the sociopolitical realm is a lay competency and their sacred duty. For, unlike the Magisterium whose competency is *"not of the world,"* the lay faithful are of the world, but nonetheless they are called to transcend that world. But such a transcendence necessarily entails a militant defense of Faith and family against the world's waging of hostilities.

The lay faithful, then, are duty-bound, both by natural and sacred law, to defend and promote natural and divine law in the public secular sphere, so as to secure a secular order propitious for the Faith and their families. Yes, in this anti-Christic day and age there must be a pronounced demarcation between Church and State, but as such there must be an even more pronounced militancy in Catholics as they undertake their sociopolitical duties. It is the lay faithful, and specifically the family man, that is fully tasked with this sociopolitical duty, which is the advancement of a new Christendom; albeit that Christendom incipiently underground and antithetically countercultural for the foreseeable future.

Due to the anti-Christic milieu of the third millennium, a new Christendom can take root only in its most authentic form, that is, within the cloistered lay realm of the family. The God-ordained head of the family is the father. As such, if a father is only concerned with taking care of his family domestically he is not taking care of his family adequately. For Christian manhood, led by familial fathers, has the sacred duty to fight the encroachment of the profane and ungodly. It is to the exact extent and degree that Christian fathers rise up, that will determine the advent of a new Christendom in the third millennium. If this patriarchal duty is shirked there is absolutely *zero* possibility of an authentic sociopolitical manifestation of the Faith, and the faithful's future will be tenuous indeed.

CHRISTIAN SOCIOPOLITICS

Any sociopolitical movement or agenda can be deemed righteous or vicious in so far as it facilitates or harms the traditional family. Thus, the sociopolitical vocation derives from the familial vocation. It is the family, according to nature, that is the basic cell of the body politic. All true Christian sociopolitical activism is then ordered to the betterment of the family. That is, Christian activism is not to be ordered toward the empowerment of the State, be it monarchic, capitalistic, socialistic, *etc.*, but rather toward the health of the family and empowerment of its authority and sacrosanct status.

As per nature and grace, the family is the essential building block of the bodies politic and ecclesiastic. As per both nature and grace, the patriarchal order—that is, a father's headship devoted to the flourishing of the feminine and familial[257]—is the most proper structure of the family. Therefore, the highest Christian political activism would promote both this patriarchal order and the sacrosanct status of the family, whose *sine qua non* heart is indeed feminine and maternal.

Christian sociopolitical activism, then, is not about restoring the royal Western monarchies, but about reinforcing the monarchy of the family; it is not about the divine right of royal families, but rather about the divine right of the patriarchal family. Nor is Christian sociopolitical activism about a reactionary socialistic "preference for the poor," for all here below are essentially poor; but rather about a God-ordained preference for the family, for all here below have families. Nor is Christian sociopolitical activism about the jingoistic group-think of nationalism that obfuscates the regions and communities of diverse and unique ethnicities and families; but rather about deeming a nation good when it facilities autonomous communities.

True Christian sociopolitics does not ascribe to the fascist unity of race and nation, but rather to the indissoluble marital unity of man and wife, and thus, family. Nor does true Christian sociopolitics ascribe to socialism's forced collectivism, but rather to the sacrificial collection of familial love. Rejecting both the *ancien régime* and other conservative regimes as well as the liberal reaction to those regimes (as seen in liberation theology), true Christian sociopolitics promotes the family as both the only God-ordained monarchy and the only God-ordained sociopolitical base community.[258]

As much as Christian sociopolitics calls for a relocation of the locus of authority from the State to the family and the individual, it is just as much against any class conflict or identity politics. For Christians there is only the classless conflict against the world, the flesh, and the devil. Nor is there the need to *identify* with anything save Faith and family, which entails *adherence* to natural and divine law. Both the family and the Church are meant to be without politics, for in the family and Church it is not a question of taking power or gaining rights but about assuming responsibility, about doing one's Christian duty, and about loving service without counting the cost. In the Christian realm it is properly never about politics but about harmony; a harmony that is not necessarily a unity of opinions but of wills; that is, it is always about the self-abnegating embrace of the Cross in doing the holy will of God.

Patriotic Piety *Contra* Nationalism

In the third millennium the erstwhile Christian nations no longer have the meaning they once did, for they have apostatized, are devoid of God, and thus illegitimate. Nostalgic ethnic sentiments and cultural reenactments do not change the fact that Western countries, and most especially those that formed the bulwark of Christendom I (such as France, Ireland, Italy, Spain, and even the late-coming Catholicism in North America) have not merely reverted to heathenism but are essentially and virulently anti-Christic; having betrayed, rejected, and are now waging war against Christ and his people. It is now a time where Christian patriotism can no longer be properly equated with nationalism but rather only with true piety. This true patriotic piety derives from the inseparable love of, and wholehearted allegiance to, Faith and family.

Due to hostile new sociopolitical paradigms, the third millennium is a time as well of new beginnings, it is a time of the clan and the small-faith community of families, and it a time when a new Christendom will be built (to the extent that it is built) solely on Christ. If any new Christian sociopolitical entities, even new countries, are to arise, they must arise anew and outside and beyond the demarcations of the past; outside and transcendent of the current sociopolitical powers-that-be; outside and in contradistinction to the world, the flesh, and the devil. It is now the time for a new Christian culture that is comprised of pastoral, that is grassroots, shoots that have made their way up among the ruins of an anti-Christic, dystopic world. It is now, in this the third Christian age, that the faithful are called to grow up and out of the childhood of ages past; to rise up fully mature, no longer holding onto props of the world, of powers and principalities, but only onto the Holy Cross.

Today, pious Christian women are called back to the holy home so as to be its *sine qua non* heart, no longer squandering their precious and irreplaceable gifts on profane entities or selling their services to the secular. Today, pious Christian men are called not to live and die for an ill-defined "God and country," but for the Holy Faith and the family, that is, for Christian women and their children. Yes, today's call to pious patriotism is ordered to a specific and living Faith and a specific and living family.

Christian piety and devotion must no longer be squandered on a supposed but baseless duty to a king, flag, or country. No longer can a romanticizing of a country's past Christian heritage evoke allegiance to that now anti-Christic country. No longer can a Christian justify a particular nationalism against a larger internationalism, for internationalism is but nationalism writ large. Rather, in the third-millennium, Christian piety, patriotism, loyalty, and devotion must be given to that which a person *can truly know and so can truly love;* and it is the Faith made tangible in the family and the community of families that one can truly know and love. It is neither countries, nor royal lineages, nor constitutions that God has immutably ordained, but rather it is the Holy Faith in grace and the sacrosanct family in both nature and grace that is God-ordained.

Catholics must not give their hearts to a State. They are called to be patriots only in so far as they are pious. A Catholic's allegiance should be both familial and universal, not national and political. For familial allegiance is grass-rooted, as charity begins in the home; and universal allegiance is just, as all men are created in God's holy image (and indeed all men have families as well). But when a people's allegiance is national and political, the flower of their own nation's familial foundation is inexorably conscripted and trampled, while the families of opposing politics or nations are inexorably incarcerated and exterminated.

Yes, Aristotle was wrong. The Greco-Roman model and political philosophy imbued the State with a sacred, albeit pagan, nature, and held it to be the only perfect society. In the erstwhile Christian era, this theory was subsequently "baptized" by adding the Church, even in her accidental and improper magisterial political power, as the only other perfect society. This modified/baptized Greco-Roman model entails the State and the Church having God-ordained authority over the people, and the Church having authority over the State. The family was said to lack self-sufficiency and so was held to be an imperfect society. As such the individuals which make up the imperfect family were tasked to depend upon and thus obey the perfect conglomerate of State and Church.

This widely adopted sociopolitical model is another example (the other herein being an acquired virtue-based morality[259]) of "Saint" Aristotle's undue influence. Indeed, the error of the Greco-Roman and subsequently Christianized sociopolitical conceptualization is personified in Aristotle's consummate hero, Socrates. For, though Socrates taught in theory that the heeding of truth is the greatest good, he lacked the courage to assert his right to do his duty to God and truth. Rather, Socrates commits the grave and cowardly sin of suicide because he could not bear the thought of being exiled from the totalitarian body politic. Such cowardliness can be attributed in part to the perverse pagan belief, which was present in both Greek and Roman society, that the State was divine. But not so in Judaic or Christian culture. Or at least not so until the Jews, murmuring against God's will, sought to have a king like the pagans did; or at least not so until the Pope, amidst the intrigues and alliances of the magisterium with princes, sought to proclaim himself king.

In truth, there are no perfect material societies here below, for matter is necessarily limiting in this fallen world. So contrary to pagan theory, lack of self-sufficiency does not belie the superiority of the family, for all here below is insufficient. In fact, the family's very insufficiency is why all other sociopolitical entities exist: they exist to fulfill the family's needs. Hence, it is the family, and not the State, that is the reason for being and end of society: that is, the family is the superior society for which all other sociopolitical societies are ordered. As such, it is the community of families, writ small or large, that is the most proper sociopolitical entity.

Providentially enough, it is the family's nemesis of

technology—a technology that can intrude itself upon the intimacy and in-the-moment interaction of the family--that is also the family's boon. For technology allows a familial self-sufficiency that was in the past only possible for families of large estates. With multiplying technology (from tractors to sewing machines to computers), as well as instant accessibility, communication, and commerce (from online shopping, to online business, to online homeschooling and libraries) the family has the additional means to do for itself without ever leaving the comforts and cloister of the home. This new self-sufficiency only emphasizes the need all the more for women to be exclusively dedicated to the home and in possession of doctoral level competencies to manage the complexities[260] of contemporary home economics. So too, this new self-sufficiency makes possible an entrepreneurship that allows men to rightly distance themselves from the status quo large corporations, for these corporations are just as satanic as their governmental partners in crime.

DIVINE RIGHTS, SACRED DUTIES, & SUBSIDIARITY

From home-grown produce, home-schooling, and cottage industries to Catholic corporations, neighborhood militias, and patriarchal governing, the family and the extended community of families can in the technologically enhanced third millennium achieve a degree of self-sufficiency, independence, and perfection that was never before possible. But this will only be actualized if responsibility is assumed by fathers as the God-ordained leaders of natural and Christian society; it will only come to fruition if mothers are enthroned as the God-ordained center and heart of natural and Christian existence; and it will only thrive if individual Christians uncompromisingly heed their God-ordained conscience informed by natural and revealed truths.

The principles of Christian sociopolitics—be these the governing principle of Christian patriarchal authority or the animating principle of devotion to Faith and family—are based themselves upon the even more basic principles of imago Dei individualism, which derives from the Psychomoral and Baptismal Vocations and the conscience informed by natural and divine laws. In fact, the principles of Christian sociopolitics, especially its governing principles of patriarchy, are properly ordered (in addition to the feminine and familial) to the facilitation of imago Dei individualism and the rightly informed conscience. These key imago Dei principles of responsibilities and rights, of duties and authority, are themselves related to the moral principle of *subsidiarity*.[261]

Subsidiarity holds that all matters of governing ought to be handled by the most basic and least centralized competent authority. The principle of subsidiarity is an immutable moral principle since it derives directly from the natural fact that man is made in the image of God. Man being made in the image of God means he is a creature who is rational and volitional, and thus is radically free and responsible. This rationality, volition, freedom, and responsibility is the essence of human personhood, and is intrinsic to the doctrine of the creation of man and his redemption. Being made in the image of God, it is the individual who is the essential moral actor, it is the individual who chooses good or evil, it is the individual who is ultimately responsible, and it is the individual who, by his own choice, is saved or damned. Thus, the principle of subsidiarity, as well as the principle of informed Catholic conscience, are of the most foundational principles of an adequate anthropology.

Authentic subsidiarity must derive from the authority of God himself, that is it is neither of the egoistic whims of the individual, nor any chauvinisms of family or ethnicity, not any in-group power-curves, and definitely not from the supposed largess of the State. Inexactly, individualism is often used to claim rights as per the dignity of the human person, but the only right the human person has is to do his duty to God, and the dignity of the human person is in his being in God's image.

Authentic individualism and its ensuing subsidiarity must be based on the understanding that human authority and rights derive from God, not the individual separate from him. So too, then, the family is not an end in itself but the primary and most effective means for facilitating true individualism. For it is the family that is foundational, and most intimate and responsive to the unique person as he goes through the stages of human development.

The family is sacrosanct in its subsidiary authority because it is in the family especially (but with true friends and mentors as well), that the drama of the individual delicately unfolds, and it is in the family that true love, understanding, and hence, formation, superlatively take place. So too, the family, like the individual, images the Triune God in its trinitarian man, wife, and child components and oneness.

Nor do rights derive from the State, but rather the State's rights, its very validity, derives solely from its facilitation of an authentic *imago Dei* individualism and the family. But in the third millennium, and at any time that despots reign, to champion subsidiarity, imago Dei individualism, and the sacrosanct family will be violently opposed by the State. It remains then up to the family, that is, the sociopolitcally structured patriarchal family, that is, the Christian patriarchal family, to champion imago Dei individuality and hence the authority of God himself.

The family in its primary God-given authority is the very last bastion against the enslavement of the *imago Dei* individual by a technologically enhanced, and hence tyrannically crazed, total State. In further accordance with subsidiarity, upholding the *divine right* of the family, and the *imago Dei* individualism it cultivates, is specifically the sacred duty of that family's patriarchal leaders. These Christian patriarchs, even though opposed not only by the State but by bureaucratic authorities in the institutional Church itself, must courageously exercise their absolute right to fulfill their duty and responsibilities to the sacrosanct family and the precious individuals, the mothers and children, that comprise it.

FUNDAMENTAL
RELIGIOUS LIBERTY

It is the Christian *qua* Christian, and not the Christian *qua* Pope that transcends the State. It is the Christian family essentially and not necessarily the Vatican that transcends the State. For specifically, it is the individual Christian via his natural and divine law informed conscience that has the absolute right to fulfill militantly his duty to God.

The right to transcend militantly the State in the fulfillment of a person's duty to God is the Catholic understanding of religious freedom. The Magisterium of the Church at one time rightly used the transcendent aspect of militancy to rebuff secular encroachment upon the divine governance of the Church. But the Church's corporate transcendence of the State as it was framed in the past is no longer the issue. The Magisterium has asserted its right and fulfilled its duty and charism to freely proclaim dogma and that dogma is unequivocal and immutable.

Today, practically and essentially, the issue of "the freedom and exaltation of Holy Mother Church"[262] is not about popes versus kings but of right versus might; of speaking truth to power; of the good being promulgated no matter the evil resisting. Succinctly, the issue of religious freedom is about the individual Christian person exercising his absolute right to do his duty to God.

Defending in either politics or warfare the sacrosanct family, *imago Dei* individualism, or religious liberty is not, then, a prerogative *per se* of the Papacy or Magisterium, but of the human person, and more so the Christian and his informed conscience. Prototypically enough, St. Peter, not to mention Our Lord Jesus Christ himself, in a *priestly kenosis* gave up what was rightfully his, as a man and as a Christian; that is, St. Peter (as well as the vast majority of popes that immediately followed him) did not exercise his inherent human and Christian prerogative but was killed by the State. However, for a Christian father, the lay leader of the family and hence Christendom, to forgo this prerogative and to go down without a fight would be a shirking of his God-given duty to provide for and protect his family.

It was the laity that bequeathed temporal sovereignty to (and subsequently had it usurped by) the papacy. And if the laity giveth, it may taketh away. When the sociopolitical power of the papacy collapsed and Pius IX was, as he characterized it, "a prisoner in the Vatican," he was certainly dismayed that the laity did not come to his aid when he called for it. But it should have been expected that there would be no popular grassroots uprising in the now exceedingly top-heavy, and in many ways top down imposed, Christendom I.[263] But that which the Lord giveth the gates of hell shall not prevail against, and that which the Lord surely giveth is the primacy of *imago Dei* individualism, the informed Catholic conscience, and the family.

While it was certainly unseemly for popes in their priestly person to claim a political status above all governmental jurisdiction, indeed to be in charge of all political jurisdictions,[264] it is right to claim this for the Church, that is all the faithful, including popes. Catholics necessarily remain both *a leaven* and *a cancer in the body politic*, depending on if the perspective is from the side of the holy angels or not.

Though it was surely providential that the papacy was free from Caesaropapist control and the coercion of the State during the Church's tender and volatile years of dogmatic formulation, this freedom is now rightly and properly located within the Christian person. In this third millennium, God again providentially actualizes these natural and divine rights in the Christian person, and the families and communities he comprises, so as to thwart the technologically enhanced oppression of the Satanic State and its corollary perverse popular culture.

Vatican II's *Dignitatis Humane* and not Boniface VII's *Unam Sanctam* is more Catholic. Religious liberty as espoused in Vatican II asserts that the State cannot coerce the family in its religion or the individual in his faith. While *Dignitatis Humane* has its glaring flaws,[265] it is not indifferentism or the denial of the sociopolitical reign of Christ (much less the reign of Boniface VII and his successors as masters of the universe) that the traditionalists decry. For in this regard, there certainly can be seen in *Dignitatis Humane* a promoting of a deeper manifestation of the spirit of the law, where the sociopolitical reign of Christ takes place first in the depths of the human heart and the recesses of the home and then manifests and advances from there, a process that certainly does not promote indifferentism.

Such a reign of Christ in the heart, and sociopolitically, does not depend on royal decrees or popular votes. God forbid that the State should be commissioned to dictate to man what is good, righteous and holy.[266] As per Vatican II's *Dignitatis Humanae*,

> This Vatican Council declares that the human person has a right to religious freedom. This freedom means that all men are to be immune from coercion on the part of individuals or of social groups and of any human power, in such wise that no one is to be forced to act in a manner contrary to his own beliefs, whether privately or publicly, whether alone or in association with others, within due limits.[267]

Specifically, the State can

> ... take account of the religious life of the citizenry and show it favor ... [but] it would clearly transgress the limits set to its power, were it to presume to command or inhibit acts that are religious.[268]

Any valid expansive or more defining teaching of the Church must always be a deepening of the letter of the law towards it spirit. Such a deepening in regards to religious liberty moves from the question of the more superficial rights of religion to the essence of religion, that is, the right of man to do his duty to God. In a truly Catholic light, *Dignitatis Humanae* can only be seen as a deepening of the law of informed Catholic conscience, a principle more fundamental than, or even fundamental to, the social reign of Christ and the rights of his Church.

Yes, once again the implementing of the deeper spirit of the law often makes the letter obsolete, but in doing so always moves towards a more militant and cross-conformed Catholicism. And what is more Catholic, a fear-driven inquisitional Catholic State or a love-emboldened Catholic standing up to the State? In the third millennium, with the State being truly satanic, the principle of religious liberty based on the law of an individual's informed Catholic conscience is the only option for the advancement of the sociopolitical reign of Christ. For it is only informed Catholic conscience, and the grassroots activism it spontaneously spawns, that will withstand mass sociopolitical indoctrination and enslavement now perpetrated worldwide by the technological empowered total State.

It is not the organizational Church, especially such as it is in the third millennium, that needs to be imbued with religious liberty so as to stand against the enslaving State but rather individual Catholics. It is individual Catholics, inspired by a naturally and divinely informed conscience, who must assert their liberty to do their duty to God. It is individual Catholics based in their nucleus of authority and existence of the family who will be able to give effective battle.

Just as it is freewheeling but coordinated guerrilla action that allows an over-matched partisan movement to fight the powerful military of an oppressive government, it is likewise only communities of Christian families coordinated under the leadership of visionary fathers that can fight the satanic powers-that-be in the third millennium. And again, it is indeed the Christian family that finds itself on the front-lines and under attack by both anti-Christic and anti-natural law assaults, and so the fight has been inexorably brought to the domestic church.

BETRAYAL & CAPITULATION

It was the lay faithful's shirking of duty in the wake of the usurpation and obstruction of those duties by the bureaucratic magisterium that in the past led to the most dire consequences for Catholic families, peoples, and nations. To be sure, the last decades of Christendom I are marked by nothing less than obscene magisterial betrayals of the lay faithful and the veritable castration of the Church Militant and Christian manhood. But the final accountability and blame must remain, not with prelates or popes, but with the lay faithful. For it was the lay faithful, and specifically the God-ordained familial patriarchs, that shirked their sacred duties and allowed their authority and competency to be usurped by both the secular and ecclesial powers.

In the latter part of Christendom I it was the alliance of the secular and ecclesial powers-that-be that destroyed the last vestiges of that Christendom still existing in the grass-roots of lay and familial Catholicism. Christendom I had increasingly become a top-heavy alliance of popes and princes, aristocrats and clerics, that kept the faithful in an infantile state. These less than fully mature faithful may have saved their own souls but could not save a failing Christendom; and thus they could not save the souls of their apostate progeny who inherited an anti-Christic world. Christendom I, at its worst, saw the alliance of the secular and ecclesial powers-that-be enter into mutual beneficial treaties that used the faithful as expendable pawns in powerbroking and politicking.

The grave harm caused by falsely equating the Church[269] with the Magisterium rather than equating the Magisterium with service unto the Church, with the identification of Catholicism with the formal ecclesial structure of the Church rather than with the essence of the Faith as lived out in the everyday intimacy of Christian existence, can be especially seen in the decaying influence of infantilism[270] on the faithful and the family. The most striking evil of this infantilism, aside from the instances of individual bullying and abuse, can be seen in the betrayal of the lay faithful by the magisterium unto the secular powers-that-be. This magisterial betrayal became increasingly and strikingly diabolical in the last decades of Christendom I. Here the magisterium sold out the faithful for a proverbial pot of parochial porridge.

Two examples from the 20th Century will suffice, though many preceded and even some are still occurring.[271] In Mexico, the Roaring Twenties was not about libertinism but liberty. Here the courageous Catholic faithful had successfully—indeed miraculously—risen under the banner of *Viva Cristo Rey* to fight for their Faith and their families against the godless masonic State. But the magisterial, and indeed aristocratic, bureaucracy somehow saw this as a threat to their own power. For these uppity *Cristeros* laymen had taken not only sociopolitics and war into their own hands but, being for the most part scandalously without the succor of priests,[272] had taken the leadership of their faith communities into their own hands as well. As always, it is only this sort of grassroots Catholicism that can be victorious in the sociopolitical realm, and miraculously victorious they were.

But alas! The magisterial bureaucracy, from the local bishops all the way to the Pope, sold the Mexican faithful out in return for a partial reinstating of ecclesial privileges, most notably a re-opening of churches (again, this indicates the disorder of thinking the faithful exist for the Mass and the parish rather than the Mass and parish existing for the faithful so that the faithful can exist for Christ). And alas even more so! The patriarchal faithful abdicated their God-given duties and, with a most unchristian and even perverse sense of infantile obedience, abdicated their authority to the magisterial bureaucracy and laid down their arms.

The magisterial bureaucracy's traitorous "1929 agreement" with the Mexican Masonic State resulted in the immediate mass executions of the militant and righteous *Cristeros* patriarchs, the raping of their women, and the murdering of their families. Indeed, *Cristero* veterans were being hunted down and killed into the 1950s. It is not known how many thousands of them lost their lives after the war had been "officially" declared over.[273]

And it was the same across the Atlantic. In 1930's Germany, the same Vatican run magisterium that betrayed Mexican faithful now betrayed the German faithful unto the neo-pagan national socialistic State. Again, in this concordance with Nazi Germany "the Church" is seen merely as her magisterial institutions. The Holy See got what it wanted, which was the appointment of bishops, the running of schools and institutions, and the securing of its wealth and properties, while the Catholic faithful, which is the only reason for the existence of the institutional church, were left to the wolves.

The German Catholic faithful[274] who were directly fighting evil in the name of Faith and family were abandoned by their prelacy, the Roman Curia, and the institutional, bureaucratic "church." As a result, even after Nazism was long vanquished from the scene, Germany remains socialistic. So too, much of the heretical theology within the post-World War II Church emanated from these Germanic lands where the faithful were betrayed.[275] It is from these most recent events, and a myriad of others before, that the Catholic faithful must learn to never again abdicate the God-given competency and duty to defend Faith and family in the sociopolitical realm.

CHARISM OF THE
CHURCH MILITANT

What will draw people to the Holy Faith for the advent of a new Christendom? It is an extraordinary pervasive attitude, subcultural manifestation, way of life, and mode of existence. That is, what will most effectively preach the Gospel is an extraordinary lived-out Christian ethos that is radical and necessarily militant and strikingly at-odds with the surrounding anti-Christic culture. Such a Christian ethos entails a disposition or attitude that is contemptuous of that anti-Christic world, along with the flesh, the devil, and especially one's own pride and sinful proclivities.

This Christian *contemptus mundi* ("contempt for the world," as well as the flesh and devil) is not an egoistic contempt. Rather this contempt for the world is a contempt of all that impedes or is opposed to the bringing about of the Kingdom. This contempt of the flesh is a contempt of all that distracts from the call to holiness and conformity to Christ Crucified. This contempt of the devil is contempt of all that is harmful to the Faith and the family and to all that is contrary to both divine revelation and natural law.

Such an integral *contemptus mundi* comes about in the assertion of the absolute right to do one's duty to God. As such, it is a contempt fully subsumed under the greater assertion, even celebration, of what is true and good. This Christian contempt requires the militant and celebratory assertion of the absolute right to do one's duty to God because not only do the world, the flesh and the devil oppose that right, but the perverse popular culture, the large corporations, and the State are opposed to it as well. The culture is a threat for it can infect and mesmerize. The corporation is a threat for it can demonetize and monopolize. The State is the greatest threat for it can confiscate, subjugate, and incarcerate through unbridled brute force.

As per paradoxical poetic justice, it is the Catholicism that was once falsely seen as inseparable from the State that must now in this third millennium be seen as irreconcilable with the State. Catholics, who once bent over backwards to show their allegiance to the State must now hunker down in opposition to that State. No, it is not *the king's good servant but God's first,* but rather *the family's good servant and God's first.* For one cannot serve two masters, especially when one of those masters is satanic.

In this anti-Christic third millennium, let Catholicism now lead the way against the totalitarian Satanic State, and let Catholics fully understand that they are necessarily seen as subversive criminals by that Satanic State. Let third millennium Catholics sorrowfully take upon themselves the opprobrium of being outlaws; for they are outside and in contempt of the secular positivistic law in their abiding by natural and divine laws.

It is this very willingness of Christians to be countercultural unto criminality that will make the Holy Faith ever more relevant to the enslaved masses, for it will offer them the freedom of the children of God and the courage to exert that freedom. For Christian freedom from external coercion and the courage to assert the absolute right to do one's duty to God is preceded and enabled by freedom from one's own egoistic bondage. The truth indeed makes a Christian free and grace gives the courage to speak truth to power.

It is the interaction of Christians with the world that manifests this sociopolitical charism of Christian liberty, which is nothing less than the charism of the Church Militant.[276]

> For our wrestling is not against flesh and blood; but against principalities and power, against the rulers

> of the world of this darkness, against the spirits of wickedness in the high places. EPH 6:12

The Christian charism of militancy is simply the mode of interaction with the world for the faithful here below. It is key to an authentic Christian ethos theology; that is, the living out of the Holy Faith in one's time and place.

The charism of Christian militancy is informed not only by the absolute right to do one's duty to God, but also by the holy virtue of piety; specifically, a Christian's love and allegiance to the Holy Faith and the sacrosanct family. Accordingly, this charism of Christian militancy is transcendent of all here below and, at one and the same time, firmly rooted in the family as the most fundamental entity here below. The transcendence of Christian militancy gives the faithful an allegiance above and beyond any state, person, or worldly concoction. Simultaneously, as per subsidiarity, the rootedness of Christian militancy ensconces the natural as part and parcel of that militancy and imbues it with the most fundamental and fiercest allegiance to family. This vertical militant transcendence and horizontal militant rooting is united in pious allegiance, thus creating in the Holy Cross it forms a fully integrated ethos of Christian existence.

The Christian sociopolitical charism of militancy is the bold liberty to do one's duty to God, that is, to Faith and family. It is this Christian charism of militancy that will empower the faithful against the perverse and totalitarian powers-that-be. The ever prayed for and advanced "liberty and exaltation of Holy Mother Church" that was once appropriated by the Papacy so as to defeat Caesaropapism will in the third millennium come to its true and full fruition in the faithful. For the Magisterium's defining of dogma made possible by its assertion of freedom is now indefectibly in place for all time, making any crisis *in* the Church impossible.

But there is an ever waxing crisis *between* the Church and the anti-Christic world, and it is specifically the laity and their Christian families that are militantly engaged on the front lines in this anti-Christic third millennium. As such, most essential to this charism of Christian militancy in the third millennium has nothing to do with the exaltation and freedom of the papacy (which is now properly obscured as the foundation under the dogmatic edifice of the Church) but with the exaltation and freedom of the Christian family.

FAITH & FAMILY

The third millennial call for the exaltation and freedom of the Church made manifest in the freedom and exaltation of the Christian family is specifically a call for the freedom and exaltation of Christian womanhood and motherhood, of Christian manhood and fatherhood, and of the Christian lay faithful. This exaltation and freedom of the Christian family will effectively bring about a new Christendom by relocating the very leadership of the Church from a top-heavy and bureaucratic curia and chancery to a grass-roots and subsidiary hearth and home.

If the Holy Faith is to thrive in the third millennium, no longer can Christians be dependent on the powers-that-be; no longer can they allow themselves to be the pawns of princes, presidents, principalities, or political powers. If there is to be any semblance of a new Christendom in the third millennium, no longer can the Holy Faith have its locus in ecclesial entities; no longer can the Faith be equated primarily with the papacy, prelature, or parish. Rather, in this third millennium, the Holy Catholic Faith must find both its dynamic leadership, primary identification, and impactive dynamics in the Christian family. This will entail creating nothing less than a grassroots Christian order that is a separate and self-sufficient power structure that has values, laws, and governance that transcends, and truly countermands, that of the perverse popular culture and the satanic State.

As such, in the third millennium Christian fathers are called to rise up in their full authority and accept their natural and divine commission to be the priest, prophet, and king of their domestic realms. These family men are called to form a confederation of Christian kings against an anti-Christic and anti-family Leviathan of ungodly power. Familial Christian patriarchy—which finds its reason for being in the love and devotion to Faith and family, womanhood, children, and to all those in need—is called to bear the brunt of militantly promulgating a new Christendom, family by family, and small-faith community by small-faith community.

And in the third millennium, the call is for Christian womanhood to be fully enshrined as the heart of Faith and family. The call is for femininity and motherhood to be honored as the jewel of not only family life but of human existence. For it is only feminine and motherly love that can integrally transform the soul of humanity by stoking the spark of imago Dei individualism, and it is only Christian womanhood that in tending the domestic hearth of familial holiness can set miraculously and unprecedentedly ablaze the communal conflagration of a new Christendom.

The bringing about of a new Christendom can only take place if done first and foremost in the family. For it is within the intimate confines of the home that reality, in the depths of its sorrows and the heights of its joys, is most readily and fully encountered. And as grace always builds upon nature, certainly Christianity is most deeply lived out within the intimacy of the domestic church.

It is in the inner stillness of the pious Christian family that a person is called to courageously venture into the center of reality which is Christ Crucified. It is the pious Christian family, both in its collective witness and in the individual Catholics it forms, that is most specifically and increasingly attacked by a hostile world. And thus it is the pious Christian family that most effectively preaches Jesus Christ and Him Crucified.[H8]

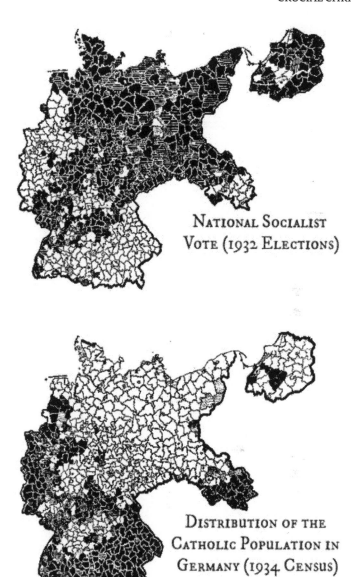

NATIONAL SOCIALIST
VOTE (1932 ELECTIONS)

DISTRIBUTION OF THE
CATHOLIC POPULATION IN
GERMANY (1934 CENSUS)

Appendix A:
National Socialistic Vote

The 1932 National Socialistic vote in Germany is shown in the dark areas of the top map on the converse page. The distribution of Catholics in Germany as per the 1934 census is shown by the dark areas of the second map. The maps are nearly an exact converse mirror image of each other depicting the total rejection of National Socialism by German Catholics and its espousal by German Protestants. The exactitude of the regional religious affiliation mapping was made possible by the historical phenomenon of principalities going *en mass* either Catholic or Protestant as per the monarch's chosen alliance.

Appendix B:
An Example of Crucial Distinction

*The following is this author's reply to his writings being cited in **John Paul II, the Theology of the Body**.[277] It is offered as an example of how crucial distinctions preserve and promote the essential truths and charisms of Catholicism. Just as Vatican I did not assert that essential papal authority was entailed in or effected by the accidental acquirement or loss of secular sovereignty (the loss of the Papal States being the very catalyst for the Council) but rather that this authority was found in a sociopolitically transcendent, and thus much greater, papal infallibility, so too does the cited essay **Karol Wojtyła and the Patriarchal Hierarchy of the Family** by not claiming that every utterance, or even formal presentation, of a pope is of papal authority result in the preservation and promotion of that same charism of papal infallibility.*

In the Vatican-approved and highly touted introduction to the definitive English collection of John Paul II's writings on gender issues (popularly termed "Theology of the Body") the esteemed scholar, translator, and author, Michael Waldstein, dedicates a full page to my essay *Karol Wojtyła and the Patriarchal Hierarchy of the Family: His Exegetical Comment on Ephesians 5:21-33 and Genesis 3:16.[278]* Waldstein writes on page 16 of the Introduction:

> One must measure the authority of TOB in accord with these findings about office, genre, and content: the authority of a text is high if (1) the Pope speaks as pastor of the universal Church, (2) in a form of teaching central to his office of bishop, and (3) on a topic central to the faith. All three of these indicators are high in TOB.

> Contrary to this evidence, some authors have dismissed the authority of TOB. In the traditionalist publication Christian Order, for example, G. C. Dilsaver argues that:

> "TOB should be considered a private theological work

by Karol Wojtyła, not part of the papal magisterium of John Paul II. Pope John Paul II has used his Wednesday catechesis conference to read much of his private theological works. Among these is The Theology of Marriage and Celibacy. In this work, Karol Wojtyła (as a private theologian, since this work was completed prior to his ascending to the papacy) introduces the novel concept of 'mutual submission' in his exegesis of Ephesians 5.24."

All the signs that surround the Wednesday catechesis and that express John Paul II's intention make it quite clear that John Paul II intended the Wednesday catechesis to be precisely this: catechesis, not the recitation of private theological works. Dilsaver simply sidesteps the plain intention of John Paul II. The only argument he [Dilsaver] offers is that this work was completed prior to his [Wojtyła's] ascending to the papacy. This argument is irrelevant. The first publication of the text was its delivery by the Bishop of Rome as a cycle of catechesis. The original or authentic text of TOB is the Italian text as delivered by Pope John Paul II and published in the official Insegnamenti series.

A position similar to Dilsaver's is proposed by Charles Curran, who likewise ignores the genre of catechesis and limits himself to the more external genre 'General Audience' used by the Insegnamenti series. [The Theology of the Body belongs to] a particular genre of teaching in the speeches given at the weekly audiences.... As such, talks to general audiences have little or no authoritative character. They are often just greetings to the various people in attendance and exhortations.... These talks...have little or no importance from the point of view of authoritative teaching. Against both Dilsaver and Curran, one should insist that TOB is a catechesis proposed by the Bishop of Rome for the universal Church on the center of Christian faith, the 'great mystery' of love (Eph 5).

While one can certainly appreciate Waldstein's attempt to discern the authoritative status of this particular selection of John Paul II's writings, Waldenstein nonetheless fails to address the actual hypothesis of my essay, nor even the specific point of the quote he uses; *viz.*, John Paul II's novel introduction, and possible heterodox construal, of the concept of "mutual submission" (explicated in my essay in question). Indeed, my assertion that John Paul II's *The Original Unity of Man and Woman* (popularly termed "theology of the body") is the work of a private theologian stems from the desire to downplay the possibly misleading or controverted elements contained therein. In identifying these elements I painstakingly (maybe even to a point of partial obfuscation) sought to employ a tone and form that was irreproachably respectful of both the papacy in general and the pontificate of John Paul II in particular. Moreover, justice requires that any comparison between the theological writings of the notorious dissenter Rev. Charles Curran's and my own requires notice that there has never been any assertion that any of my theological writings are suspect as to their orthodoxy. However, Waldstein's presentation is apt to give the impression that both Curran's and my positions are equally unorthodox, albeit on polar ends of the spectrum. Indeed, as explicated in my essay in question, this position is the only possible orthodox position.

The essence of my essays, *Patriarchal Hierarchy of the Family; A Constant Teaching of the Church, and Karol Wojtyła and The Patriarchal Hierarchy of the Family: His Exegetical Comment on Ephesians 5:21-33 and Genesis 3:16.*, were first presented as a double lecture at the Pontifical Institute on Marriage and Family in the Spring of 1991. At the time, I was in the last months of master work and enrolled in a class on *Wojtyła's Original Unity of Man and Woman* by a co-founder of the Institute, the late Msgr. Lorenzo Albacete. During an earlier lecture being given by Albacete, I raised a question about the apparent conflict between what was said in the John Paul II's *Original Unity* writings and what I discerned to be the teaching of the Church on the patriarchal hierarchy of the family. Albacete (who had during the course of my studies become an extracurricular friend) graciously offered to let me lecture at the next week's double class to present my position. I accepted and further researched the issue during the ensuing week.

By accessing scriptural and magisterial writings, it was quickly discernible that John Paul II's writings on the subject of patriarchal hierarchy did indeed appear to contradict previous magisterial teachings. But how could this be? Like many of my generation, for me, Pope John Paul II, was the touchstone of orthodoxy (as Peter should be) amidst a sea of heterodoxy, a sea especially turbulent in my own native Archdiocese of Los Angeles. I gave the double lecture the following week, and my findings were not substantially challenged by either students or the professor—nor has it been subsequently. Indeed, at the end of the lecture, Msgr. Lorenzo Albacete, the erudite champion of Vatican II and a foremost expert on the writings of John Paul II, thanked me kindly and, shrugging his shoulders, said, "All I can say is that these writings are those of a private theologian, and therefore do not partake of the papal charism of infallibility." This solution left the papal authority unscathed while still allowing the truth to prevail; a solution I hence used in my published essay.

The authority Waldstein wishes to imbue the *Original Unity* writings with is based on discerning what Pope John Paul II's supposed inner intent was in the absence of any stated intent. Thus Waldstein's recourse to the interpretation of "signs":

> All the signs that surround the Wednesday catechesis and that express John Paul II's intention make it quite clear that John Paul II intended the Wednesday catechesis to be precisely this: catechesis, not the recitation of private theological works.

Of course catechesis broadly varies in authority from mere theological opinion to de fide statements. But

Waldstein's view of these writings as "a catechesis proposed by the Bishop of Rome for the universal Church on the center of Christian faith" imbues them with an authority that is as close to *ex cathedra* as possible (though specific words that express intent are required for *ex cathedra* teachings).

Though Waldstein is surely an able and well-intended defender of the Church, the position he advocates that imbues a very high degree of authority to these writings issued by John Paul II during his pontificate may have the eventual effect of undermining that particular pontificate, the papacy as a whole, and the general teaching authority of the Church. For Waldstein's position entails *the rejection of a constant authoritative teaching of the Church in favor of contradictory teachings of controverted authority.* Indeed, his position could be used to justify those who dismiss or reject modern pontificates (such as *sedevacantists* or other schismatic traditionalists) because they expect a pope to be too infallible, as well as by those who reject all pontificates (such as modernists and assorted dissenting progressives) because they accept no infallibility.

In light of the fact that the familial patriarchal hierarchy is an infallible teaching, it seems prudent to construe private writings of John Paul II that in some way seem to contradict this infallible teaching as those of a private theologian in order to uphold the very authority of the papacy that the Church was graced to have John Paul II hold.

Such a position not only maintains the constant teachings of the Church but surely brings out the stated intent of the Holy Father's writings on the subject. As I write in my conclusion to the essay,

> When John Paul II's writings on familial patriarch are read in the contextual harmony with previous magisterial pronouncements on the subject, they must be viewed as having the primary intent of eradicating that which has in the past masqueraded as a Christian patriarchy. John Paul II's writings, then, can be seen as paving the way for the establishment

of an authentic familial Christian patriarchy. Such a patriarchy will be purified of all brutish dominance and worldly power and based purely and firmly on Christ and his commission of authority, as per the constant traditional spirituality, exegesis, and teaching of the Church.

WORKS CITED

Acta Apostolicae Sedis: Commentarium Officiale, Annus XXXV, Second Series, vol. X, 193. *Typis Polyglottis Vaticanis*, 1943.

Address of Pope Paul VI During the Last General Meeting of the Second Vatican Council. December 7, 1965.

Ahn, K., et al. "538 A.D. and the transition from Pagan Roman Empire to Holy Roman Empire: Justinian's metamorphosis from chief of staffs to theologian." *International Journal of Humanities and Social Science*. Vol. 7, no. 1 (2017): 44–85.

Aquinas, Thomas. *The Summa Theologiae of St. Thomas Aquinas*, 1a, q. 12, a. 4; 1a2ae, q. 55, a. 1; *1a2ae, q. 65, a. 2, c.;* 1a2ae, q. 91, a. 2; 2a2ae, q. 19, a. 2; *2a2ae,* q. 104, a. 5.; Suppl. 3ae, app. 2, a. 2. Second and Revised Edition. Translated by the Fathers of the English Dominican Province. 1920.

Augustine, *City of God,* Book I.

Bailey, David C. *Viva Cristo Rey!* Austin: University of Texas Press, 1974.

Bailey, Michael D. "Pope John XXII." *History Publications*, 56. Iowa State University, 2006.

Bainvel, Jean. "Devotion to the Sacred Heart of Jesus." *The Catholic Encyclopedia*. Vol. 7. New York: Robert Appleton Company, 1910.

Benedict XVI. *Angelus Address.* June 22, 2008.

Benedict XVI, *Theological Highlights of Vatican II,* rev. ed. (Paulist Press, 2009).

"Bérulle, Pierre de." *Vincentian Encyclopedia*. November 26, 2017.

"Binary process." *Farlex Partner Medical Dictionary*. 2012.

Brownson, Orestes Augustus. *Brownson's Quarterly Review: January, 1851-October, 1851*. Vol. 5. No. II, a. IV. Metcalf and Company, 1851.

Canons and Decrees of the Council of Trent, Session XIII, Chapter II, § *On the Reason of the Institution of this Most holy Sacrament,* trans. Theodore Alois Buckley (London: George Routledge and Co., 1851).

Canons and Decrees of the Council of Trent, Session XXII, Chapter V, § *On the Solemn Ceremonies of the Sacrifice of the Mass.*

Canons and Decrees of the Council of Trent, Session XXII, Chapter I, § *On the Institution of the Most Holy Sacrifice of the Mass.* Chapter II, § *That the Sacrifice of the Mass is Propitiatory both for the Living and the Dead.*

Catechism of the Catholic Church, a. 1324; 1776; 2214.

Clippinger, Walter G. "Eloi; Eloi; Lama; Sabachtha; Eli; Eli; Lama Sabachthani." *International Standard Bible Encyclopedia.* Edited by James Orr. Wm. B. Eerdmans Publishing Co., 1939.

De Montfort, Louis. *True Devotion to Mary.* 1712 (French).

Decrees of the First Vatican Council, Session III, Canon 4.3. April 24, 1870.

Decrees of the First Vatican Council, Session IV, Chapter 1.3. July 18, 1870.

Dilsaver, G. C. *Psychomoralitics: The Soul-Deep Alternative to the Failed Mental Health Professions,* 88; 96-97; 112;   139ff; 153; 160-162. Imago Dei Press, 2017.

Dilsaver, G.C. *Celebrating God Given Gender: Masculinity and Femininity per Nature and* Grace. Imago Dei Press, 2016.

Dilsaver, G.C. *Imago Dei Psychotherapy,* 144-145. *Catholic University of American Press,* 2009.

Dilsaver, G.C. *The Three Marks of Manhood.* TAN Books, 2010.

Fleming, David A. *The Fire and the Cloud: An Anthology of Catholic Spirituality,* 272-273. New York: Paulist Press, 1978.

Garrigou-Lagrange, Reginald. "Ch. XXIII: Angelic Nature and Knowledge." *Reality: A Synthesis of Thomistic Thought,* 166. St. Louis, Mo.: Herder, 1950.

Gilmartin, Thomas. "Good Friday." *The Catholic Encyclopedia.* Vol. 6. New York: Robert Appleton Company, 1909.

Guercio, Gelsomino Del. "What did Paul VI mean by saying 'the smoke of Satan has entered the Church'?" *Aleteia.* July 6, 2018.

Holy See Press Office. "Tiara." 2001.

John Paul II. *Apostolic Letter on Reserving Priestly Ordination to Men Alone.* No. 4. May 22, 1994.

John Paul II. *The Theology of the Body: A New Translation based on the John Paul II Archives.* Translation, index, and introduction by Michael Waldstein. Boston: Pauline Books & Media.

John Paul II. *Vatican Address.* October 1, 1979.

John XIII. "Pope John's Opening Speech to the Council." *The Documents of Vatican II,* 712-713. Edited by Walter M. Abbott, S.J. New York: Herder and Herder / Association Press, 1966.

Jones, Kenneth C. *Index of Leading Catholic Indicators*, 8-9. St. Louis, Mo.: Oriens Publishing Company, 2003.

Lamont, John R.T. "Tyranny and sexual abuse in the Catholic Church: A Jesuit tragedy." *Rorate Caeli.* October 28, 2018.

Leo XIII. *Apostolicae curae.* 1896.

"Letter to Father Charles Curran." Congregation for the Doctrine of the Faith, July 25, 1986.

Martin, Colin and Parker, Geoffrey. *The Spanish Armada: Revised Edition,* 252. Manchester, UK: Mandolin, 1999.

McHugh, John and Callan, Charles, trans. *Catechism of the Council of Trent for Parish Priests,* 218-219; 258-259; 352. New York: Joseph F. Wagner, Inc., 1947.

McMahon, Joseph. "Perpetual Adoration." *The Catholic Encyclopedia.* Vol. 1. New York: Robert Appleton Company, 1907.

Nabuco, Joaquim, ed. *Ius Pontificalium: Introductio in Caeremoniale Episcoporum.* Tornaci: Desclée et Socii, 1956.

Newman, Henry. *Certain Difficulties felt by Anglicans in Catholic Teaching II,* 248. London: Longmans Green, 1885.

Nicene and Post-Nicene Fathers. Second Series. Vol. 1. Edited by Philip Schaff and Henry Wace. Buffalo, NY: Christian Literature Publishing Co., 1890.

Nicene and Post-Nicene Fathers. First Series. Vol. 7. Edited by Philip Schaff. Buffalo, NY: Christian Literature Publishing Co., 1888.

Paul VI. *Apostolicam Actuositatem*. Chapter IV. No. 20. November 18, 1965.

Paul VI. *Dignitatis Humane*. No. 2, 3, 13. December 7, 1965.

Paul VI. *Guadium et Spes*. Chapter III. No. 38. December 7, 1965.

Paul VI. *Lumen* Gentium. Chapter II. No. 11. November 21, 1964.

Paul VI. *Perfectae* Caritatis. No. 4. October 28, 1965.

Pinsent, Andrew. "Thomas Aquinas on the Passions." *Notre Dame Philosophical* Reviews. February 7, 2010.

Pius IX. *Beneficia Dei*. No. 3. 1871.

Pius IX. *Ubi Nos*. 1871. No. 1, 12-14.

Pius XI. *Casti Connubii*. December 31, 1932.

Pohle, Joseph. "Actual Grace." *The Catholic Encyclopedia*.
Vol. 6. New York: Robert Appleton Company, 1909.

Porphyry. *Introduction (or Isagoge) to the Logical Categories of Aristotle*, 609-633. Vol. II. Chapter V. Translated by Octavius F. Owen. 1853.

Ratzinger, Joseph Cardinal. *Principles of Catholic Theology: Building Stones for a Fundamental Theology*, 393. Translated by Sister Mary F. McCarthy. San Francisco: Ignatius Press, 1987.

Sheen, F.J. *God and Intelligence in Modern Philosophy: A Critical Study in the Light of the Philosophy of Saint Thomas*, 139 London: Longmans & Green, 1938.

"The Jesuits in America." *Life Magazine*. October 11, 1954.

Thornton, John F. and Varenne, Susan B. *The Essential Pope Benedict XVI: His Central Writings & Speeches*. New York: Harper Collins, 2007.

Thurston, Herbert. "Visits to the Blessed Sacrament." *The Catholic Encyclopedia*. Vol. 15. New York: Robert   Appleton Company, 1912.

"To the Members of the Society in Portugal, Rome, March 26, 1553." *Ignatius of Loyola: Letters and Instructions*. Edited by John W. Padberg, et al. St. Louis, Mo.: Institute of Jesuit Sources, 1996.

Von Mises, Ludwig. *Bureaucracy*, 101-103. New Haven: Yale University Press, 1944.

Weber, Nicholas. "Swedenborgians." *The Catholic Encyclopedia.* Vol. 14. New York: Robert Appleton Company, 1912.

Wiltgen, Ralph. *Rhine Flows into the* Tiber. TAN Books, 1991.

Wojtyła, Karol. *Original Unity of Man and Woman: Catechesis on the Book of Genesis.* Boston, Mass.: St. Paul Editions, 1981.

INDEX

A

B

C

D

E

F

G

H

I

M

O

P

R

Religions

S

T

V

W

---

[1] God's providence at the turn of the third millennium, paradoxical as it may be, can be readily discerned in the deconstruction of the Papacy: from the down-to-earth, non-monarchical Pope John XXIII, who came from "peasant stock"; to Pope Paul VI's relinquishing of his Tiara, as unseemly as the donation to the United Nations was; to a Pope John Paul II's celebrity status, rock stardom though it may have been; to Pope Benedict's shocking abdication, for reason still in doubt; to the follow-up dismantling of the monarchical papacy by Pope Francis, though this dismantling be engendered by the undermining of confidence in conservative and traditionalist monarchical papist tendencies.

[2] An ethos is a disposition, character, or fundamental values peculiar to a specific person, people, corporation, culture, or movement.

[3] See footnote 261.

[4] Evangelical is here used, regardless of Protestant co-opting of the term, since it refers specifically to the evangelical counsels of poverty, chastity, and obedience. The use of the term "religious" for those in the evangelical state denotes that those in the familial (i.e., lay) state are somehow not religious! The term "consecrated" for those in the evangelical state discounts the consecrated state of all Catholics via baptism, confirmation, and non-sacramental consecrations, such as the consecration to the Blessed Virgin Mary.

[5] Due to the term "psychological" being no longer equated with its traditional and etymological meaning, viz., "study of the soul," the term "psychomoral," with its connotations of the rational and volitional moral act, is used to designate the true study and treatment of the soul.

[6] See Chapter VIII, § *Seeker of the Truth.*

[7] See Chapter I, § Third Millennium Technarcistic Man.

[8] January 20, 1990

[9] Paul VI, *Guadium et Spes*, Chapter III, no. 38 (7 December 1965).

[10] Benedict XVI, *Theological Highlights of Vatican II*, rev. ed. (Paulist Press, 2009). This is Joseph Ratzinger's personal reflections on Vatican II, at which he was a *peritus* or theological expert (and a quite progressive one at that).

[11] Joseph Cardinal Ratzinger, *Principles of Catholic Theology: Building Stones for a Fundamental Theology,* trans. Sister Mary F. McCarthy (San Francisco: Ignatius Press, 1987), 393.

[12] In 1986, Ratzinger, as the Cardinal Prefect of the Congregation for the Doctrine of the Faith, forbade Charles Curran, the most notable disciple of *peritus* Bernard Häring, from teaching at any Catholic institution, declaring him no longer "suitable nor eligible to exercise the function of a professor of Catholic theology." See "Letter to Father Charles Curran" (Congregation for the Doctrine of the Faith, July 25, 1986).

[13] Technarcism: a reality distorting narcissism enabled by technology. See Chapter II, § *Third Millennium Technarcistic Man.*

[14] See Preface, § *Psychomoral Foundation.* For a full explication of the clinical science of psychomoralitics see the textbook *Psychomoralitics: The Soul-Deep Alternative to the Failed Mental Health Professions* (Imago Dei Press, 2017).

[15] St. Augustine (354-430) standardized the Latin term *re-ligare*, with *ligo* (bind, connect) prefixed with *re-* (again).

[16] Here are included as well, to one extent or the other, all the apostolic confessions and even those non-sacramental confessions that may still maintain an orientation towards Christ Crucified.

[17] A pristine example of third millennium Technarcistic Man may someday be discovered by paleontologists underneath layers of ever new and improved electronics that are riddled throughout with childproof vials of psychotropics and miles of red-tape. The archaeologists may well remark that Technarcistic Man seems to have

lived and died without any signs of trauma, apparently remaining blissfully unaware throughout his mortal existence.

[18] The spiritual nature of the *imago Dei* intellect causes both angels and men to have immortal souls. See Chapter X, § *Mortality & Contingency*.

[19] As will be explicated in subsequent chapters, such a crucial Christian ethos, in its eschewing of all ecclesial politics as non-essential or even contrary to Christianity, welcomes the radical deconstruction of the papacy of all its princely and political powers; the remanding of the Magisterium to its essential role of explicating (but now preserving, more so, than defining) the Deposit of Faith; the reorientation of the episcopacy and priesthood to its essential ministry of service; and the equating of the Church with her truths and with those that adhere to those truths.

[20] See Chapter IX, § *Purgative Love*.

[21] But though experiencing the separation of damnation, Christ was not damned, for even in his darkest hour he never loved the Father one *iota* less, and damnation is but choosing not to love God. See Chapter VII, § *Our Lord Jesus Christ*.

[22] The doctrine of Mary as *Co-Redemptrix* is one of the very few beliefs that could still be dogmatically defined. Co-Redemptrix refers to a subordinate but essential participation by the Blessed Virgin Mary in redemption. Co-Redemptrix denotes that she gave free consent to giving life to the Redeemer and thus gave him the enfleshment necessary for his sacrifice. Co-Redemptrix also denotes that the Blessed Mother, in her absolute compassion for Christ, was one with him in his passion.

[23] See Chapter VII, § *Our Lord Jesus Christ*.

[24] Compunction is "habitual sorrow for sin," and is the *sine qua non* catalyst for advancement in the spiritual life.

[25] Testimony of St. Peter's martyrdom is extensive, including Origen, Eusebius of Caesarea, St. Clement I of Rome, St. Ignatius, and St. Irenaeus. According to rich tradition, Peter was crucified on the Vatican Hill upside down because he declared himself unworthy to die in the same manner as the Lord. See Eusebius, *Church History*, Book III, Chapter I, trans. Arthur Cushman McGiffert. From *Nicene and Post-Nicene Fathers*, Second Series, vol. 1, ed. Philip Schaff and Henry Wace (Buffalo, NY: Christian Literature Publishing Co., 1890).

[26] See Chapter VII, § The Crucial Natural Vocation and Chapter VIII, § A Soul that Magnifies the Lord.

[27] See Chapter VIII, § *Our Lord Jesus Christ*.

[28] See Chapter V, § Ecclesial Kenosis Continued.

[29] *Aggiornamento:* "bringing up to date." Aggiornamento was used to mean throwing open the doors of the Church in a desire to dialogue with the outside world. It was the name John XXIII gave to his pontifical program in a speech of January 25, 1959. "Aggiornamento," *Wikipedia* (17 January 2021).

[30] *Ressourcement:* "return to the sources." Proponents of *nouvelle théologie* "adopted a systemic openness to dialogue with the contemporary world on issues of theology" and advanced new endeavors in "biblical exegesis, typology, art, literature, and mysticism." "Nouvelle théologie," *Wikipedia* (29 January 2021).

[31]K. Ahn, G. Damsteegt, E. de Kock, S. Kim, J. Kwon, K. van Wyk, et al., "538 A.D. and the transition from Pagan Roman Empire to Holy Roman Empire: Justinian's metamorphosis from chief of staffs to theologian," *International Journal of Humanities and Social Science*, vol. 7, no. 1 (2017): 44–85.

[32] And woe be to any who should challenge this papal audacity. Not only did Boniface imprison and kill his saintly predecessor, Celestine V, who had abdicated the papacy due to its corruption but he sought a similar fate for the King of France, Philip IV, and the Habsburg Emperor, Albert I. Boniface VIII was constantly engaged in waging ruthless political and actual battles in his advancement of papal power. A further example of this ruthlessness can be seen in his dealings with the recalcitrant Colonnas clan and their associated families. In 1298 the Colonnas, who began by opposing Pope Boniface's aggression to overtake their fiefdom, finally chose to surrender peacefully to him due to his assurances that they would be shown mercy, and be spared any punishment. However, Pope Boniface deceived them and, to show an example to all future generations of what happens to those that would oppose the totalitarian power of the papacy, ordered the utter destruction of the Colonnas family's city of Palestrina. Palestrina, known for its pristine preservation of ancient Roman architectural structures, was razed to the ground and its fields salted, as the Ancient Roman's had infamously done to Carthage. Only the city's cathedral did Boniface leave standing.

[33] *Ius Pontificalium: Introductio in Caeremoniale Episcoporum,* ed. Joaquim Nabuco (Tornaci: Desclée et Socii, 1956).

[34]Holy See Press Office, "Tiara," (2001).

[35] The Crusaders insured this by sacking Constantinople on the way to the Holy Land.

[36] Orestes Brownson (September 16, 1803—April 17, 1876) wrote:

"[Savonarola's] protest against Paganism, which was in the latter half of the fifteenth century reappearing in literature and art, was not misplaced nor uncalled for. That he exaggerated the danger is possible; that he carried his invectives farther than was necessary is also possible; but that he was right in opposing the paganizing tendency of his time, as well as correct in his literary and artistic principles. . . Certainly we are not among those who object to the study of the ancient classics or the ancient models of art, and if that study were wrong, or even hazardous to the scholar or the artist, the highest authority in the Church would long since have officially condemned it; but that in the time of Savonarola it had become excessive, and led to the depreciation of the labors of Christian scholars and artists, there can be little doubt. . . ." (Citation below).

[37]Orestes Augustus Brownson, *Brownson's Quarterly Review: January, 1851-October, 1851*, vol. 5, no. II, a. IV (Metcalf and Company, 1851). Reprinted in the Classic Reprint Series (Forgotten Books, 2018).

[38]   Though the Counter-Reformation was only mildly successful, the concurrent conquering of new lands afforded fertile grounds for missionary efforts and the loss of much of European Catholicism was equally compensated for, at leastwise in numbers, by newly baptized (if not always completely converted) peoples.

[39]   This hijacking of the Vendée cause by prelates and nobles was elucidated upon by Charles-Louis Chassin (1831—1901), whose eleven volumes of historical documents supporting this thesis are considered the definitive collection on the War in the Vendée.

[40]   See Chapter XIV, § *Betrayal & Capitulation*, for other more recent, and equally tragic, lay abdications.

[41]   Hence the politically motivated elevation of Joan d'Arc (c. 1412 – 30 May 1431), who is bizarrely the darling of both feminists and traditionalists alike, is telling. Joan, who as far as the currency of saints go is quite minor, might have been considered quite the towering saint if instead of perpetrating a war between Catholic nations she had facilitated a peace. But Joan's bolstering up of the deeply decadent French monarchy and setting it and France at violent odds with England inevitably made possible not only the schism of England but the French Revolution. England became susceptible to its eventual schism in its separation from and animosity towards France, who was still the eldest daughter of the Church and a main source of Catholicity for England. If the kingdoms of England and France had remained united or at least allies, schism would have entailed the loss of France and been much too costly for Henry VIII. So too the decadent Royalty of France, purported to be supported by God and his Church due to the private revelations of Joan, led to the reconstitution of the *ancien régime* of Church and Crown, which the French Revolution was indiscriminately dead set against. Finally, the French Revolution would not have succeeded if a Catholic England

had come to the military aid of Vendée.

[42]   Guy Fawkes (13 April 1570 – 31 January 1606) was a convert to Catholicism and a member of the Recusant English Catholics that fought against the tyranny of the British Crown. He was executed for his involvement in the failed Gunpowder Plot of 1605.

[43]   See maps in *Appendix A*. As per the fruit of this unholy alliance between State and Church, one can see the horrid ramifications in the direct correlation between the principalities that opted for Protestantism and those that voted for the National Socialist German's Worker Party. Though this correlation does explicate Catholics, who at least then knew neo-paganism when they saw it in Nazism, the aforementioned selling out of the Catholic faithful by the Magisterium of Church nonetheless deflated their movement. see Chapter XV, § *Lay Faithful Competency*.

[44]Ribadeneira, "Letter to Don Juan de Idiáquez," *Monumenta historica societatis Iesu, LX*, (December 1588), 105-111; quoted in Colin Martin and Geoffrey Parker, *The Spanish Armada: Revised Edition* (Manchester, UK: Mandolin, 1999), 252.

[45]   The Jesuits, themselves autocrats to the end, first advanced the cause of papacy and crown. But with the fall of monarchies and the subsequent ascent of vicious military juntas, the Jesuits themselves would become insurgents. The Jesuits "Liberation Theology" was righteously named, and even rightly proposed small faith communities. However, liberation theology betrayed true liberty and orthodox theology in proposing a new socialistic order that was equally draconian to those of the past, and it once again betrayed the common faithful, and the God-given small faith community that is the family, in its insertion of political/ecclesial cells that were controlled by a State party apparatchik, even preferably a priest/apparatchik. Thus, liberation theology is a mere morphing of the power structure that had been that of the *ancien régime's* unholy union of Crown and Papacy.

[46]   Pope Pius IX described himself as a "prisoner in the Vatican" (It.: *Prigioniero del Vaticano*; Lt.: *Captivus Vaticani*) following "the capture of Rome by the armed forces of the Kingdom of Italy on 20 September 1870." See "Prisoner in the Vatican," *Wikipedia* (9 January 2021).

[47]Pius IX, *Ubi Nos*, no. 1, 12-14 (1871).

[48]Pius IX, *Beneficia Dei*, no. 3 (1871).

[49]   But alas! Paul VI would surrender it to nothing less than the new usurping "magisterium" of the universal league of secular states, the United Nations.

[50]Decrees of the First Vatican Council, Session IV, Chapter 1.3 (18 July

1870).

[51] As with the *tiara,* might much of the other ecclesial regal trappings (such as the mighty mitre or the absurd *cappa magna)* of Church prelates, be done away with, or at least parred down? The bishop's mitre, for instance, grew from a humble skullcap to an ostentatious tower, its height and ornamentation increasing in direct correlation with the monarchical posturings and claims of the Magisterium. Indeed, ecclesial regal trappings have become parodies of themselves. In 2018, the New York Metropolitan Museum of Art exhibited the gaudiest renditions of ecclesial garb in its "Heavenly Bodies: Fashion and the Catholic Imagination." While some conservative Catholics protested the exhibit, did they protest too much? Doesn't defending such accidentals only reinforce the worldly belief that these mere trinkets are of the Church's essence?

[52] *Decrees of the First Vatican Council,* Session III, Canon 4.3 (24 April 1870). As will be seen, Vatican II's apparent attempt to so imbue dogma with a different sense was precluded by its twin, but firstborn, council.

[53] For example, Poland, Lithuania, Austria, Hungry, and Northern Italy.

[54] "An estimated 100,000–260,000 civilian casualties were caused by chemical weapons during the conflict and tens of thousands... died from scarring of the lungs, skin damage, and cerebral damage in the years after the conflict ended." "Chemical weapons in World War I," *Wikipedia* (26 January 2021).

[55] The Church condemned the immorality of the 1920's with Pius XI's encyclical *Casti Connubii* (31 December 1930). See *Papal Encyclicals Online.*

[56] The heroic myth of the Poles waging the last doomed cavalry charge of history against mechanized Panzer tank divisions roaring across the border of Poland, though not true, expresses in a poetic way this last fully Catholic and thus medieval nation going against the emerging post-Christian Satanic State. And in truth, the aristocratic cavalry officers of Poland were arrested and murdered en masse by the Nazis. And in truth, the Poles were the most effective and courageous of the underground resistance in World War II. In fact, the men of Poland fought gallantly against the technological German invasion, as expatriated Polish men were heavily involved in the formal Allied armies.

[57] The atomic bombing of Japan was ordered by a 33rd degree Mason, President Harry S. Truman.

[58] In recognizing the irredeemability of the West's anti-Christic culture, Christian's are able to realistically, and thus efficaciously,

begin to build a new Christendom amidst the dystopic ruins. See Chapter XIV, *New Christendom*.

[59]   When capitalized, the term *Magisterium* herein refers to the teaching authority of the Church; when not capitalized, the term *magisterium* herein refers to the bureaucratic power structure of the Church.

[60]   Catholic Action is "the organized work of the laity that is performed under the direction or mandate of a bishop in the fields of dogma, morals, liturgy, education, and charity." The Editors of Encyclopaedia Britannica, "Catholic Action," *Encyclopaedia Britannica* (2 December 2019).

[61]   Pius Xl, *Letter "Quae Nobis" to Cardinal Bertram* (13 November 1928). From *Acta Apostolicae Sedis: Commentarium Officiale*, Annus XX, vol. XX (Typis Polyglottis Vaticanis, 1943); quoted in Paul VI, *Apostolicam Actuositatem*, Chapter IV, no. 20 (18 November 1965).

[62]   For example, the unchristian ecclesial identity-political movements such as *We are Church*, and *Voice of the Faithful*.

[63]   Single Catholics are incorporated into the extra liturgical functions of a parish by being in various degrees incorporated into individual families. Without such incorporation into individual families, "parish family" remains but a platitude.

[64]John XIII, "Pope John's Opening Speech to the Council," *The Documents of Vatican II*, ed. Walter M. Abbott, S.J. (New York: Herder and Herder / Association Press, 1966), 712-713. Given on October 11th, 1962.

[65]Joseph Cardinal Ratzinger, *Principles of Catholic Theology: Building Stones for a Fundamental Theology*, trans. Sister Mary F. McCarthy (San Francisco: Ignatius Press, 1987), 393. Epilogue will be found on pgs. 367-393.

[66]   Vatican II's liberal "Rhine Alliance" had as its core the Germanic bishops and their *periti*, and were joined by other liberals. The "English Alliance" had great influence due to the international geo-political dominance of the United States. This English speaking alliance, especially due to the Americans, was generally conservative but overly optimistic and unscholarly, and thus would, for the most part, allow the Rhine fathers to set the ideological agenda. The more traditional Italian Curia Alliance, which was joined by other traditionalists, especially French but some English blocs as well, would be neutered with the death of John XXIII and election of Montini. The remaining designated traditional/conservative bloc of bishops, the International Alliance, was made up of individual conservative bishops from around the world, who because of their lack of homogeneity were not an effective countermeasure to the Rhine Alliance. (At the time of Vatican II, the prelates of third world

countries had little influence, but subsequently have proven to be more orthodox than the prelates from Europe and America.)

[67]   Paul VI, *Lumen Gentium* (21 November 1964).

[68]   The issue of informed Catholic conscience versus the bureaucratic elements of the Church is indeed the question, albeit lopsided, of both an ideological traditionalism and liberalism; with traditionalism doing violence to the conscience part and liberalism doing violence to the Catholic part.

[69]   PS 20:7

[70]   In traditional and conservative circles this militancy has been thwarted by a compartmentalized liturgicalism, a castrating clericalism, and non-radical conservatism.

[71]   For more on hidebound traditionalism, see Chapter XI, § *Spectrum of Orthodoxy* and § *Spectrum of Orthopraxy*.

[72]   The replacing of preaching the Gospel with the advocacy for social justice was dubbed the "consistent ethic of life" or the more biblical term "seamless garment." Social justice against a myriad of opined social ills, such as capital punishment, economic injustice, racism, national borders, and unjust war. Citing New Testament principles such as forgiveness and reconciliation as common—that is not specifically Christian—denominators, the social justice gospel seeks, again, to create alliances with secular powers and interests.

[73]*Ubi Nos*, no. 13.

[74]Paul VI, *Dignitatis Humane*, no. 13 (7 December 1965).

[75]Discorsi of John XXIII (1962), 583; quoted in Address of Pope Paul VI during the Last General Meeting of the Second Vatican Council (7 December 1965).

[76]Address of Pope Paul VI During the Last General Meeting of the Second Vatican Council (7 December 1965).

[77]   "We would say that, through some mysterious crack—no, it's not mysterious; through some crack, the smoke of Satan has entered the Church of God. There is doubt, uncertainty, problems, unrest, dissatisfaction, confrontation." Paul VI, June 29, 1972. See Gelsomino Del Guercio, "What did Paul VI mean by saying 'the smoke of Satan has entered the Church'?" *Aleteia* (6 July 2018).

[78]   Hence, the abiding clericalism and episcopal arrogance that transcends both conservative and liberal priests and prelates.

[79]   Note well, that Peter, and all those ordained to be ministers of her treasury of truth and grace, are, in so far as they are functioning as

ordained ministers, likewise called to give up even those things that are rightfully man's.

[80]   *Libido dominandi* (Lt.): "The desire to dominate." See St. Augustine, *City of God,* Book I.

[81]   The Roman Curia's clericalistic culture is legendary, and its likes may never be seen again. This Roman curia was populated by the brightest, or at least the most conniving and linguistically astute. Indeed, linguistically, the lack of Latin literacy that has increased since Vatican II has deprived this clerical cabal of its own special and nuanced language, which in itself might be the best valid defense of the vernacular.

[82] Ludwig Von Mises, *Bureaucracy* (New Haven: Yale University Press, 1944), 101-103. Mises (29 September 1881 – 10 October 1973), a secular Jew raised in *ancien régime* Catholic Austria, was the leading advocate of the School of Austrian Economics. Mises was economic adviser to Otto von Habsburg, the Christian Democratic politician and claimant to the defunct Catholic throne of Austria and the Holy Roman Empire.

[83]   For instance, Catholic Charities (which is deficient in both Catholicity and charity) is the 5th largest social services institution in the United States. "In 2010, Catholic Charities had revenues of $4.7 billion, $2.9 billion of which came directly from the United States government," and the balance coming from other State, local, and corporate entities, topped off with donations from parish collections (*viz.,* diocesan annual appeals). "Catholic Charities USA," *Wikipedia* (12 December 2020).

[84]   See Chapter XIII, § *Priesthood.*

[85]   "Hubris," *Wikipedia* (12 January 2021); See The Editors of Encyclopaedia Britannica, "Hubris," *Encyclopedia Britannica* (18 May 2017).

[86]   In addition to this author having being a seminarian in both minor and major seminaries, and having taught in seminaries, he has worked professionally with countless seminaries, monasteries, evangelical houses, and individual priests.

[87]   Mainstream priestly recruitment programs, such as the widespread *Quo Vadis* program, emphasize what can be gained by becoming a priest, thus appealing to those that may desire a relatively easy path to privilege and prestige.

[88] Aristotle, *Rhetoric,* 1378b; quoted in "Hubris," *Wikipedia.*

[89]   As per this author's clinical work as a psychomoralist and adviser to various priestly societies, including the major traditional ones, it

must be noted that seminary rectors and faculty, much less bishops, do not adhere to objective standards of psychosexual normalcy in their admittance of men for ordination. Deficient and even aberrant psychosexuality is often tolerated if the man is able to remain chaste. However, *nota bene,* that the largest traditional priestly fraternity, the *Society of Pius X,* though rife with a virulent clericalism (that has inherently resulted in the sins of hubris, demands for blind obedience, severe bullying, and an unaccountability for even some sexual abuses), has at least remained relatively free from priests with homosexual tendencies. This is due in great part to its founder's intolerance of any such tendencies in his seminarians and priests; so much so that Monsignor Marcel Lefebvre banned the wearing of the biretta for being too foppish. On the other hand, some other prominent traditional societies do seem to pride themselves on their foppishness; for instance, on the degree of lace intricacies that adorn their surplices.

[90] The precipitous fall of many Jesuits from Catholicism to Marxism is a fruit of this pride-based obedience. This pride base was also responsible in great part for their stupendous accomplishments. The Jesuits were heralded as nothing less than supermen even by the secular press; for instance, Life Magazine had a feature photo spread on the Jesuits' many accomplishments: "The Jesuits in America," *Life Magazine (11* October 1954).

[91]"To the Members of the Society in Portugal, Rome, March 26, 1553," *Ignatius of Loyola: Letters and Instructions,* ed. John W. Padberg, et al. (St. Louis, Mo.: Institute of Jesuit Sources, 1996).

[92]Alphonsus Rodriguez, *Practice of Christian and Religious Perfection* (Seville: 1609); quoted in John R.T. Lamont, "Tyranny and sexual abuse in the Catholic Church: A Jesuit tragedy," *Rorate Caeli* (28 October 2018).

[93]Rodriguez.

[94] "The Society of Priests of Saint Sulpice was founded in France in 1641 by Father Jean-Jacques Olier (1608–1657), an exemplar of the French School of Spirituality" (for a critique of this school see Chapter XII, § *Devotionalism).* "Society of the Priests of Saint Sulpice," *Wikipedia* (31 December 2020).

[95]John R.T. Lamont, "Tyranny and sexual abuse in the Catholic Church: A Jesuit tragedy," *Rorate Caeli* (October 28, 2018).

[96]Children should rightly be read as adolescent males, since they were vastly the victims of homosexual degradation.

[97] Lamont.

[98] Maybe even more outrageously, these same traditional priests are known to assert that it is not the parents who are responsible for the

souls of their children, or not the father who is charged with leading his family, but rather that they as pastors of the communal parish have ultimate responsibility and headship, an assertion that goes hellishly against both piety and subsidiarity.

[99] All creation exists as analogous being of Supreme Being, that is, while not sharing in God's nature, that is, creation by definition is not divine, having similarity in function. This analogous being with Supreme Being ranges from the simplest particle of matter having the similar function of mere existence to the *imago Dei* persons, that is, the angels and humans, having the similar function of rationality and volition.

[100] Here individualism is taken as a transcendent ideal that goes beyond a person's mere individuality. Thus, both egoistic individualism and *imago Dei* individualism are the same categorically but diametrically opposed definitively.

[101] See Preface, § *Psychomoral Foundation*. For a full explication of the clinical science of psychomoralitics see the textbook *Psychomoralitics: The Soul-Deep Alternative to the Failed Mental Health Professions*.

[102] Henry Newman, *Certain Difficulties felt by Anglicans in Catholic Teaching II* (London: Longmans Green, 1885), 248. Newman further wrote: "I shall drink to the Pope, if you please, still, to conscience first, and to the Pope afterwards." Newman used the term "Vicar of Christ" pointedly so as to address those opponents of his conversion to Catholicism who misunderstood, as did and do many Catholics, the primary locus of authority in the Catholic Church as being in the papacy, that normally, though apparently misleadingly, has this term applied to it.

[103] St. Augustine, *A Sermon on Love*. See St. Augustine, *Homily 7 on the First Epistle of John*, trans. by H. Browne. From *Nicene and Post-Nicene Fathers*, First Series, vol. 7, ed. Philip Schaff (Buffalo, NY: Christian Literature Publishing Co., 1888).

[104] See next Chapter, § *What is Truth?*

[105] See Chapter XI, § *Spectrum of Orthodoxy*.

[106] See Chapter XI, § Spectrum of Orthodoxy.

[107] See Chapter V, § Heretical Authoritarianism.

[108] Much of these heretical strains have been introduced under the guise of private revelation.

[109] Thus, under the dual aspect of clericalism and infantilism, the faithful, especially the fathers of families who by nature and grace are called to lead the community, abdicate their roles to usurping priests. Indeed, the fathers, who are the God-given leaders of the

Christian community, are effectively castrated. Thus, the past fall of Christendom I, the continued loss of Catholic culture and society, and the unchecked rise of anti-Christic powers.

[110] Thomas Aquinas, *The Summa Theologiae of St. Thomas Aquinas*, second and revised edition, trans. Fathers of the English Dominican Province (1920), 2a2ae, q. 104, a. 5.

[111] See Chapter XII, § *Devotionalism.*

[112] Psychomoralitics, 160-162.

[113] See Chapter VIII, § *Receptive Virtue.*

[114] An atypical act of the pride is one that appears humble.

[115] See Chapter XII, § *Devotionalism*, and Chapter XIII, § *Evangelical Authenticity.*

[116] See Chapter XII, § *Devotionalism.*

[117] "The path of maturation and psychomoral well-being entails the psyche increasing in its receptivity, assenting to, and choosing of reality in both breadth and depth. This requires that the psyche be unencumbered by a dominant ego in its subjective and reality-rejecting orientation. From the highest faculty of the psyche comes the ability to rationally choose and fully accept objective reality even when that reality is not in accord with, or threatens harm to, the subjective good of the ego. But so too, it is the psyche that can choose to acquiesce to the ego and allow the domination of the ego's defenses, thus choosing a lower subjective good of the ego over the objective good. The crucial psychomoralitic point is at this juncture of choice between the objective higher good and the subjective egoistic good. The intensity of this psychomoralitic point is determined by the degree that the choice entails the attainment of either the objective good or the subjective good to the detriment of the other." *Psychomoralitics*, 96-97.

[118] But while the *imago Dei* is an analogous manifestation of the Trinity, it is only in the Christian state of sanctification that the Trinity actually indwells in the soul.

[119] This heresy of material monism is a denial of the hylomorphic composite that is a definitive cardinal truth of natural law and the Christian faith.

[120] "Psychomoral passions of the ego are brought about by either the negative stimuli of humiliation or the positive stimuli of aggrandizement. Psychomoral passions of the psyche are brought about by either the negative stimuli of sorrow or the positive stimuli of joy. The same impacting reality or stimuli can cause different and even conflicting passions and emotions to be elicited from the three

elements of body, ego, and psyche." *Psychomoralitics*, 88.

[121] "Because for the human intellect an atheistic position entails a logical absurdity, and even an agnostic position entails the possibility of a logical absurdity, those that hold such positions necessarily do violence to the human reasoning process; and hence to the human concept of truth; and hence to the good and being itself; and hence to the human person as a truth seeker. Positing that God does not exist renders the human person as a *seeker of truth, good, and beatitude* empty and tragic indeed; leaving nothing deeper within a person than this emptiness, nor anything loftier outside a person than the sought after but illusory divine chimera. And therein lies the urgency of the ultimate quest to answer the ultimate dilemma, a quest into even an apparent emptiness." *Psychomoralitics*, 88.

[122] Sanctification necessarily entails temptation. For it entails loving God and humbly accepting one's deficiency or pridefully turning from God because he makes one realize one's deficiency and loving oneself/hating God for making one deficient. This temptation entails the choice to either suffer well or reject one's inherent creaturely deficiency.

[123] "Both psychomoralitics and existential stoicism correctly hold that a person cannot fight certain realities, specifically those deepest of realities, those ultimate concerns. But the solution stoicism proffers is to not be bothered by these deepest and most impacting of realities. If these realities become too bothersome or insistent, that is if they no longer can be effectively ignored, then suicide is an option. Existential stoicism, then, is a high-functioning ego coping mechanism that protects the ego from ultimate reality. Very strong, and apparently virtuous people, may function on this level. They are focused on what they can do; they are often high achievers. But existential stoicism is a practiced selectivity of reality. It defends against the realities that a person cannot do anything about. But these ultimate realities are indeed ultimate, and openness to them is essential to entering into the full drama of human existence and to experiencing true human flourishing. Yes, these ultimate realities are the most devastating: the present reality of the irreversible past, its guilt, failure, and all the loss of the good now gone; and the present reality of the irresistible future, its suffering, death and all the loss of the good now had. Resigning to things one cannot change is rational, but not being bothered by these things, these ultimate realities, is not. To hold, "If I can't do something about it, it doesn't matter," is the stoic's ideological coping defense of the ego. This defense is the arrogant, prideful refusal to be overwhelmed, even if it means taking one's life once one can no longer keep up the stoical pretense." *Psychomoralitics*, 153.

[124] In an existential, experiential, and precognitive manner.

[125] Hilary of Poitiers (310 – 367 AD).

[126] See Chapter I, § Third Millennium Technarcistic Man.

[127] "Virtue denotes a certain perfection of a power. Now a thing's perfection is considered chiefly in regard to its end. But the end of power is act. Wherefore power is said to be perfect, according as it is determinate to its act. Now there are some powers which of themselves are determinate to their acts; for instance, the active natural powers. And therefore these natural powers are in themselves called virtues. But the rational powers, which are proper to man, are not determinate to one particular action, but are inclined indifferently to many: and they are determinate to acts by means of habits, as is clear from what we have said above (I-II:49:4). Therefore human virtues are habits.... Good use of free-will is said to be a virtue, in the same sense as above (Reply to Objection 1); that is to say, because it is that to which virtue is directed as to its proper act. For the act of virtue is nothing else than the good use of free-will." *Summa Theologiae,* 1a2ae, q. 55, a. 1.

[128] Aquinas does not even regard acquired virtues, that is, those obtained by our own repeated good actions, as being proper virtues at all, but only virtues in a restricted sense: "Only the infused virtues are perfect, and deserve to be called virtues simply..." *Summa Theologiae 1a2ae, q. 65, a. 2, c.* "Unlike acquired virtues, infused virtues are unified by *caritas* (divine friendship), they can be received by anyone, they can co-exist with contrary acquired dispositions, they can be gained immediately by divine infusion and they can be lost immediately by one seriously evil action." Andrew Pinsent, "Thomas Aquinas on the Passions," *Notre Dame Philosophical Reviews* (7 February 2010).

[129] "The passions have been traditionally categorized as love, desire and repugnance, delight and loss, hope and despair, daring and fear, and anger. This list can be expanded by delineating the plethora of "feeling" adjectives both positive and negative. But no matter the delineation, the chief passion is always love and the other passions are derivatives of this *chief passion.* The derivative passions come from either love of egoistic/subjective good or love of psychic/objective good. Love, then, is the chief passion, being the *sine qua non* of all the other passions." *Psychomoralitics*, 112.

[130] The infused virtues infuse themselves, whereas the psychomoralitic virtue of receptivity allows for the infusing of reality.

[131] Psychomoralitics defines virtue and applies the terms *avenues* and *defenses* more strictly and succinctly than that which is commonly regarded as *virtue* or *vice* and the psychomoralitic continuum does not necessarily correlate with a continuum of apparent virtue and vice.

[132] For example, in acquired virtue courage is the mean virtue, cowardice its deficient vice and recklessness its excessive vice.

[133] See Chapter VII, § Our Lord Jesus Christ.

[134] The ability to delay gratification can often hamper the deep psychotherapeutic process. See *Psychomoralitics*, Chapter 8, *Coping*, 139ff.

[135] The ego, or pseudo-self, as per psychomoralitics, is the complex of pride, self-love, and its defense mechanisms.

[136] It is the Triune God who is Supreme Being, Supreme Truth, and Supreme Good; from whence all being, truth, and good analogously derive.

[137] This natural maturation and decreasing of the egoistic self is the abnegation of pride and its defensive secretions which besmirch the *imago Dei* essence of the human person.

[138] Though St. John the Baptist was born without sin, he was conceived in original sin and thus not without its effects. St. John's original sin was removed *in utero*. Thus, only his, Christ's and the Blessed Mother's birthdays are celebrated. Though St. John the Baptist received a singular remission of original sin in anticipation of the Crucifixion of Christ, he is still deemed the last and greatest of the Old Testament prophets. Though the effects of original sin need not necessarily lead to actual sins, as can be supposed to some extent in the case of St. John, they are nonetheless imperfect and thus mar the image of God.

[139] Actual grace is very apparent in, even possibly the *sine qua non* of, receptive virtue.

[140] While acquired virtue is vulnerable to semi-Pelagianism, receptive virtue is not. This is because acquired virtue is indeed acquired by human effort, whereas receptive virtue is not an acquirement but an acquiescence.

[141] Note well, the theological ethos of crucialism is based upon the clinical intervention of Thomistic psychomoralitics. For a person who has not adequately gone through a gradual maturation (a common occurrence in the third millennium) and does not have the requisite acquired virtues, the natural foundation of Christian holiness can be remedied by Thomistic psychomoralitics. With an emphasis on receptive (versus acquired) natural virtue, psychomoralitics effects transformative maturation, and especially in those that have maturation disorders (symptomatically present in most of the "mental disorders") and acquired vices.

[142] In many non-Catholic sects, the ardency—most often evaluated as per the emotionality exhibited—a person wills in his claiming of

Jesus Christ as his savior determines the efficacy of that claim.

[143] "Before the Council of Trent, the Schoolmen would seldom distinguished actual grace from sanctifying grace. But, in consequence of modern controversies regarding grace [see immediately below § *Controversy on Efficacious Grace*] it has become usual and necessary in theology to draw a sharper distinction between the transient help to act (actual grace) and the permanent state of grace (sanctifying grace). . . . Actual grace derives its name, *actual*, from the Latin *actualis* (*ad actum*), for it is granted by God for the performance of salutary acts and is present and disappears with the action itself." Joseph Pohle, "Actual Grace," *The Catholic Encyclopedia*, vol. 6 (New York: Robert Appleton Company, 1909).

[144] See Chapter 7, § Dehumanizing Obedience.

[145] Glory taken as an intrinsic quality of God's splendor is infinite, and thus cannot become greater; but glory taken as a quantitative manifestation of this intrinsic glory in his creatures can be increased, and infinitely so because of its intrinsic quality.

[146] To conceptualize the specific dynamics of purgation or damnation it is necessary to understand the topography of the soul. As per the Thomistic topography of psychomoralitics, that which is to purgated away from the image of God is the pseudo-self. The psuedo-self is the combined complex of the ego, its passions, and coping mechanisms. Most often a person, and by definition those of the technarcistic bent, identifies the pseudo-self with his essential self. However, it is the subjugation and reduction of the pseudo-self that brings out the essential and authentic self of the psyche; that is, the *imago Dei*.

[147] See Chapter 2, § Suffering is not a Mystery.

[148] Michael; (Heb.) מיכאל / מִיכָאֵל

[149] This preternatural deficiency is seen in Adam's poverty of being "alone," which God pronounced as "not good." GN 2:18

[150] *Summa Theologica*, Suppl. 3ae, app. 2, a. 2.

[151] Contrary to pietistic depictions, the damned do not cry out for mercy, do not desire heaven or God, but rather, as per the intrinsic dynamics of damnation, choose in the singular and eternal moment to hate God for prideful love of self.

[152] *Agonia* (Gk.) means "a struggle unto death," referring specifically to a wrestling match unto death as it was practiced in the ancient Greek world.

[153] 2COR 5:21

[154] In the average physically and psychomorally healthy human, much less the perfect physical and psychomoral human who is Jesus Christ, it is only the most extreme stress, and even then it is very rare, that can cause the involuntary nervous system reaction of *hematidrosis* or bloody sweat.

[155] Christ's intact human volition is not given up or reduced in any degree but rather wills to do the will of the Father.

[156] "The first two words, *Eloi, Eloi,* whether in Hebrew or Aramaic, have sufficient similarity to each other and each sufficient similarity to the name itself to warrant the jeer that Jesus was calling upon Elias, or the sincere supposition of those who might not fully understand the language, that he was actually calling on Elias. The forms *lema* and *lama* used in Matthew and Mark respectively (Westcott and Hort, The New Testament in Greek) represent the various possible forms, the first the Aramaic, and the second the Hebrew. The various readings and translations of the latter word, sabacthani, only add confusion to an effort at ultimate explanation of the real statement." (*italicization* added). Walter G. Clippinger, "Eloi; Eloi; Lama; Sabachtha; Eli; Eli; Lama Sabachthani," *International Standard Bible Encyclopedia*, ed. James Orr (Wm. B. Eerdmans Publishing Co., 1939).

[157] A psychomoral binary process involves a simple assent or dissent. It is "a random event with two exhaustive and mutually exclusive outcomes." See "Binary process," *Farlex Partner Medical Dictionary* (2012).

[158] The palliative use of psychotropics and narcotics should aim at alleviating pain *so as to* allow the most recollected and conscious death as possible. However, psychotropics and narcotics are now heavily used to avoid all agitation of soul, which not only disallows the final priceless moments of the dying with their loved ones, but disallows preparing for and entering into the final salvific purgation of death.

[159] "Only a philosophy that upholds a spiritual faculty can explain even the possibility of knowledge." F.J. Sheen, *God and Intelligence in Modern Philosophy: A Critical Study in the Light of the Philosophy of Saint Thomas* (London: Longmans & Green, 1938), 139.
Aquinas divides the intellect according to specific powers or faculties. The first is a material entity called the potential intellect, which receives sense experience from the world. The potential intellect includes common sense faculty, memory, imagination, and the cogitative faculty. The second is a spiritual entity called the actual intellect, which has the power to abstract the form from beings encountered through sense experience. The third, also spiritual, is called the acquired intellect, which is the power to reflect on the facts and upon its own operations. In addition, both the actual and acquired intellects require a causal power to actualize their potential;

this is called the agent intellect.

[160] "[The rational creature] has a share of the Eternal Reason, whereby it has a natural inclination to its proper act and end: and this participation of the eternal law in the rational creature is called the natural law." *Summa* Theologica, 1a2ae, q. 91, a. 2.

[161] Aquinas succinctly delineates the types of fear: "Accordingly if a man turn to God and adhere to Him, through fear of punishment, it will be servile fear; but if it be on account of fear of committing a fault, it will be filial fear, for it becomes a child to fear offending its father. If, however, it be on account of both, it will be initial fear, which is between both these fears." *Summa Theologiae*, 2a2ae, q. 19, a. 2.

[162] Benedict XVI, *Angelus Address,* (June 22, 2008).

[163] See G.C. Dilsaver, Celebrating God Given Gender: Masculinity and Femininity per Nature and Grace (Imago Dei Press, 2016).

[164] Psychomoral is a term that refers to the realm of spirit and soul, that is, to the specific difference of the human person in God's image.

[165] "Accident is that which is present and absent without the destruction of its subject. It receives a two-fold division, for one kind of it is separable, but the other inseparable, e.g., to sleep is a separable accident, but to be black happens inseparably to a crow and an Ethiopian; we may possibly indeed conceive a white crow, and an Ethiopian casting his colour, without destruction of the subject." Porphyry, *Introduction (or Isagoge) to the Logical Categories of Aristotle*, vol. II, Chapter V, trans. Octavius F. Owen (1853), 609-633.

[166] As per psychomoralitics, the *humiliation* of reality becomes *humbling*, or effects an increase in humility, only if one says *"yes"* to the reality.

[167] "There are three orders of knowledge: human, angelic, divine. The object of knowledge in general is intelligible reality. The proper object of human intelligence is the intelligible being of sense objects, because the human intellect has as its proportioned object the lowest order of intelligible reality, the shadowy reality of the sense world. By opposition, then, the proper object of angelic intelligence is the intelligible reality of spiritual creatures. Hence, the proper intelligible object of each particular angel is that angel's own essence, just as God's proper intelligible object is his own divine essence." Reginald Garrigou-Lagrange, "Ch. XXIII: Angelic Nature and Knowledge," *Reality: A Synthesis of Thomistic Thought*, (St. Louis: Herder, 1950), 166. Lagrange refers here to the *Summa*, 1a, q. 12, a. 4.

[168] Humiliation before the Fall was not yet possible since Adam and Eve had not yet turned away from God in apostatizing pride, with

such pride being that which humiliation affects.

[169] Humility is the antidote to pride; and pride is not only the primordial sin, but also is the primordial precursor of all essential mal-being, ego-reactivity, and the superficial symptomology of so-called "mental disorder." Humility is the basis for maturation and essential well-being. See G.C. Dilsaver, *Imago Dei Psychotherapy* (*Catholic University of American Press*, 2009), 144-145. Also, see G.C. Dilsaver, *Psychomoralitics: The Antidotal Alternative to the Failed Mental Health Professions (Imago Dei Press*, 2017).

[170] See Celebrating God Given Gender, Chapter 4, § Maternal Sweetness.

[171] John Paul II, *Vatican Address* (1 October 1979).

[172] For a full explication of the definitive teaching on Christian familial patriarchy see G.C. Dilsaver, *The Three Marks of Manhood* (TAN Books, 2010).

[173] *Catechism of the Council of Trent for Parish Priests*, trans. John McHugh and Charles Callan (New York: Joseph F. Wagner, Inc., 1947), 352.

[174] See Celebrating God Given Gender, Chapter VI, § *The Sacredness of Sexuality.*

[175] While a woman with a promiscuous disposition is an abnormality both in regards to nature and grace, a man with a promiscuous disposition is not abnormal within nature; therefore, he must do violence to this nature within grace.

[176] *Church is subject to Christ*: The Church, then, is ever obedient to Christ and can never fall from him, but remain faithful to him, unspotted and unchanged, to the end of the world.

[177] *The Original Unity of Man and Woman* was written by Karol Wojtyła as a private theologian before he ascended to the papacy but was read during his Wednesday audiences. Thus, it is important to note that even in its unadulterated form, and read by Wojtyła when he held the papacy as John Paul II, *Original Unity of Man and Woman* remains the work of a private theologian and not a magisterial pronouncement (See Appendix B).

[178] This accepted humiliation diminishes the pride and self-love that make up the pseudo-self. See *Psychomoralitics.*

[179] For example, on April 11, 2005, Joe Solmonese, the chief executive of the pro-abortion Democratic activist group *Emily's List* (which finances the political campaigns of pro-abortion Democratic women) moved sideways to become president of the *Human Rights Campaign*, the largest of the homosexual pressure groups. The pro-abortion National Organization for Women (NOW) supports all aspects of

the homosexual agenda, including same-sex "marriage," hate crime laws, and persecuting the Boy Scouts for barring homosexuals as scoutmasters. The feminist pro-abortion/homosexual relationship is incestuous indeed, but thankfully barren and damned.

[180] Again, "If anyone [*e.g.*, popes and/or councils] says that it is possible that at some time, given the advancement of knowledge, a sense may be assigned to the dogmas propounded by the church which is different from that which the church has understood and understands: let him be anathema." *Decrees of the First Vatican Council*, Session III, Canon 4.3 (24 April 1870).

[181] See Chapter VII, § The Primacy of Informed Conscience.

[182] Not just ecclesial authority, but sociopolitical authority as well. See Chapter XII, *New Christendom*.

[183] See Chapter VI, Perversions of Power.

[184] The grace of being incorporated into her is tangibly done via baptism and all, when validly baptized, become members of the Church, and they will remain members of the Church until they somehow abjure.

[185] See Chapter XIV, § Patriotic Piety Contra Nationalism.

[186] A society is "a voluntary association of individuals for common ends, ... a community, nation, or broad grouping of people having common traditions, institutions, and collective activities and interests." See "Society," *Merriam-Webster.com Dictionary* (Merriam-Webster).

[187] *Acta Apostolicae Sedis: Commentarium Officiale*, Annus XXXV, Second Series, vol. X (Typis Polyglottis Vaticanis, 1943), 193ff. See the Vatican website.

[188] Let traditionalism/progressivism also admit of subcategories such as Jansenism/humanism, liberalism/conservatism, and fatalism/eudaemonism.

[189] The pristine and most essential example of salient/radical orthodoxy is the Christological one. It is neither Christ as not consubstantial with the Father (Arianism et al.) nor Christ as only apparently human (Monophysitism et al.), but Christ as hypostatically one in his divinity and humanity that is the most earthshaking position.

[190] For example, the virtue of courage has as its deficient vice cowardice and its excessive vice recklessness, and it is recklessness that is more akin to courage than cowardice. In fact recklessness is often an overcompensation for cowardice.

[191] John Paul II, *Apostolic Letter on Reserving Priestly Ordination to Men Alone*, no. 4 (22 May 1994).

[192] In the ancient days there was no special liturgy at all, much less communion services. The earliest Roman Ordines, dating from about A.D. 800, according to Duchesne, state "the exact order of the ancient Synaxes without a liturgy," *i.e.* the order of the earliest Christian prayer meetings did not celebrate the liturgy proper, *i.e.* the Mass. The Good Friday custom of unveiling and adoration of the Holy Cross was introduced into the Latin Rite in the seventh or eighth century. Thomas Gilmartin, "Good Friday," *The Catholic Encyclopedia*, vol. 6 (New York: Robert Appleton Company, 1909).

[193] The only apostle present, St. John, is considered not as priest but in his essential vocation as one of the faithful, and only within the essential relational context of human and Christian existence of the family: "When Jesus therefore had seen his mother and the disciple standing whom he loved, he saith to his mother: Woman, behold thy son. After that, he saith to the disciple: Behold thy mother. And from that hour, the disciple took her to his own." JN 19:26

[194] On Good Friday, remaining totally cloistered at home in abject worship and intimate penitential union with Christ Crucified may be deemed more proper than going out in public, even if but to a chapel. For it is in the home that the Cross is to be most frequently and intimately embraced throughout the year.

[195] See Chapter III, § *Portentous Papal Pretenses*. While in Avignon, as per the French royal proclivities, John XXII, who vigorous fought against the radical poverty of the Franciscans, lived quite lavishly and royally (as did the other Avignon popes).

[196] "Throughout his pontificate, John XXII also exhibited a marked concern over matters of sorcery, divination, and demonic invocation. The pope feared magical assaults and assassination attempts on his own person, and he used charges of heresy, sorcery, and idolatry as political weapons against his enemies....His bull on this matter, *Super illius specula* (Upon His Watchtower), remained an important part of the legal apparatus against practitioners of sorcery for the remainder of the Middle Ages." Michael D. Bailey, "Pope John XXII," *History Publications* (Iowa State University, 2006), 56. John XXII himself was charged with the heresy (mild as it was) for holding that the beatific vision was not enjoyed until after the general judgment, for which he is said to have repented of on his deathbed.

[197] Joseph McMahon, "Perpetual Adoration," *The Catholic Encyclopedia*, vol. 1 (New York: Robert Appleton Company, 1907).

[198] Herbert Thurston, "Visits to the Blessed Sacrament," *The Catholic Encyclopedia*, vol. 15 (New York: Robert Appleton Company, 1912).

[199] As the Roman Church's fixation on the Eucharist is a reaction to the heresy of Protestantism, the Eastern Church's fixation on icons is a reaction to its own heretical iconoclasm. But while the Roman fixation on the Eucharist is somewhat logical even if syllogistically erroneous, the Eastern fixation on icons lacks any basis in logic.

[200] Canons and Decrees of the Council of Trent, Session XXII, Chapter II, § That the Sacrifice of the Mass is Propitiatory both for the Living and the Dead.

[201] Lumen Gentium, Chapter II, no. 11. (Lt.) Sacrificium eucharisticum, totius vitae christianae fontem et culmen, participantes, divinam Victimam Deo offerunt atque seipsos cum Ea.

[202] Vatican II collegiality has only increased the bureaucratic powers of the episcopacy and the chancery, as can be witnessed in the Magisterium's unresponsiveness to the abuse of the faithful in the post-Vatican II sacerdotal scandals. In sum, in the wake of Vatican II, with the teachings and authority of the Church herself watered-down, the authority of the bishops, and even popes, was no longer constrained by those teachings but rather intentionally increased so as to be able to override those teachings.

[203] Catechism of the Council of Trent for Parish Priests, trans. John McHugh and Charles Callan (New York: Joseph F. Wagner, Inc., 1947), 218. The Council also declared: "Our Savior, therefore, when about to depart from this world unto the Father, instituted this Sacrament, in which he, as it were, poured forth the riches of His divine love towards man, making a remembrance of his wonderful works; and He commanded us, in the participation thereof, to venerate His memory, and to show his death until He come to judge the world. And He also willed that this sacrament should be received as the spiritual food of souls, whereby may be nourished and strengthened those who live with His life, who said, He that eateth me, he also shall live by me; and as an antidote, by the which we may be freed from daily faults, and preserved from mortal sins. He willed, furthermore, that it should be a pledge of our glory to come, and of everlasting happiness, and thus be a symbol of that one body of which He is the head, and to which He would fain have us, as members, be united by the closest bond of faith, hope, and charity, that we might all speak the same thing, and there might be no schisms among us." Canons and Decrees of the Council of Trent, Session XIII, Chapter II, § On the Reason of the Institution of this most holy Sacrament, trans. Theodore Alois Buckley (London: George Routledge and Co., 1851).

[204] The words of institution are not synonymous with the words of consecration. It is semantically and logically obvious that the only words essential for confecting the Eucharist are "this is my Body" or "this is (the Chalice of) My Blood." For whatever Our Lord God says, "it" comes necessarily into being; e.g. "Let there be light, and there was

light." GN 1:3

[205] Tied to the newly emphasized Eucharistic devotion was the even more novel and controversial devotion to the Sacred Heart. The Congregation of Rites refused to authorize devotion to the Sacred Heart in 1729 due to a wariness of devotional compartmentalization, which was graphically represented in the center of the Sacred Heart devotion: the artistic dismembering of the Sacred Heart from its embodiment in the anatomically whole Christ. See Jean Bainvel, "Devotion to the Sacred Heart of Jesus," *The Catholic* Encyclopedia, vol. 7 (New York: Robert Appleton Company, 1910).

[206] See Chapter IV, § *Parishism & Catholic Action.*

[207] In addition to its beginnings as a Catholic counter-response to Protestant spirituality, devotionalism also coincided with the great popularity of all forms of spiritism and dabblings in necromancy and the paranormal; and, in Catholic circles, with a great uptake in private revelations of all sorts. As per spiritism, Emanuel Swedenborg (1688–1772) purported direct communication with God, spirits, and angels. Even otherwise orthodox Catholic writers, such as Robert Hugh Benson (1871–1914) also manifested an unhealthy fascination with the paranormal. See Nicholas Weber, "Swedenborgians," *The Catholic Encyclopedia,* vol. 14 (New York: Robert Appleton Company, 1912).

[208] See below, § Efficacy & Sufficiency of the Holy Mass.

[209] See Chapter VII, § *Receptive Virtue.*

[210] David A. Fleming, *The Fire and the Cloud: An Anthology of Catholic Spirituality* (New York: Paulist Press, 1978), 272-273.

[211] "Pierre de Bérulle is considered as the leader of this movement, and he was joined by people like Charles de Condren, Jean-Jacques Olier, and Jean Eudes." It was priests and women who were the leaders of this French school of spirituality, and thus it lacked the familial father's masculine militancy and real-life practicality. As a result, this movement did little to impede, and maybe even facilitated, the withering away of Christendom. See "Bérulle, Pierre de," *Vincentian Encyclopedia* (26 November 2017).

[212] See Chapter XIII, § Evangelical Authenticity.

[213] See Preface.

[214] See Chapter IV, § *Parishism & Catholic Action.*

[215] See below § Continued Compartmentalization.

[216] Canons and Decrees of the Council of Trent, Session XXII, Chapter V, § *On the Solemn Ceremonies of the Sacrifice of the Mass.*

[217] The actual documents of Trent which addressed the Protestant heresy against the Mass never compartmentalized the Mass, but rather always referred to its transcendence to Christ Crucified. See below § *Compartmentalization of Mass & Eucharist.*

[218] See Chapter V, § *True Reform.*

[219] Is in fact utterly irredeemable. See Chapter XIV, *New Christendom.*

[220] There was a providential inculturation by Catholicism of classical culture, since it was a union of the secular and sacral. In Greco-Roman paganism and sociopolitics the State was seen as sacral. However, the pervasive embrace by conservative and traditional Catholics of "classical education," as if such an education is a *de fide* Catholic education, has no basis.

[221] While triumphalist themes, such as on Easter and Pentecost Sundays, of exaltation are liturgically proper still even they remain ancillary to the crucial theme of Christ Crucified and a broken spirit and contrite heart.

[222] *Catechism of the Council of Trent for Parish Priests*, trans. John McHugh and Charles Callan (New York: Joseph F. Wagner, Inc., 1947), 258-259.

[223] Canons and Decrees of the Council of Trent, Session XXII, Chapter I, § On the Institution of the Most Holy Sacrifice of the Mass.

[224] *Catechism of the Council of Trent for Parish Priests*, trans. John McHugh and Charles Callan (New York: Joseph F. Wagner, Inc., 1947), 218-219.

[225] As per psychomoralitics, intimacy entails the psychic passions, whereas sentimentality entails the egoistic passions. Thus, intimacy, as opposed to sentimentality, always entails some ego-abnegation.

[226] In St. Louis De Montfort's treatise on *True Devotion to Mary* he states that whenever Our Lady's devotees say 'Mary' she says 'Jesus.'

[227] Even when a Christian is blessed to consecrate himself to the Blessed Virgin Mary as her very slave, in properly doing so he is trusting absolutely in her maternity and, being caught up in rapturous love for her, gives her his entire person. Such a slavery of love is absent of all servile fear.

[228] In the late 1950's and early 1960's, there were more masses being said, more priestly and evangelical vocations, more churches and parochial schools being built than ever in the history of Christianity. (A practice for the most overtly pious of lay Catholics was to attend three back-to-back-to-back daily masses: one in preparation for communion, one for reception of communion, and one in

thanksgiving.) Yet, as witnessed by the late 1960's precipitous fall of those cultures most overtly Catholic, underneath it all there was an extensive rotting and evil was advancing.

[229] The receiving of extreme unction and viaticum on a Christian's deathbed is a singular signal grace of salvation, though it is the sacramental confession that remits mortal sin.

[230] It is the ultimate end of the crucial natural vocation to manifest God's image in the ego-abnegation of maturing reality, as a burnt offering unto the Lord God for his greater manifest glory. All other natural vocations, be they incarnational, familial, or sociopolitical, are ordered toward this *imago Dei* manifestation.

[231] Ontology is the philosophical study of being.

[232] Yes, the Holy Mass and Eucharist can be overemphasized when that emphasis compartmentalizes these from their *raison d'etre* "leavening" effects in the greater context of Christian life. See Chapter XII, § *Compartmentalization of Mass & Eucharist.*

[233] Even the Anglican orders, which were the closest to the Catholic ones, were, in keeping with the constant position of the Church, pronounced "absolutely null and utterly void" by Leo XIII in the papal bull *Apostolicae curae*, no. 36 (1896).

[234] Is there the occasion that a Christian is alone and not part of, that is at least close friends with, a family or families? Yes, but this is an anomaly and not the ideal. And no, the nebulous "parish family," which only has existence at parish functions does not suffice, but may in fact give a false sense of comfort for those Christians who fall between the gaps of familial community.

[235] See Chapter X, § *The Feminine Charism.*

[236] Sisters: In 1965, there were 180,000 Catholic nuns. By 2002, that had fallen to 75,000 and the average age of a Catholic nun is today 68. In 1965, there were 104,000 teaching nuns. Today, there are 8,200, a decline of 94 percent since the end of Vatican II. Evangelical Orders: In 1965, 3,559 young men were studying to become Jesuit priests. In 2000, the figure was 389. With the Christian Brothers, the situation is even more dire. Their number has shrunk by two-thirds, with the number of seminarians falling 99 percent. In 1965, there were 912 seminarians in the Christian Brothers. In 2000, there were only seven. Kenneth C. Jones, *Index of Leading Catholic Indicators* (St. Louis, Mo.: Oriens Publishing Company, 2003), 8-9.

[237] Within a four month period of Vatican II's last session in addition to *Perfectae Caritatis*, the Synod of Bishops was established, *Dignitatis Humanae* (Decree on Religious Liberty) and *Dei Verbum* (Dogmatic Constitution on Divine Revelation) were approved, and

other incomplete works of lesser import were wrapped up: *viz.*, the decrees *Christus Dominus* (On the pastoral office of bishops), *Optatam Totius* (On education for the priesthood), *Gravissimum Educationis* (On Christian education), *Apostolicam Actuositatem* (On the Role of the Laity), and *Nostra Aetate* (On the Jews).

[238] Vatican II, *Perfectae* Caritatis, no. 4 (28 October 1965).

[239] See Chapter V, § *True Reform*.

[240] This is an "overt quantifiable limit," for the Christian state finds its final perfection in absolute, and thus unquantifiable, abnegation.

[241] This, of course, includes conveniences and entertainment, and especially electronic entertainment or conveniences.

[242] Chapter VI, § Dehumanizing Obedience.

[243] Chapter IX, § Crucial Christian Receptivity.

[244] See Chapter VII, § Individualism as Prerequisite for Relational Communion.

[245] See Chapter VII, § Individualism as Prerequisite for Relational Communion.

[246] So too, the most tender station of the Cross is Jesus' meeting of his Blessed Mother on the way to Calvary, as well as the tradition of the *pieta* where Our Blessed Lord's lifeless, but still divine, body being taken down from the cross is cradled in the arms of his Blessed Mother.

[247] During the Middle Ages, a limited yet sanctioned practice was to the lifetime enclosure of a person (usually women) within tiny cells no larger than 12 x 15 square feet, without doors or any means of ingress or egress, and with very small windows. Typically, the cell was attached to a church.

[248] In Roman law, the *pater familias* was the father or "oldest living male in a household, and exercised autocratic authority over his extended family." "Pater familias," *Wikipedia* (21 January 2021).

[249] See Chapter XVI, § Sociopolitical Lay Competency.

[250] As a clinical observation, there is a disturbing but common phenomenon in families that have had a child, often an eldest daughter, enter the monastery and then have the remaining siblings or the parent's marriage itself be overtaken by dysfunction, mal-being, and evil. This can be attributed directly to the false and perverse notion of chastity that promotes not celibacy but a vicious and impious familial alienation. The remedy, and indeed reverse dynamics of familial thriving, peace, and holiness, is to be found

when an evangelical life is properly understood, with the Rule itself facilitating this, as an integral extension of and vivifying element within the evangelical's family of origin.

[251] Baptism can be validly administered by anyone, Christian or not, who intends to do what the Church intends and adheres to form and matter.

[252] The only military chaplains postbellum of the Civil War to ever receive the Medal of Honor have been Catholic priests, which at present are five and counting.

[253] Corporal works of mercy: to feed the hungry; to give water to the thirsty; to clothe the naked; to shelter the homeless; to visit the sick; to visit the imprisoned or ransom the captive; to bury the dead. Spiritual Works of Mercy: to instruct the ignorant; to counsel the doubtful; to admonish the sinners; to bear patiently those who wrong us; to forgive offenses; to comfort the afflicted; to pray for the living and the dead.

[254] And thus for priestly celibacy to efficaciously subordinate the self, a healthy psychosexuality is necessary.

[255] The new Latin Mass fraternities of priests seem to have as a working charism the *perfection of the priest*. But this is quite misguided. For in saying perfecting the priest, they refer to perfecting and actually elevating the man who is the priest. This is not in accord with the true nature of priesthood. For the priesthood is already perfect in Jesus Christ. The only need for the man who is priest is to decrease himself so as to allow the priesthood not to be obfuscated by himself.

[256] See Chapter V, § Ecclesial Kenosis Continued.

[257] True Christian patriarchal order is counterbalanced by its promotion of *imago Dei* individualism (see Chapter VII, § *Imago Dei Individualism*). For, it is for the good of the individuals—the wives, mothers, children, and extended members of the family—to which patriarchy is ordered. So too, the Christian patriarchal order promotes the primacy of the informed Catholic conscience, for it derives its moral authority from being in accord with Christian truth. Thus, the Christian patriarchal order is at one and the same time monarchic and individualistic.

[258] It is, therefore, the family and not the base communities of liberation theology that is God-ordained. Surely, it is from the family that any true grassroots Christendom will arise. As Joseph Ratzinger said, the base communities of liberation theology where not a grassroots movement among the poor, but rather, a creation of Western intellectuals, *viz.*, "an attempt to test, in a concrete scenario, ideologies that have been invented in the laboratory by European

theologians" and thus in a certain sense itself a form of "cultural imperialism." So too, liberation theology carried on the clericalism of the past, the only difference being is that its Jesuit priest leaders now aligned with the proletariat rather than the aristocracy. See John F. Thornton and Susan B. Varenne, *The Essential Pope Benedict XVI: His Central Writings & Speeches* (New York: Harper Collins, 2007).

[259] See Chapter VII, § *Ego-Abnegating Receptive Virtue.*

[260] Multitasking is a characteristically feminine aptitude.

[261] The moral principle of subsidiarity is of natural law. It has been increasingly cited and promoted by pontiffs since Leo XIII. While the Holy Magisterium has no special, much less infallible, political competency, it does have a competency, and an infallible one, in the enunciation of morals. The Magisterium's repeated advancement of the moral principle of subsidiarity as one of the essential elements of all governing must be accepted by all Catholics, though any suggested political application of that moral principle need not be. Also see the works of Oswald Nell-Breuning, S.J. (March 8, 1890 – August 21, 1991).

[262] From the Leonine Prayers that were prescribed to be recitation at the foot of the altar after Low Mass from 1884 to 1965.

[263] See Chapter IV, § *Dethronement.*

[264] See Chapter III, § *Portentous Papal Pretenses.*

[265] See Chapter V, § *Christian Rights.*

[266] Though the State clearly should never be the final arbitrator of what is truly human, of what is moral or immoral, of what is righteous or vicious, that is exactly what it now postures to be via its mental health system. Indeed, the Mental Health System seeks to usurp the Church as today's *de facto* moral magisterium. For the State Mental Health System claims total authority over the practice and study of "psychology." But the State, and most especially today's godless and corrupt State, can never control the real practice and "study of the soul," and in fact its mental health system does not even recognize the soul as a real entity.

[267] Dignitatis Humane, no. 2.

[268] Dignitatis Humane, no. 3.

[269] See Chapter XI, *Ecclesial Existence.*

[270] See Chapter VII, § *Dehumanizing Obedience.*

[271] These dynamics continue as to this writing, with a papal concordant being made with Communist China and the recognition

of its State- controlled Patriotic Catholic Church and the betrayal of the true Church which is both dissident and familial.

[272] There were heroic notable exceptions, e.g., Blessed Miguel Pro.

[273] See David C. Bailey, *Viva Cristo Rey! (Austin:* University of Texas Press, 1974).

[274] For instance, Claus Philipp Maria Schenk Graf Von Stauffenberg, who was the Catholic war hero who led the failed 1944 plot, code-named "Valkyrie," to kill Adolf Hitler and overthrow the neo-pagan and socialistic Nazi regime.

[275] See Ralph Wiltgen, *Rhine Flows into the Tiber* (TAN Books, 1991).

[276] The Church Militant (*Ecclesia militans*) consists of Christians on earth; the Church Penitent (*Ecclesia poenitens*), also called the Church Suffering (*Ecclesia dolens*), consists of those Christians currently in Purgatory; and the Church Triumphant (*Ecclesia triumphans*) consists of those in Heaven.

[277] John Paul II, *The Theology of the Body: A New Translation based on the John Paul II Archives,* translation, index, and introduction by Michael Waldstein (Boston: Pauline Books & Media).

[278] This essay is included in *The Three Marks of Manhood*, and can also be found at: http://www.christianorder.com /features /features_2002/features_jun-july02_bonus_1.html

---

[H1]I capitalized this because it is the beginning of a quote.

[H2]Apocalyptic?

[H3]Added comma and "to" before "choose"

[H4]This sentences switches from singular "person" to plural "creatures."

[H5]Use either/or

[H6]Use either/or

[H7]Suggest "because he is" instead of "for his being."

[H8]This was never capitalized anywhere else.